MIRACLE PRAYER

Nine Steps to Creating Prayers That Get Results

Susan Shumsky, D.D.

CELESTIAL ARTS
Berkeley | Toronto

Celestial Arts
an imprint of Ten Speed Press
P.O. Box 7123
Berkeley, California 94707
www.tenspeed.com

Distributed in Australia by Simon and Schuster Australia, in Canada by Ten Speed Press Canada, in New Zealand by Southern Publishers Group, in South Africa by Real Books, and in the United Kingdom and Europe by Airlift Book Company.

Cover design by Katy Brown
Interior design by Lynn Bell, Monroe Street Studios

Library of Congress Cataloging-in-Publication data on file with the publisher.

First printing, 2006
Printed in the United States of America

1 2 3 4 5 6 7 8 9 10 — 10 09 08 07 06

DEDICATION

This book was written with great love for those who have not given up hope that their dreams might come true. It is dedicated to the despondent and demoralized, who have struggled for so long to achieve their desires, to no avail. Yet, even though everything around themselves tells them otherwise, with a faint glimmer of faith, they have clung desperately to their heartfelt aspirations. Never, never, never give up.

ACKNOWLEDGMENTS

I am grateful for everyone who made this book possible. Thanks to everyone at Celestial Arts, especially Jo Ann Deck, for believing in this book, and to Veronica Randall, for bringing it to completion.

Thank you to our dearly beloved departed Dr. Peter Meyer, my Prayer Therapy mentor. Thanks to our adored departed Rich Bell, who wrote many of the healing prayers in my books. I am grateful to Prem Raja Baba for opening my eyes to the real power of the subconscious mind. Thanks to James Van Praagh for your support in getting this book published. I give thanks to all the New Thought ministers who have graciously and generously invited me to their churches and conferences to speak.

But most of all, I am grateful to Jeff and Deborah Herman. Thank you for standing by me always, through thick, thin, and everything in between.

CONTENTS

MIRACLE CONSCIOUSNESS

As a child, I held great appreciation for the miracles of life. In every part of creation I saw a wonderland of forms and phenomena. Looking at a flower or leaf, a tree or bird, I contemplated the God-essence within it. While riding the city bus, I appreciated the beauty shining through every face: bright bouncy children, ancient wrinkled faces—all races, all ages, all colors—a garden of flowers in the landscape of God's love.

I received great realizations of truth as an artist. I remember attempting to translate a landscape or a person onto paper. However, the longer I gazed at an object, the more I realized it was impossible to accurately paint it. That is because every object is an infinity in itself. There is endless detail in God's creation. No one can represent that boundlessness with the inadequacy of an artist's tools.

As I grew up, I sought to recapture something of that childlike joy of Spirit. I began an amazing spiritual quest that took me all over the world. This search culminated in a profound opening to the sublime presence of God within. With the help of the effulgent beings of light, in constant communion with me, I regained appreciation for commonplace things that express God's wonders. Through daily revelations from God within, I have understood how anyone can create miracles through trusting the "still small voice" within and following its guidance.

The advantage I bring to this work is that I was not born with any extraordinary abilities but discovered the inner life through patient, dedicated study and practice for forty years. Because I have walked this pathway myself, I can assist others in developing some of the abilities I have achieved.

I am on a journey. I have not arrived at a destination where no further progress is to be made. I assume you are on a similar path, and I know this book can help you materialize greater good for yourself and others. It can also inspire you to make some remarkable choices that you may not have considered before. So keep an open mind to what you are about to receive, and continue to awaken your soul to the Spirit of God.

With love, Dr. Susan Shumsky, June 1, 2006

HOW TO USE THIS BOOK

This book is part of a teaching called Divine Revelation®, a body of knowledge inspired by divine guidance, to assist you in developing spiritually and realizing God. My first book, *Divine Revelation*, is the foundation of this teaching. Therefore, it is suggested that you also study and digest that book, so that you can fully appreciate the work brought forth here. You will find more information at www.divinerevelation.org.

Miracle Prayer offers a complete system for discovering and ascertaining your deepest, heartfelt desires, and for manifesting them. You will learn how miracles occur and how you can invite miracles into your own life. You will use the law of karma to your advantage and overcome your own "mental law," which has bound you to limitation.

You will learn unique, step-by-step methods of prayer and affirmation that heal negative influences and beliefs and thereby transform your life. By reading this book and using its techniques, you can become a master-manifestor and miracle-maker.

Take time to do the exercises and to use the affirmations and prayers in your daily life. Do not rush through this book or attempt to read it in one sitting. Instead, use it as a textbook to study and practice the methods. It takes time to develop prayer power, so be patient with yourself. Trust that you are on the right path, guided by Spirit, and filled with the light of God. This book will help you enter the flow of divinity and ride the current of God's love.

When reading this book, come with an open mind and heart. If you are receptive to the possibilities, your life can be transformed profoundly and dramatically.

PART I

MAKING LIFE MIRACULOUS

1 EVERYDAY MIRACLES

ANYONE WHO DOESN'T BELIEVE IN MIRACLES ISN'T A REALIST.
—*Billy Wilder*

Why does a seemingly capricious deity answer prayers for some people and not for others? Why do some prayers remain unfulfilled? Is our technique of prayer ineffectual? Are we praying amiss?

Some people who attempt to pray give up in defeat, concluding that prayer does not work for them. They assume that only the fortunate few, perhaps those with extreme purity in their hearts, or excessive faith in their souls, can pray successfully. But God seems to turn a deaf ear to ordinary folks.

As a child I tried to pray and hoped God would respond. But it seemed the more I prayed, the more God refused to listen. I came to the conclusion that either God does not exist, or else I am not worthy for God to acknowledge me. This childhood experience was so disheartening that I totally lost touch with how accessible God can be.

It was not until 1986, when I learned a powerful method called "Scientific Prayer," that I realized that anyone who can learn a few simple principles is capable of praying successfully and getting startling results.

Even though many people are not getting winning results from prayer, there are millions who have used a proven prayer technique that is effective, practical, and highly successful. By reading this book, you will learn and practice this extraordinary method.

This book offers a unique process of Scientific Prayer that will help you get the positive outcome you are seeking. This system is based on the teachings of "New Thought," which is, in turn, the foundation of the human potential movement. New Thought teachings were developed by such illumined souls as Ernest Holmes (1887–1960), founder of the Church of Religious Science and author of *The Science of Mind*, and Charles (1854–1948) and Myrtle (1845–1931) Fillmore, co-founders of the Unity Church.

New Thought, a nonsectarian philosophy, proposes that all causes are internal forces, and all difficulties can be overcome by metaphysical means, such as prayer and affirmation. "Spiritual Mind Treatment," in which mind is considered primary and causative, is the principal method of healing used in New Thought.

Although prayer and affirmation have become increasingly popular, many people do not know how to pray effectively. They read books or attend churches that inspire them to pray, yet they do not know how to put the words together that comprise a powerful, masterful prayer. While many people have studied principles of prayer and affirmation, they have not received basic training in the art of prayer.

This book offers a new, systematic approach to prayer. It helps anyone create miracles in daily life through a simple nine-step Scientific Prayer method. This system offers a source of inner strength and self-confidence unavailable in other teachings.

Although this book addresses the need to develop prayer power, it does not assume prior experience in the field. Anyone can easily comprehend and apply these simple methods that can be used in everyday life. These field-proven techniques have been tested and verified by millions of people from all backgrounds and religions, who have experienced significant benefits.

PRACTICAL SOLUTIONS

Throughout forty years of teaching meditation and prayer techniques, I have often heard the following complaints, to which this book provides practical solutions:

1. **"I have tried prayer and affirmation, but it just doesn't work for me."**
   In this book you will learn unique, simple prayer and affirmation techniques that anyone can do and get positive results.

2. **"My negative thought-patterns, habits, and conditioning prevent me from fulfilling my desires."**
   In Part V you will find specific healing affirmations and prayers that help you overcome negative patterns.

3. **"I feel frustrated that I cannot fulfill my desires."**
   By reading this book, you will discover what your soul is longing to fulfill, and you will realize how to achieve those true desires of your heart.

4. **"I want to fulfill my true purpose, but I don't know what it is."**
   Using a simple technique in this book, you will get in touch with your true life plan and purpose and how to express it.

5. **"I am offended by rules and regulations, cults, and coercive organizations."**
   The universal techniques in this book impose no restrictions and are compatible with other religious philosophies, lifestyles, and personal beliefs.

6. **"I don't want to work at difficult, strict, hard-to-follow disciplines."**
   This book is easy to understand, logical, and practical, with simple methods requiring no previous experience, background, training, or knowledge.

BENEFITS YOU CAN EXPECT

Here are a few of the many benefits you can receive through practicing the methods in this book. Included are testimonials from people who have used these techniques to create miracles in their lives:

1. **Taking control of your destiny.**

   Janet Ponce, a cosmetologist from Las Cruces, New Mexico, reports: "I felt like a ship without a rudder. My life had no particular direction. Since I joined a prayer circle and learned Scientific Prayer, my life has been on track. Now I feel I am the captain of my ship and can steer my own course."

2. **Setting clear goals and fulfilling them.**

   An engineer from San Diego, Anthony Hague, says: "Thank you for teaching me how to establish clear-cut objectives that I can work to achieve. Through praying to manifest my goals, I was able to start my own consulting business, which has become a very successful company with several employees."

3. **Getting in touch with your true heartfelt desires and divine purpose.**

   An artist from Dallas, Sharon Bordic, reveals: "For many years I was seeking to know my life purpose. By discovering my divine plan in Susan Shumsky's workshop at Unity Church, I had a revelation that changed my career path. I went back to art school and have been painting again. This new direction is like a ray of sunshine for my life."

4. **Enjoying better relationships with family, friends, and coworkers.**

   Jacob Unger, from Point Roberts, Washington, says: "I have been using the methods of spiritual healing and am surprised at the result. My friends seem to relate to me on a more clear level, honoring my integrity and quality of being. They are less possessive and more tolerant and unconditionally loving toward me. My relationships are changing for the better. They're more clear, mature, and the muddy emotional imbalances are less."

5. **Enjoying a sense of inner happiness in everyday life.**

   Andrea Lasko, an administrative assistant from Denver, reports: "Since I started using the prayers from Dr. Shumsky's workshop at the Energy Medicine conference in Boulder, I have undergone a major shift in how I see myself and my relationships. I am amazed by how much joy I have discovered in the little miracles of life. Thank you for this beautiful teaching."

6. **Being more self-reliant and less dependent on others.**
   James Tan, an architect from San Diego, says: "I feel less controlled by other people. I feel that if someone is trying to control me, I now have a way that I can be detached from that."

7. **Enjoying greater self-love, self-acceptance, and inner power.**
   Lorene Spencer, a cancer patient from Lansing, Michigan, writes: "I am learning how to finally love myself, heal myself, and overcome this loneliness. I've been saying the healing prayers and affirmations daily. I really feel like I have power within me—feeling something great inside."

8. **Learning to pray for yourself and for others and getting positive results.**
   A mother from Ontario, Canada, Juliet DiFranco, says: "Since taking your workshop at Christ Church Unity, I have been using the prayers and find greater harmony at home and at work. Especially when I pray for my kids, I notice immediate benefits. My prayers have healed everything from physical ailments to problems at school. Thank you for changing my life."

9. **Dwelling in the joyous, comforting, loving presence of God.**
   Grace Suzuki, a teacher from San Francisco, says: "One thing I've experienced is a feeling of invincibility. When we know the healing prayers, we know we are protected by the light of our being; then there's no reason to fear, no matter where we go, no matter who we happen to be with. This is a wonderful sense of security."

10. **Experiencing God's grace at work in your everyday life.**
    Doina Barkhaus, a teacher from Phoenix, Arizona, writes: "For

the leap in spirituality I gained in one day at Dr. Shumsky's 'Expect Miracles' workshop, I would have had to attend church for 100 years. Upon awakening the next morning, I was so much lighter! I had let go of all my religious conditioning—my preconceived notions of what God is. I was lifted to a new level. I realized, I AM a divine being! I AM a part of God, and it's okay to say that. I realized how limiting my life has been, and I'm ready to cut through! I know what to pray for, what the block is, and what to do. I am ready to let it go. A lot of obstacles were removed."

11. **Creating miracles in your everyday life.**

    From Portland, Oregon, Jason Reynolds, a consumer advocate, writes: "I am a long-time meditator. I call myself a God junkie, and my prayer life is frequently ecstatic. In the last two years, I have had great luck praying for people with cancer. In eight of nine cases so far, the tumors have disappeared in God's perfect light. I am astonished each and every time. Also blown away by God's generosity. One thing about the spiritual journey: it is never dull! Infinitely expansive love for our Infinite Creator."

GIFTS OF THIS BOOK

This book is written to open untold possibilities to everyone who is led to it. It is a guidebook to fulfilling your personal desires and an introduction to the field of miracles. Lovingly brought forth under the guidance of the Holy Spirit—the spirit of wholeness within—it will help you use your inner God-given power, which is your birthright, to fulfill your dreams and manifest your divine purpose.

This book tears down old idols, eliminates useless concepts, and abolishes habitual, damaging thought processes. Therefore, it is designed to effect the true transformation that you seek as an aspirant of the living God.

It is not for those unwilling to learn, to grow, and to take a few risks. It is not for anyone content to be hypnotized by previously held, false beliefs that have kept you in bondage.

> To grow in prayer is to grow in awareness of what's real. We free ourselves from denial, from illusions, from addictions.
>
> —THOMAS E. CLARKE

This book is meant as a gift of love from a God of love. Those who wish to cling to a God of wrath and punishment may find little comfort in these pages. However, if you have held such a belief so far but are open to the possibility of something new, then this book is a gift to you with blessings of the Almighty.

Those who are exhausted with the world, downtrodden and weary of struggling to find fulfillment, to you this book may be a great awakening and a treasure. Therefore, be open to possibilities that await you in the jewels of your inner precious crown of life, God's gift for you.

WHY I WROTE THIS BOOK

I have practiced spiritual disciplines since 1967, when I learned to meditate. My first spiritual mentor was Maharishi Mahesh Yogi, enlightened master from India, guru of the Beatles and Deepak Chopra, and founder of Transcendental Meditation. In 1970, on the banks of the Ganges River in India, Maharishi personally trained me to be a meditation teacher. I lived in his ashrams (learning institutions) in secluded areas, including the Himalayas of India and the Swiss Alps, for twenty-two years, and I served on his personal staff for seven of those years.

Under Maharishi's tutelage, I used to meditate up to twenty hours a day. I would go into my room and not emerge for eight weeks at a time. Meals were left outside my door. I sometimes observed silence and did not utter a word for four months at a time. I fasted for up to two months at a time. I practiced total celibacy. I was an introvert, and that is definitely an understatement.

After spending twenty-two years with my eyes closed, I had a profound realization. Even though I was fortunate to enjoy amazing spiritual experiences in daily meditation, I was not expressing spirituality in my outer personality. Exceedingly arrogant, I believed my guru was the only guru, his teaching was the only way to realize God, and his disciples were superior human beings on a higher mission. No one could tell me anything—I knew it all. Little did I know how little I knew.

Happily, I was introduced to a wonderful New Thought system—Teaching of Intuitional Metaphysics, founded by Dr. Peter Meyer, co-author of *Being a Christ!* Dr. Meyer's techniques helped me attain direct communication with the "still small voice" of God within and to use the power of the spoken word in prayer in order to heal others and myself.

I began teaching Divine Revelation® seminars, and students had such miraculous experiences that I was inspired to offer these seminars in print. *Divine Revelation* was the first book published. This, my fifth book, *Miracle Prayer*, offers a practical program to help you fulfill your purpose and create miracles in everyday life.

I am pleased and grateful to now give this precious teaching to you. For Scientific Prayer has definitely transformed my life, and it can transform yours. You have the God-given power to dream, and your dreams are real and worthy. Let God's love and miracle-power help you fulfill your dreams. If you can dream miracles, and you can believe in miracles, then you can achieve miracles. Believe in yourself now and begin to realize your destiny. Trust in God's grace to be your guide on this journey to fulfillment. You are the driver. Let God be your co-pilot.

Let us now get started on this miraculous voyage.

2 MIRACLES— OR MADNESS?

IF YOU CAN DREAM IT, YOU CAN DO IT.

—*Walt Disney*

Can you create miracles in your life and fulfill your dreams and ideals? Or are miracles the exclusive property of great souls and saintly beings? In this chapter you will discover how miracles and wonders can happen to you through your own inner connection with Spirit.

MIRACLES OF THE PROPHETS

Our society believes that when we talk to God, it is called "prayer." But when God talks to us, it is called "schizophrenia." If you told a psychiatrist that you were having two-way conversations with God, and that God spoke to you in your mind, he would doubtlessly diagnose you with psychosis.

Yet, the ability to communicate with God is well documented in every religious tradition. Prophets of every religion have received inner revelations, which then became the world's great scriptures. In every age, mystical experiences of God contact have been reported.

> Prayer is simply a two-way conversation between you and God.
>
> —BILLY GRAHAM

Saints such as Joan of Arc were considered heretic or insane, as are those who claim to know God today.

If a long-haired, bearded, robed, wandering prophet appeared today, seeing visions of God in burning bushes, turning rivers into blood, parting seas, raising the dead, or feeding five thousand people from five loaves and two fishes, how would he be accepted?

I have met saints from India whom I have seen perform miracles. One of them was locked in a New Jersey penitentiary for a seven-year term. Another has not entered the United States since 1985 due to subpoenas and the threat of indictments in American courts. We all know what happened to Jesus and his Apostles as well as Socrates, Mahatma Gandhi, Martin Luther King, and other spiritual leaders.

What did these extraordinary people do that aroused such vehement opposition? Because of their supernormal abilities, and perhaps due to their inability to keep these abilities concealed, they were harshly persecuted.

Their powers, considered "works of the devil," included:

1. Hearing the "still small voice" of God and receiving direct revelations.

2. Seeing spiritual visions from God, which gave teaching, prophesy, and wisdom.

3. Communicating mentally and spiritually with animals and other life-forms.

4. Performing miraculous feats, such as levitating, walking through walls, superhuman strength, supersensory perception, and disappearing.

5. Possessing mastery over nature's elements, such as changing the weather, parting the seas, precipitating objects, taming animals, and removing earthbound spirits.

6. Acquiring miraculous knowledge, such as knowing ultimate truths, ancient history, past lives, hidden objects, mind-reading, and prophecy.

7. Healing the sick through entirely spiritual means, even from a distance.

8. Bringing the dead back to life.

9. Achieving mastery over life and death by attaining immortality.

11

I DO NOTHING OF MYSELF

What is the key to achieving miracles, wondrous powers, and superhuman feats? The answer to this question was clearly stated by a Nazarene who was highly successful at performing miracles:

"The Son can do nothing of himself, but what he seeth the Father do: for what things soever he doeth, these also doeth the Son likewise."[1]

"For I have not spoken of myself; but the Father which sent me, he gave me a commandment, what I should say, and what I should speak…whatsoever I speak therefore, even as the Father said unto me, so I speak."[2]

"I do nothing of myself; but as my Father hath taught me, I speak these things."[3]

"The words that I speak unto you I speak not of myself: but the Father that dwelleth in me, he doeth the works."[4]

In these passages, Jesus declared that he was incapable of making miracles without God. Through his inner connection with Spirit, he could perform any miracle. Yet, it was not the person of Jeshua ben Joseph (Jesus) who did these amazing works. It was God within him. Jesus was a simple channel for God to reveal through him, to speak, heal, walk, and live through him. Jesus gave breath to the life of God through his existence. He was an instrument for God to express through him continually.

Jesus fully expressed his higher self. However, everyone can realize and express the higher self within. On that level of being, with your God-self doing the work, you can perform any miracle and fulfill any desire. You can be a perfect vehicle for God to work through you.

"Let this mind be in you, which was also in Christ Jesus: Who, being in the form of God, thought it not robbery to be equal with God."[5]

MAKING MIRACLES

Deep within is your divine, sacred self, a perpetual instrument of God. However, most people have not awakened their higher self in conscious awareness.

ROAD MAP TO YOUR INNER LIFE

OUTER LIFE (Material World)	**BODY**	Environment
		Physical Body
	MIND	Conscious Mind
		Subconscious Mind
		Facade Barrier (False Belief in Separation from God)
INNER LIFE (Spirit World)		Etheric (Soul) Self
	SPIRIT	Christ Self
		"I AM" Self
		God Self
		Cosmic Self
ABSOLUTE PURE CONSCIOUSNESS (Present Everywhere)		

Please refer to "Road Map to Your Inner Life" on page 13. On this chart, various dimensions of Spirit are listed. All these levels of reality dwell deep within you. These aspects of your spiritual self are always "one with the Father." Thus, there is no separation between you and God.

You can learn to contact and communicate with God within. Once you fully develop your ability to be a conduit for God, there is nothing you cannot do. For it is not your limited egoic self who is acting. It is your God self within, unlimited by space, time, and causation.

"The things which are impossible with men are possible with God." [6]

It would appear that the extraordinary works of Jesus are not attainable by average individuals. However, Jesus would disagree. He indicated that he was a wayshower—an ideal from whom people could gain inspiration. I believe his mission was to demonstrate that everyone is capable of attainments, wonders, and miracles:

> With God all things are possible. [7]
>
> —JESUS CHRIST

YOU HAVE GOD WITHIN YOU

Jesus himself stated, *"The kingdom of God is within you."* [8] and, *"Seek ye first the kingdom of God, and his righteousness; and all these things shall be added unto you."* [9] The kingdom of heaven is indeed within you and within every particle of creation, for God is omnipresent. If you make that kingdom your first priority, then you can receive the blessings of God and do the works of God.

YOU CAN RECEIVE BY ASKING

Jesus said, *"Ask, and it shall be given you; seek, and ye shall find; knock, and it shall be opened unto you: For every one that asketh receiveth; and he that seeketh findeth; and to him that knocketh it shall be opened."* [10] Every one of you is capable of receiving all that you seek, just by asking.

YOU CAN DO EVEN GREATER WORKS

He promised that *"greater works than these shall he do."* [11] You can do all the things that Jesus did and even greater works than he.

YOU ARE PERFECTION WITHIN

He said, *"Be ye therefore perfect, even as your Father which is in heaven is perfect."* [12] You are perfection at the depth of your being, and you can attain any goals that you seek and perform any miracles.

YOU CAN BECOME PERFECT

He promised, *"The disciple is not above his master: but every one that is perfect shall be as his master."* [13] You can perfect yourself and become like Jesus, and do all the works that he was capable of doing.

YOU CAN DO GOD'S WILL

He said, *"Not every one that saith unto me, Lord, Lord, shall enter into the kingdom of heaven; but he that doeth the will of my Father which is in heaven."* [14] You have been promised the kingdom of heaven by doing the will of God, not by idolizing Jesus.

YOU CAN RECEIVE POWER AND KNOWLEDGE

He told his disciples, *"Ye shall receive power, after that the Holy Ghost is come upon you."* [15] And he said, *"The Comforter, which is the Holy Ghost, whom the Father will send in my name, he shall teach you all things."* [16] You have been promised power and inner teaching by your direct connection to the Holy Spirit within.

YOU ARE DIVINE LIGHT

He stated, *"Ye are the light of the world...Let your light so shine before men, that they may see your good works, and glorify your Father which is in heaven."* [17] You are that divine light, and you are capable of all good works, glorifying God by performing them.

15

Anyone wanting to attain full mastery of the Christ consciousness may well gain inspiration from the life of Jesus. The Christ within Jesus made him all that he was. That same Christ power, within you, can make you all that you can be. Perhaps you have not yet developed the faith to fully attain the magnificence of Jesus' example, but you can certainly begin to fulfill your heart's desires and true purpose.

IDOLATRY VS. PERSONAL POWER

Purportedly, the only people allowed to do miraculous works are great sages, saints, prophets, holy men (I emphasize the word "men") who lived at least two thousand years ago in some faraway land. Ostensibly, there was only one divinely revealed book ever written, and since then, apparently, God has gone mute.

Blind followers of religious dogma take false comfort in believing that the power of God was granted solely to great prophets and not ordinary individuals. Thus they abdicate the burden of responsibility that would arise from possessing the kind of enormous power enjoyed by the ancient prophets.

Such belief in personal powerlessness causes humanity to be enslaved by idolatry—worshipping a faraway, unattainable, anthropomorphic deity rather than realizing the presence of God within self, within all beings, and within all life. Idolatry perpetuates the relinquishment of personal accountability.

Belief in any external deity beyond your reach is a form of idolatry. You are worshipping an *idol* instead of exemplifying an *ideal*. What if the prophets of old had squandered their lives idolizing an external power rather than mastering the power within? Could they have called forth the great currents of cosmic energy by which they performed miracles? No. History would never have recorded their names.

Take your archaic, anthropomorphic God out of the sky and implant it firmly in the rich soil of your heart, at the center of your being. That is where

God belongs—and where God already dwells. *"The kingdom of God is within you."* [18] *"Ye are gods, and all of you are the children of the most High."* [19]

The Christ consciousness is within you. Accept the inner awareness that fathoms who you really are. Realizing your supreme self will bring much greater delight to God than a lifetime of praise and worship.

Saint Paul said: *"For as many as are led by the Spirit of God, they are the sons of God…we are the children of God. And if children, then heirs; heirs of God and joint-heirs with Christ."* [20] You are a child of the living God, and Jesus is your elder brother. Thus, your birthright is to glorify God by living your full, divine potential—to possess the spiritual gifts that Jesus displayed and "greater than these."

"Eye hath not seen, nor ear heard, neither have entered into the heart of man, the things which God hath prepared for them that love him. But God hath revealed them unto us by his Spirit: for the Spirit searcheth all things, yea, the deep things of God." [21]

INVITATION TO THE MIRACULOUS

Does God intend for only special, "enlightened" saints, sages, seers, prophets, and "godly" people to make miracles? I believe that miracles are not reserved for an elite cadre of saintly snobs who have signed an exclusive contract with God. You too can accomplish amazing feats, simply by believing. An innocent mind, quiet and serene, has the supreme faith to perform *"greater works than these."* [22]

Through meditation, you can develop that kind of faith. You have the power to *"be still and know that I AM God."* [23] You can quiet your mind and hear the divine voice. By trusting and following that inner voice, your faith develops as your higher self guides you to the miraculous. (Refer to my book *Divine Revelation*.)

You have the potential for greatness. Your version of greatness may look quite different from anyone else's. It may be the greatness of loving your children or of helping those in need. It may be the greatness of healing the sick or creating works of art. Whatever your gift for greatness, that is your unique expression of miracles in action.

Miracles are thought to belong to the realm of the utterly fantastic and arise from incredible circumstances. But feast your eyes on God's glorious creation. Isn't a small bud or a tiny ant a miracle? Isn't this glorious universe of innumerable luminous spheres the greatest miracle? In fact, every time you take a breath or your heart beats, a miracle occurs. Miracles are everywhere. Simply open your eyes to them. The extraordinary is indeed ordinary.

> There are only two ways to live your life. One is as though nothing is a miracle. The other is as though everything is a miracle.
>
> —ALBERT EINSTEIN[24]

It seems ordinary to paint a picture or play the piano. But did these talents come without effort, practice, or faith? Painting a picture and playing a piano are no less extraordinary than levitating, disappearing, or faith-healing, yet they *seem* less extraordinary, simply because you have never met someone capable of so-called miraculous feats. What seems miraculous for some is taken for granted by others.

The definition of *faith* is to have an assured expectation of a particular outcome. Through faith you can do anything. *"All things, whatsoever ye shall ask in prayer, believing, ye shall receive."*[24] Nothing is impossible. You are not a small, insignificant creature. You have tremendous power that can be tapped. Within yourself is the spark of life that created you, with the ability to fulfill any desire and perform any miracle.

Are you surprised at this capacity? As Jesus proclaimed, *"He that believeth in me, the works that I do shall he do also; and greater works than these shall he do."*[25] You are unlimited. Whatever you conceive in your mind, you can achieve. Whatever you see in your vision, you can materialize. Your only limitation is your imagination.

God is always within you, waiting to manifest your every thought. You are a co-creator with the creator of this universe. You bring into being, through your imagination, the substance of God. That eternal substance is simply slowed down into material form to take shape as things of this world.

The purpose of this book is to help you raise your consciousness, awaken your latent abilities, and draw upon divine substance to fulfill your desires instantaneously. All this and more are possible with God.

Read this text and hear this message of love. You have the power within you. Now is the time to use it.

TWO STEPS TO EASY MIRACLES

This book will help you achieve your desires. What are you doing now to fulfill these goals? In fact, you are creating your future right now in each moment. Every thought you think, every word you speak, and every deed you do—these are the seeds that sprout into your future destiny. You create everything already.

You can make a life of grace, majesty, well-being, joy, and glory. Or you can manifest suffering and unhappiness. You are the captain of your ship, and the rudder is your free will. You have the capacity to create whatever you want, because that is exactly what you are doing right now, through your freedom of choice.

I have discovered an astonishing secret in my travels—a key to fulfilling your most precious desires. I am about to reveal this secret. But first, I must tell you a painful story. Before my first book *Divine Revelation* was published, I endured a terrible accident. My leg was crushed by an extremely heavy eight-foot-tall iron gate. In fact, it was nearly severed in half and barely escaped amputation. I experienced a fair amount of suffering for several years, and I ended up financially devastated.

When I signed the contract with Simon & Schuster to write *Divine Revelation*, I had planned to use the money from a court settlement related to the injury in order to pay for my nationwide book tour. But no settlement came. In fact, several years later, I still waited for the settlement.

What did I do in this dilemma? I went into meditation and asked guidance from my higher self. The answer I received was that I need not worry—the money would come. With total blind faith I planned an expensive book tour and then started out on the road in a Ford E350 van—with no money. Astonishingly, as I began to move around the country, money manifested at every turn.

Whenever I asked for guidance from my higher self, I received messages to continue to travel and to invest in various expensive promotional activities. Then I would say in a clear, strong voice, "Dear God, since you want me to do all of these things, please SHOW ME THE MONEY!" And the money always came. Often it came at the eleventh hour and fifty-ninth minute. Sometimes it came through bizarre circumstances. But it always came.

What did I learn from this? My two-step technique for creating miracles:

FIRST STEP: ASK GOD FOR GUIDANCE.

Why is this first step essential? Simply because if you do not ask God for guidance, then you might spend years beating your skull against a stone wall, accomplishing nothing. The first step to fulfilling desires is to discover what highest wisdom to desire in the first place. For example, if you think you want to be an actor, but your true soul's purpose is to become a carpenter, then you will subconsciously sabotage your acting career at every turn. Your higher self knows best. You just need to catch up with your inner wisdom.

In this book, you will discover your true soul's purpose. Once you have made this breakthrough, only then are you ready to fulfill your deepest desires. This book will help you discover how to cooperate with God in order to reach your goals.

SECOND STEP: ASK GOD TO GIVE IT TO YOU,
AND MAKE IT HAPPEN.

Pray for it. Demand it. Set it as a goal. Make an absolute, firm decision to follow your guidance, and follow through with action. Then expect miracles to occur.

In this book, you will learn everything you need to know about fulfilling your ideals through the powerful method called Scientific Prayer. By the time you have finished reading this book, you will have all the tools you need to create and live a miraculous life, in which your loftiest dreams come true.

Imagine how happy you will be when you have the self-assuredness that comes from knowing you are on the right path, fulfilling your God-given destiny. This is a very profound status to attain, and you are about to embark on this journey right now. This book is your ticket for this great adventure.

Enjoy the ride!

3 YOU ARE NOT A VICTIM

HE THAT MAKES HIS BED ILL, LIES THERE.

—*George Herbert*

*W*ho or what controls your life? What forces create your destiny? Is it determined by genetics, upbringing, or outer situations? This chapter will answer these questions in a way that you may have never considered before.

WHO HAPPENS TO YOU?

You can perceive your life in one of two ways: (1) that you are in charge of your life, or (2) that life is "done to" you. If you subscribe to the first viewpoint, then you are a "creator"—a master of your destiny. If you believe the second, then you are a "victim"—a sufferer of predetermined fate.

Victims believe things "happen to them," due to vicissitudes of fate, karma, or luck, or due to outer circumstances, such as parents, upbringing, or social status. In contrast, creators know they have unlimited inner power. They realize that life does not "happen to them." They only "happen" to themselves.

Are you a creator, or are you a victim?

You have an inner power not influenced by outer circumstances—the power of God. With this power at your command, you can do anything— and I mean *anything*. You are not a victim of social conditions. You can rise above all these. Your inner power can be tapped and used anytime. It only requires some effort and practice to master it.

Self-mastery means taking charge of your life by consciously creating your pathway and making miracles. You may have no interest in parting the Red Sea or walking through walls. But you are definitely interested in everyday miracles, such as being happy, fulfilling your heart's desires, and living prosperously and joyously. Therefore, you may wish to take command of your destiny.

YOU ARE RESPONSIBLE

Does some outside force control you? Is an evil, unseen god or karmic lord plotting nefarious tribulations to punish you? Is your fate determined by chance or accident? In truth, there are no accidents. You are not prey to winds of providence. Everything that happens to you is caused by you—by nothing else.

Lord Buddha said, *"All that we are is the result of what we have thought… If a man speaks or acts with an evil thought, pain follows him, as the wheel follows the foot of the ox that draws the carriage… If a man speaks or acts with a pure thought, happiness follows him, like a shadow that never leaves him."* [1]

In other words, you are 100% responsible for your destiny. You have created your own happiness or unhappiness. Therefore you are not a victim. Nor have you ever been a victim. Your life is not determined by any outside force. You create your own destiny by your thoughts, speech, and actions. *"For as he thinketh in his heart, so is he."* [2]

MUSCLE-TESTING EXPERIMENT

Let us do an experiment to demonstrate this reality. First, drink a full glass of water and take several deep breaths. Then, with your nondominant hand, create a circle between your pinky finger and your thumb. In other words, if you are right-handed, connect the tip of your left thumb with the tip of your left little finger. If you are left-handed, connect your right thumb tip with your right pinky fingertip.

Then, with your dominant hand, make a little duck by pressing your thumb pad to your index finger pad. That means, if you are right-handed, connect your right thumb to your right index finger pad. Your three other fingers will be free.

Now place your "duck-beak" made by your thumb and index finger of your dominant hand into the circle made with your nondominant hand. Your "beak" should stick up into your nondominant palm beneath the thumb and little finger of your nondominant hand.

As you remain in this position, say the following affirmation in a strong, clear voice: "I AM a mighty, powerful, spiritual being."

Then, press the pinky finger and thumb of your nondominant hand together in a circle and resist pressure, as you apply an equal degree of pressure with your dominant hand, opening the duck-beak and trying to pull the circle apart, as though your duck is opening its mouth. Press the duck-beak against the circle with steady, continuous pressure, without forcing. As you resist the pressure with your nondominant hand, you will find it difficult to open the circle with your duck-beak. This is called "muscle-testing" or "muscle-checking."

Now relax your hands. Say the following affirmation aloud and clearly, as though you really mean it: "I AM unworthy, inadequate, useless, and shameful."

Then muscle-test again by pressing your dominant hand's duck-beak against your nondominant hand's circle, while you resist with equal pressure. You will find your circle will open easily, like a scissors, under the pressure of your duck-beak.

Now relax your hands again and say the following affirmation in a strong, clear voice: "I AM divinely protected by the light of my being." Once more, when you practice muscle-testing, your circle will have strong resistance to your duck-beak. It will not open.

What did you learn from this experiment? You might draw several conclusions:

1. Positive affirmations and truth statements strengthen your muscles. Negative affirmations and false statements weaken your muscles.

2. You are responsible for your own strength or weakness by virtue of your thoughts, words, and deeds.

3. The effects of positive and negative affirmations and statements are immediate.

4. You create your own reality.

DETERMINISM: FACT OR FICTION

Are you the beneficiary of preordained fate and fortune? Unfortunately, a sickness runs rampant today, perpetuated by fatalistic psychics, astrologers, and fortune-tellers. This is the disease of determinism, which says your destiny is already written. This idea is sustained by predictions of your future and by the belief in "karma," the effect of past actions that "control you."

How often do you hear the following statements?

"You can't change the stars."

"I guess it was meant to be that way."

"I guess it was for the best."

"It was supposed to happen like this."

"I cannot control my destiny."

"My destiny is already written."

"Maybe I wasn't supposed to have it."

"Perhaps I wasn't supposed to do it."

"Maybe God doesn't want me to have it."

Do you ever hear yourself saying such declarations of utter victimization? Such a fatalistic philosophy says that you have no control, no free will, and no choice. Your fate has already been chosen, and you are acting out a prearranged script.

WHO IS THE BOSS?

Who is in charge of your life? Are you in the audience, passively observing your life? Or are you on the stage? I contend that you are not only the actor playing the starring role, but also the playwright. You are not only in the play, but you have also written the script. You are the director and producer. You have authored everything that has happened, and that will happen. No force determines your future other than your own free will.

You might disagree with this. It is certainly not a popular idea, since it suggests that you can blame no one else for your problems. You might believe that external forces shape your future, such as environment, social status, race, sex, family, and education. But the truth is all of these aforementioned factors were caused by you. You have freedom to choose, in each moment, what your future will be, and your choices are nearly limitless.

Before birth, your soul calculated what would be wise to accomplish in this life. You then chose your parents accordingly. At the same time, your parents chose you. You determined your parents' race, health, economic status, nationality, and so forth, most conducive to your life path. You chose your own birth time and place, physical attributes, and all other conditions, such as education, career, marriage, and so forth.

At every step, you make choices, and on the basis of those choices, you make new choices. Your every decision is determined by free will—

nothing else. It is futile to blame others, for you freely choose everything. Those choices are based on what you believe you need, based on past experiences. You have caused every fortune or misfortune.

As a result of using the prayer methods in this book, Barbara Gianino from Fairfield, Iowa, says: "I used to blame my unhappiness on how I was raised, my parents, the job situation, or other situations in life outside of myself. Now I recognize that I am responsible for what I experience. I draw to myself these things because of my belief system. And if I don't like something, I recognize that I can change this. I simply now know how to ask for any error-belief in my subconscious mind to be healed and that the truth replace that."

YOU CAN DO IT

This book is about overcoming past habits and creating the life you envision. In order to achieve dominion, it is essential to heal past ideas about who you think you are. Your limited self-image has prevented you from fulfilling your heartfelt ideals. By realizing your true identity as an unlimited divine being, you can make miracles. You have all the power of nature at your command, and you can wield it.

You can do miraculous works, for *"greater works than these shall he do."*[3] You can achieve the desires of your soul. No matter how impossible it may seem now, you can do it. Do not be afraid to do it. But remember, of yourself you can do nothing—God is the one that performs miracles. By allowing God to do the work, you can accomplish anything.

In this book, you are given tools to help you create miracles. However, your success in using these tools is entirely dependent on how you apply them. There must be a willingness to succeed. Like any other skill, such as learning to swim, it takes not only knowledge, but also practice. You can learn the theory of swimming by reading a book, but you cannot actually swim until you get into the water. The knowledge of swimming contained in a book is dead until you give it life by jumping into the pool.

Similarly, the Divine Revelation and Scientific Prayer methodologies, explained in my books, can come to life by practicing them. By taking inspiration from these words and transforming these words into practice, you can bring these words to life. Then knowledge breathes life.

DARE TO DREAM

Who are you, and why are you on Earth? You were not thrown onto this planet arbitrarily. You have a divine purpose and a destiny that is calling you, even now.

You are a mighty, powerful, spiritual being. You have undoubtedly heard this before. Maybe you have read spiritual books about your unlimited potential. Yet, perhaps you have not realized that power. Perhaps your own greatness eludes you. Maybe you belittle yourself, thinking others are better than you. But you are no greater or less than anyone else.

Everyone is given a gift from God—free will. You can use that gift to uplift yourself and others. You can make a difference, and you are here for a specific, spiritual purpose.

As a child you probably had a vision of what you could contribute to the world when you grew up. Perhaps you saw yourself as a healer, maybe a homemaker, a parent, teacher, or businessperson. Perhaps you conceived of traveling to foreign lands or serving in government. You may have envisioned yourself as an artist or writer. Maybe you dreamt of working in religion or a charity. Possibly your dream was vast and far-reaching, such as world peace, spiritual enlightenment, God-realization, salvation, or planetary healing.

Whatever your dream, for some of you, that dream was shattered by grief or scattered in the wind by necessities of fate. Your beloved dream may have vanished, and with it, your hope and optimism. Your spirit may have died young, along with your dream. Perhaps some of you continue sleep-walking in "quiet desperation," pretending it does not matter, convincing yourself that you dare not dream for more. But your true vision, your desire to live the purpose you were born to fulfill, still burns in your heart.

That flame of hope is God's call to wake up and realize who you truly are—a powerful, magnificent being of infinite love and light. Nothing is too great for you to accomplish. You are unlimited. You do not have to abandon your dream, no matter what your seeming limitations or chronological age. With faith and perseverance, you can manifest it. You were born to realize and to fulfill your destiny.

Let us now take a test with no grade or studying. This test is very easy. Get out a paper and pen and answer one question:

Imagine for a moment that you have unlimited resources of money, people, assistance, time, and freedom. You have everything you want, and you can do anything in the world. There is no limit. Let your imagination soar to realms far beyond your normal vision. What would you do in this situation?

Do not write an essay on what possessions you would acquire; instead, write what you would do with your time. Once you have written it, read it over and add anything you may have missed. *Do not* read the next paragraph until you have finished writing your paper.

Now close this book and go write your paper.

AN AMAZING SECRET

Now, here is an amazing secret: This paper can completely transform your life. It is an exposé about your true desires and higher purpose. You have gotten in touch with an unlimited part of yourself and have graduated to unbounded thinking.

Written on this paper is your divine plan and purpose that you desire to accomplish in this lifetime. It may seem impossible to fulfill this now. You may feel undeserving or restricted. But you *can* start fulfilling it right now, today. And, furthermore, you *already* have all the resources you need to fulfill it. Because this dream comes from your higher self, it is within your grasp. Even if you think you have no means to actualize it today, if you would take just *one* step in the direction of achieving it, God would begin to support you to achieve it.

That one step may involve getting more education or traveling to a different area. It may mean letting go of something holding you back. You might even have to let go of a dead-end relationship. In order to take that first step, you might be criticized for being unrealistic and naive. Your family or friends may laugh at you.

You may be concocting a multitude of excuses preventing you from doing it. But there is nothing stopping you, except your pathetic excuses. Let go of the idea of not being ready, of not having enough, of not being enough. Free yourself from the incessant wheel of procrastination and false justification.

Almost everyone who takes a risk is afraid at first. You can be afraid and yet start anyway. Do you want to spend the rest of your life fulfilling other people's dreams or your own? Get your priorities straight and live with a sense of urgency.

Start on your dream today. With a spark of faith, take the first step to fulfill your higher purpose. It takes courage to take that step, but it is definitely worth taking. Ask God to assist you in fulfilling it. Jump off that cliff. When you jump, you know that God will catch you—or you will have to learn how to fly real fast!

In the next section of this book, some myths about karma will be dispelled. And you will discover how karmic law can be overcome through the law of grace.

THE MYTH OF KARMA

4 WHAT IS KARMA?

*H*ave you struggled to fulfill your desires by forcing, cajoling, or coercing, and yet the result never appeared? Have you tried affirmations or prayers and then concluded, in defeat, "It just doesn't work for me"? To uncover the secret of achieving desires and creating miracles, it is important to first understand the "law of karma."

In this chapter, we will consider and answer the following questions:

1. What does the word *karma* mean?
2. What is the law of karma and how does it function?
3. How does karma affect you?
4. "Who" or "what" gives so-called "karmic retribution"?
5. How does karma affect you from past incarnations?

THE COSMIC BOOMERANG

So what is karma, anyway? A popular definition is as follows: Whatever you do will be paid back to you as retribution. In other words, if you kill someone, then someone will kill you. Does this actually happen? Surprisingly, the answer is no.

Karma is a Sanskrit word that simply means "action." That is all it means. It does not mean that good deeds are rewarded while bad deeds are punished. There are no karmic debts from past lives to punish you in future lives. Nor do karmic courts or trials judge, sentence, or execute you in vengeance, ad infinitum.

So how does the law of karma actually work? Whatever you think, say, or do produces far-reaching consequences. If you drop a rock into the center of a pond, ripples on the surface radiate outward from that pebble in concentric circles. When these circles reach the pond's outer shore, they then travel inward, converging toward the center. Similarly, even your imperceptible thoughts affect the universe more profoundly than you could imagine. Your every thought, word, and deed affects the entire universe and then affects yourself in unfathomable ways.

Every moment you radiate either harmonious waves of thought energy, or inharmonious waves. Positive feelings create an *aura* (energy field) that attracts positivism by the Law of Magnetic Attraction, a law that states, "Like attracts like."

 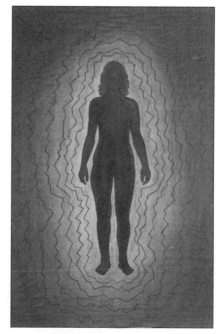

Please refer to the figures on the previous page. In the illustration on the left, a peaceful woman emits positive, balanced, harmonious, orderly emotional vibrations. In contrast, the woman on the right vibrates inharmonious, jagged, irritable, negative, chaotic thoughts and emotions. The ripples of these thought vibrations radiate in all directions. However, the effect of these thoughts does not stop at the edge of the auric field (energy field that permeates and surrounds the body). The effect travels throughout the universe. Then, according to the Law of Magnetic Attraction, it returns to the sender, exactly as it was sent. Harmonious thoughts produce harmonious, peaceful, beneficial results. Inharmonious thoughts produce inharmonious, disorderly, harmful, possibly even violent results.

"Give, and it shall be given unto you; good measure, pressed down, and shaken together, and running over, shall men give into your bosom. For with the same measure that ye mete withal it shall be measured to you again." [1]

You may have learned, *"As ye would that men should do to you, do ye also to them likewise."* [2] This Golden Rule is a universal truth, but it does not mean that if you do something bad, then something bad will be done to you. Many people believe that unfortunate events are punishment for past "evil" actions. Is this true? Not so.

The true meaning of the Golden Rule is: Love everyone and treat everyone as precious, for everyone is a part of God and is precious to you as yourself. If you are motivated by love rather than fear of retribution from a karmic judge and executioner, then you are truly living in accord with the Golden Rule.

You have the choice in every moment to create harmonious, loving, life-supporting waves of thought and energy or inharmonious, negative, life-damaging waves. Your life is the result of the quality of vibrations you project into the universe.

DISPELLING KARMIC MYTHS

The law of karma is the law of consequences of action. This is also the law of cause and effect, stated in scientific terms as Sir Isaac Newton's third law: "Forces always originate in pairs, equal in magnitude and opposite in direction." This law is often quoted as, "Every action has an equal and opposite reaction."

Saint Paul declared a similar law, *"Whatsoever a man soweth, that shall he also reap."*[3] Most people interpret the law of karma as the belief in good and bad deeds, reward and punishment, sin and damnation, evil and vengeance, transgression and retribution. "Karmic debts," due to evils, sins, and crimes, purportedly recycle from incarnation to incarnation.

Karmic retribution is supposedly administered through trials, judgments, and sentences in karmic courts. When you do something bad, then the same bad thing will happen to you. When you do something good, then the same good thing will happen to you. Do you think this is true? Not so. In reality, all the following beliefs are false:

1. Good deeds will be rewarded.
2. Bad deeds will be punished.
3. There is karmic payback, either in this life or future lives.
4. God punishes sin with damnation.
5. God's justice is meted out as retribution and vengeance.
6. You get back the punishment that you "deserve."

Surprisingly, the truth is that there are no:

◆ Karmic debts.
◆ Karmic courts.
◆ Karmic trials.
◆ Karmic judges.

◆ Karmic lords.

◆ Karmic retribution.

Now you will discover how the law of karma really works and how you can use it to your advantage to fulfill your deepest desires.

AS YOU BELIEVE

The true meaning of the law of karma is as follows: *"As thou hast believed, so be it done unto thee."* [4] This means whatever you *believe* will happen is exactly what will happen. It is that simple.

Your belief determines your destiny. If you believe you deserve punishment due to past "evil" deeds, then you will be punished, for *"it is done unto you as you believe."* If, on the other hand, you believe God is all-loving, all-forgiving, and does not punish or exact retribution, then you will not be punished, for *"it is done unto you as you believe."*

If you believe you are poor, then you will be poor. If you believe you are wealthy, you will be. If you believe you are lonely, you will be. If you believe you are happy, you will be, for *"it is done unto you as you believe."*

"It is done unto you as you believe" presumes that you create your destiny, not a karmic lord or Saint Peter's angels sitting in the sky recording your "sins" in a big book, conjuring up punishments to deliver in your next incarnation. You are not a marionette, and God is not a puppeteer. Because you have free will, you have absolute control over your own path, experiences, and future.

What determines, for instance, the wellness of your body? Your beliefs determine it. If you believe you get a cold every spring, and if you declare repeatedly that you get a cold every spring, then that cold will arrive every spring, just like clockwork. You will prove it to yourself, according to your belief. Similarly, if you believe you can never lose weight, then you will find it difficult to lose weight, no matter how hard you try. If you believe you cannot get a good relationship or a decent job, then you will not. If you believe you cannot buy a house, then you will not buy one, even when given the opportunity.

Victims would object to *"it is done unto you as you believe,"* since they are invested in the idea that some outside force controls them, and their fate is determined by a punishing, condemning God. Or they indulge in the belief that their fate is controlled by chance and happenstance.

As a perceptive individual, you might ask, "How can mere belief manifest anything? Believing that you are a king does not make you king. Similarly, if you believe you will get sick, how can that make you sick? Isn't belief mere imagination?" These questions are valid, because the word *belief* is often defined as a mood or imaginary musing. However, your life is nothing more than the outpicturing of your deepest imagination. Lord Buddha declared, *"All that we are is the result of what we have thought."* But what kind of "thought" is Lord Buddha referring to? What "belief" is indicated in the Biblical quotation, *"As thou hast believed, so be it done unto thee"*[5]? Is it your conscious or your subconscious thought?

The meaning of the word *belief* in this context means "a complete conviction, an assured expectation of a particular result." Your deepest convictions are not in your conscious mind. Rather, they are in your subconscious mind. You might not even be aware of them. Your conscious beliefs are what you *think* you believe. Your subconscious beliefs and deepest convictions are what you *really* believe.

For example, it may be far-fetched to have a complete conviction, in your subconscious mind, that you will become king or president of your country. Without that conviction, you would not become king or president. On the other hand, it may be entirely plausible to have a full conviction that you will become a professor, a doctor, a stockbroker, a mother, a chef, a physician, or another profession. That conviction makes your dream a reality.

The karmic law can be used to your advantage. Why? Because your deepest convictions determine your destiny, and all that is needed is to change those beliefs.

YOUR SUBCONSCIOUS TYRANT

What is the difference between conscious and subconscious beliefs? Let us first define *conscious* and *subconscious*. Your conscious mind is the mental apparatus with which you operate. Right now you are reading this book and sitting, most likely, on a chair, couch, or bed. You are conscious of the words on the page and of sounds, sights, and smells around you. That is your conscious, waking mind, also known as your "attention."

ASPECTS OF MIND	CONSCIOUS MIND (What You Think You Believe)	Mental Faculty Thought Judgment Intellect Reasoning Discrimination Sensory Awareness Attention
	SUBCONSCIOUS MIND (What You Really Believe)	Beliefs Habits Traits Tendencies Conditioning Patterning Brainwashing Memories Experiences Impressions Self-image Emotions

Your subconscious mind, on the other hand, is an impartial computer bank that indelibly records everything you experience. For example, if your schoolteacher said you were a brilliant student and would go far, that experience made an impression on you. If your father said you were a bad child and would never amount to anything, that negative experience left a deep psychological scar. When you were a teenager, perhaps you fell in love with someone who abandoned you. You were devastated and felt undesirable. This wound left a severe, permanent mental blemish.

Similarly, every experience gestates in your subconscious mind and adds to a set of beliefs. The sum total of your beliefs constitutes your ego-identity. When you confront any new situation, such as starting a relationship, changing jobs, or buying a house, you unconsciously reference your subconscious computer bank, and, based on your set of beliefs, you act.

Consider an example: Fred wanted to own a Jaguar. So, he cut out a picture of a Jaguar from a magazine and pasted it on his bedroom wall, because he attended a seminar about posting pictures on his walls to fulfill his desires. Next, Fred said affirmations about his Jaguar. "My Jaguar is coming to me," "I have a Jaguar now," and so on, because he attended a seminar about affirmations. Fred waits for his Jaguar to fall out of the sky and plop onto his driveway.

However, Fred has a deep conviction hidden within his subconscious mind. This conviction began in childhood, when his parents continually complained, "We never have enough, we always have an old, broken-down car, we can't afford a decent car." As a result of his upbringing, Fred's deep, unconscious belief is that he deserves an old broken-down Hyundai.

What Fred *thinks* he believes differs from what he *really* believes. Consciously, Fred *thinks* he believes that he deserves a Jaguar. Yet, subconsciously, he *really* believes that he deserves an old Hyundai. So, what will Fred get? The Hyundai. Because his deepest, unconscious belief determines what he gets.

In this case, Fred's subconscious mind is his master, and his conscious mind is its slave. If you are ignorant of the power of your subconscious beliefs, then those beliefs control you. You are then subject to experiences that you have not consciously chosen and do not consciously desire. This is rather a dismal picture, isn't it? It is depressing to think you could be entirely enslaved by unconscious beliefs. How can you escape this predicament? Can you take control of your destiny rather than being tyrannized by your subconscious mind? Let us consider some possibilities.

How about reprogramming your subconscious mind? Eva, the owner of a New Age center in Toronto, bought expensive subliminal audiotapes to lose weight. She gained twenty pounds listening to the tapes. Why? Because, as the tapes broadcasted affirmations, Eva's subconscious mind fought each affirmation. Listening to the tapes just amplified her negations. Her subconscious mind won each battle—and evidently won the whole war. With subliminal tapes, the muck and mire of your subconscious mind could stir and flood to the surface. Reprogramming the subconscious mind may not be as easy as you think.

What other ways can you attempt to escape the relentless supremacy of your subconscious mind? Have you tried hypnotic suggestion? Have you attempted to release past traumas? Many methods are available for transforming past beliefs. Still, people complain that it is difficult-to-impossible to remove subconscious beliefs. These deeply held habits, which have ruled your destiny for lifetimes, do not disappear overnight.

My experience is that the best way to overcome subconscious programming is to make a profound, fundamental change in your life—to trade in your old, limited ego identity for a new, unlimited identity.

IDENTIFICATION

Your ego is a set of beliefs about yourself that you have come to accept and own. When a person asks, "Who are you?" then you might answer, "My name is so-and-so. I am such-and-such race. I am this tall and have these color eyes and this color hair. I live in this house and have this job. I own this car. I have this education and this bank account." In other words, you define yourself by past experiences.

The term *identification* means that you identify yourself in a limited way, usually by physical characteristics. You cram yourself into an ego identity box that defines you within confines of small boundaries. This limited identity determines how you experience life.

Your ego-identity is who you *think* you are. Yet, who is it that you really are? Indeed, this question is elementary. The answer is in nearly every spiritual book you have ever read, "I AM love, I AM light, I AM a child of God, I AM a part of God." Of course you know who you are—at least you *think* you know. But do you *really* know?

Do you *experience* who you really are? Or is it an intellectual exercise to say the words, "I AM love, I AM light, I AM a child of God"? Do you directly experience who you really are, or are you kidding yourself? When confronted, you might have to admit your incapacity to know, on the deepest level, who you really are.

Many spiritual books and teachers extol the experience of knowing who you really are, but they do not provide direct experience. This could be likened to a description of a strawberry: "This beautiful strawberry is a gorgeous red color, with little yellow specks and a beautiful bright green stem. It is so juicy, luscious, sweet, and yummy." Yet, until you hold that strawberry in your hand, and then bite into it and eat it, you will never know what a strawberry is.

> Knowledge is of two kinds, that which is heard, and that which is felt directly in the heart; The heart yields not full fruit until it comes home to the soul by some experience.
>
> —ARABIAN MAXIM

Similarly, identifying yourself as limitlessness, as boundlessness, as "I AM that I AM," as a God-being, comes from direct experience, not intellectualization. "*Who are you?*" cannot be fathomed in this ordinary waking state of consciousness. It can be known when directly experienced within, in meditation. Once you attain higher consciousness, then you can know by direct revelation, "I AM God, I AM Light, I AM Love, I AM Truth, I AM the resurrection and the life, I AM perfection everywhere now."

True unification with God releases limited, previously held beliefs about yourself and expands your old ego-identity box. Now is the time to trade in your old box for a new one—a box without sides, top or bottom, infinitely large, flexible, and unbounded. This new box identifies you as God within, which brings freedom, enlightenment, and unbounded awareness in bliss-consciousness.

When you change the way you see yourself, then the way you see the world changes. The world around you changes. How you see others changes. The way others see you changes. Your capacity to fulfill your desires increases. Letting go of old, undesirable subconscious beliefs becomes viable.

Indeed, the only way your subconscious mind can permanently change is from such a fundamental transformation of your inner identity.

"WHO AM I?" EXERCISE

Let us do an exercise now. Take out a piece of paper. On the top of the page, write the words, "Who AM I?" Then, on the left side of the page, write "Who I Think I Am," and on the right side, write "Who I Really Am." On the left side of the page, make a list of how you identify yourself. On the right side, list the appropriate correlates that indicate who you really are. Your paper might look something like this:

WHO AM I?	
WHO I THINK I AM	**WHO I REALLY AM**
1. My name is Jane Anderson.	1. My true identity is Spirit within.
2. I am 5' 5" tall and have blue eyes.	2. I have a light body without boundaries.
3. I live in Springfield, Missouri.	3. I live in the heart of God.
4. I have a husband and three children.	4. I am a child of God.
5. I went to California University.	5. I have unlimited knowledge and wisdom within.
6. I am an office administrator.	6. I fulfill my purpose by doing God's will.
7. I have $26,000 in my bank account.	7. I am always richly provided for.
8. My life is difficult and challenging.	8. My life is filled with wonders and miracles.

When you experience yourself as who-you-*really*-are, rather than who-you-*think*-you-are, then you identify with your true nature of being—your God self. You can then overcome limitations and operate from a new level, from the divine will rather than egoic will. This new level of consciousness brings peace, comfort, and divine direction.

No longer do you operate with a limited identity that caused lack of fulfillment. Now you have the support of the almighty creator, the one power that manifests all good, abundance, grace, glory—God the good, omnipotent. Unifying with that power brings spontaneous fulfillment of all desires. As captain of your ship, you can make your heartfelt dreams come true.

Cease to identify yourself with race, clan, name, form, and walk of life. These belong to the body, the garment of decay. Cease to follow the way of the world, cease to follow the way of the flesh, cease to follow the way of tradition. Get rid of this false identification and know the true Atman [God self].

—LORD SHANKARA

THREE TYPES OF KARMA

As you learned earlier, the word *karma* means "action." The law of karma is the law of consequences of action: action-and-reaction or cause-and-effect.

TYPE OF KARMA	INTENSITY OF KARMA
SANCHITA The mountain of Karma	**DROODHA** Heavy tendencies
PRARABDHA A portion of the mountain of Karma for this incarnation	**ADROODHA** Light tendencies
KRIYAMANI AND AGAMI The Karma that is created moment by moment	**DROODHA/ADROODHA** Medium tendencies

Please refer to the illustration on page 44. The sum total of all your past thoughts, words, and actions is called *sanchita karma* in Sanskrit. That is a big mountain of impressions held in your subconscious mind—an indelible record of every experience you have ever had in this or any past life. When you take birth, you break a chunk off the mountain in order to accomplish your path and purpose for this lifetime. This chunk, *prarabdha karma*, based on your beliefs, choices, and habits, determines your life experiences.

There is another factor, however—your free will, which finds creative solutions to karmic situations. Your ability to conceive those solutions is *agami karma*. You implement those choices through *kriyamani karma*, which you create each moment with every thought, word, and action. You can mitigate or change future events by free will. Yet, your free will is limited by your past experiences and resultant self-image.

For example, Roger was raised in a poor family, had a low-paying job, and considered himself a second-class citizen. His boss invited all his employees to a party at an opulent mansion. A beautiful woman drove up in an expensive car, unescorted. She slinked out of her car and breezed by Roger, smiling welcomingly. Roger was stunned that this gorgeous woman appeared to be flirting with him. But a nagging voice inside said, "She can't be attracted to you." Though he wanted to ask her to dance, he did not. Paralyzed by shyness, he missed the opportunity and drove home alone, demoralized. Roger created kriyamani karma corresponding to his prarabdha karma—his past beliefs about himself.

However, Roger could have conceived of a better solution. He could have used agami karma to transform his unworthiness into self-confidence and then used kriyamani karma to act in accord with that higher opinion of himself. He could have created new kriyamani karma—a wonderful new relationship with an attractive woman.

Your prarabdha karma is of three types: *droodha, adroodha,* or *droodha/adroodha.* These three types are the measure of severity, or intensity of your belief pattern concerning a certain area of life. Droodha is defined as difficult to overcome, like a line etched into stone. Adroodha is easy to overcome, like a line drawn in the sand. Droodha/adroodha is in between, like a line etched on wood.

For example, suppose that maintaining loving relationships is easy for you. Imagine, however, that it is difficult for you to make money. Then, in the area of money, you would have negative droodha karma. Each person's karmic setup is unique. Some find it easy to manipulate certain areas of life that others find difficult.

Imagine going out to the store and buying a quart of milk. Now imagine a starving person in an impoverished area, squatting on the dirt, not knowing where to get the next meal. Would it be easy for that person to get that quart of milk? No. For that person, negative droodha karma prevents it.

It is easy to fulfill desires that are easy to fulfill. It is difficult to fulfill desires that are difficult to fulfill. Simple, but true. You can easily get what you believe you can get. I have never met a person who prays for things that they can obtain without effort. They only pray for things that they doubt they can achieve.

ASTROLOGY

Do you believe your fate is determined by the stars? Not so. Your astrology chart does *not* shape your destiny. *You* do. *You* shape your *own* stars. Are you surprised? Here is the truth about astrology.

Your soul precisely calculated your birth time and place in which the planets aligned in a configuration that perfectly reflected your set of beliefs. The moment you took your first breath, the planets formed a specific pattern in the sky. This map of your set of beliefs and choices for this incarnation (your "mental law") is called your horoscope.

Some gifted astrologers are capable of reading this map accurately. They can foresee the exact timing of events. But they are not reading the influence of stars. Rather, they are reading the choices you made by incarnating at a particular time and place, under a particular pattern of stars. Such remarkable astrologers can read the blueprint of *"it is done unto you as you believe."* They can foresee what would be *"done unto you"* if you were to continue to foster the same beliefs as at your moment of birth.

Your astrology chart is a catalog of your beliefs that can be read like a book. It indicates, for instance, what type of mother and father you chose, according to your beliefs. It states whether you chose to have children, according to your beliefs. It shows what your marriage and your spouse would be like, according to your beliefs.

Your astrology chart is an accurate map of the experiences you have chosen for this incarnation—your prarabdha karma. Those choices can change any moment. You have complete control over your astrology chart. It does not control you. You can change the mental law that you had at birth into a new set of laws. Thereby you can create a new destiny.

WHAT ARE YOUR CHOICES?

Life is much simpler than you might think. You can make one of two choices in each moment. You can either: (1) do things that make you happy, or (2) do things that make you suffer. It is that simple.

You may argue that you have no control over your happiness or suffering. However, if you are not in control, then who is? You have freedom of choice and are fully responsible for everything that happens. Get over the idea that you are a victim. Your life is simple. You can walk the path of happiness and love, or suffering and fear. You are in charge of your destiny, and you create heaven or hell on Earth by your choices. You can choose light or darkness, happiness or suffering.

You are in charge, so choose wisely.

In the next chapter, you will discover the mental laws that have governed your life and how you can change them.

5 YOUR MENTAL LEGISLATURE

IF YOU DO NOT BELIEVE YOU CAN HAVE IT ALL, THEN YOU GET TO
CHOOSE HOW MUCH LESS THAN ALL YOU WILL HAVE."
—*Unknown*

*W*hat are the beliefs that govern your life? What are the laws that determine who you think you are, based upon false notions about yourself? In this chapter, you will discover the mental laws that have shaped your destiny. You are not restricted by these laws, yet you believe yourself to be.

STATUTES OF YOUR MENTAL LAW

Who-you-*think*-you-are is not who-you-*really*-are. Who you *think* you are is a limited being, controlled by beliefs, rules, and laws invented by your mind. Who you *really* are is a magnificent being of divine light, love, and unlimited power.

You have created a subconscious set of beliefs—your "mental law." The statutes of this mental law are built of false mental constructs about who you think you are. These beliefs stem from both internal and external influences. Past and present negative environmental influences can and do prevent you from fulfilling your divine purpose. As a result of these influences, you may find yourself frustrated, unhappy, and incomplete.

INTERNAL INFLUENCES
You may have internalized and accepted indoctrination from authority figures and institutions from your past. These influences become part of you

INFLUENCES WITHIN AND AROUND YOU	
INTERNAL INFLUENCES	Societal Brainwashing Educational Brainwashing Religious Brainwashing Parental Brainwashing Memories Past Experiences Concepts and Ideas Thought Forms Belief Systems or "isms"
ENVIRONMENTAL INFLUENCES	Pressure from Loved Ones Peer Pressure Societal Beliefs Media Hype Environ-mental Static Race-mind Consciousness Collective Unconscious

when you allow them to occupy your subconscious mind. Then you own these beliefs, or more precisely, they own you. Here are some examples:

Educational institutions say, "Do not think for yourself; do not have original ideas; think linearly and not intuitively: the mind is superior to the heart; do not think outside the bounds of academia."

Religious organizations say, "Our religion is the only way to heaven; you were born in sin; our scripture is the only truth; you are condemned to hellfire and damnation if you do not follow our religion."

Parental brainwashing may have said, "Be a nice little child; do not be loud; girls never get angry; boys never cry; boys never act like sissies; children should be seen and not heard; you are a bad child; you will never amount to anything."

Our society says, "Follow our rules and be 'normal'; people with money, status, celebrity, and power are superior; college-educated Caucasian males are superior; other people are inferior."

Your past memories and experiences may have taught you, "You are unworthy; you are a failure; you are incompetent; you are an idiot; you are ugly; you are not good enough; you are unpopular; you are poor; you are fat; you are shameful."

These influences crystallize into thought-forms (belief patterns that take concrete shape) that make up two aspects of your subtle body: your mental body (mind) and facade body (ego). You can read more about your subtle body in my books *Exploring Auras* and *Exploring Chakras*.

ENVIRONMENTAL INFLUENCES

Environ-mental influences include negative, draining vibrations and thought-forms in your surroundings. Here are a few examples:

Family members may pressure you to act in ways they "approve of." They may say, "Be like us; conform to our beliefs; wake up and get real; do not follow ridiculous dreams; you cannot possibly succeed in chasing impossible fantasies."

Media hype says, "Youth is valuable and old age is worthless; women are unattractive unless they are rail-thin, long-legged, and large-breasted; our product will make you glamorous, sexy, rich, and attractive; our product will bring you happiness."

The collective unconscious mind of humanity brainwashes you to believe: "Men are superior to women; women do not deserve equal pay; women are weaker; women are taken advantage of; it is a man's world; rich people exploit the poor; poor people never get an even break; rich people are not spiritual; spiritual people must be poor; power and money make people superior."

"Environ-mental static" is an oppressive feeling in your surroundings, such as claustrophobia in a crowded subway, sports event, or concert, or creepy vibrations in an old building, home, theater, hospital, mental institution, bar, educational institution, or prison.

The collective mind or "race-mind" (collection of beliefs of the human race) is an aggregation of dense, conditioned beliefs that blocks people from their life purpose. Thankfully, this dirty, thick, thought-form cloud has been thinning over the past fifty years, due to prayers, meditations, and intentions of so many people worldwide. However, we still have a long way to go before humans can instantaneously fulfill their desires in an atmosphere of support, love, joy, and freedom.

YOUR INNER JUDGE AND JURY

The "race-mind" or "mass consciousness" perpetuates beliefs of reward and punishment, retribution and vengeance. From childhood, these beliefs implanted fear and guilt in your mind. Parents and society taught you conditional love, judgment, and condemnation. Didn't you learn that "good" children are rewarded, while "bad" children are punished?

This belief in good-and-bad/right-and-wrong is likely so ingrained that you do not think twice about it. In fact, your most driving motive may be the need for approval as a "good" child. Once your outer judges (parents, teachers, church, society, loved ones, and peers) are absent, then your inner subconscious condemner takes over to dispense rewards and punishments. You become your own inner judge and jury.

You are thinking tens of thousands of thoughts every day. If the majority is characterized by condemnation, guilt, and blame, then the result is obvious, for *"it is done unto you as you believe."* Your daily experience would be self-inflicted punishment along with a few rewards thrown in for rare "good deeds."

Do you punish yourself with self-destructive, self-sabotaging attitudes? Even at this instant, are you condemning yourself because you think I just pointed out how "bad" you are by creating such experiences?

YOUR INNER SHERIFF

How does your subconscious judge and jury function? It compares your every action with subconscious, idealistic, unrealistic models that you previously labeled "good" or "bad." These models are based on learned experiences and judgments. Your complex unconscious computer calculates your every action and files it under "good" or "bad." If your action is deemed "good" by your inner jury, then a prize is awarded by your inner judge. If it is considered "bad," then a punishment is imposed by your inner sheriff.

Your prize or reward may be a feeling of love, happiness, joyfulness, or euphoria. Or you may receive a material reward, such as money, gifts, honor, praise, or fame. Your punishment may be a feeling of depression, guilt, confusion, anger, fear, or sadness. Or it may appear as illness, violence, theft, poverty, accident, loss, or death.

Because *"it is done unto you as you believe,"* you subconsciously request reward or punishment. Then it is delivered by the law of cause and effect, which fulfills every subconscious order. Your demand for reward or punishment attracts the "justice" that you unconsciously feel you deserve. This dispensation is either meted out immediately or it may be delayed, even until a future incarnation.

How Judgment Occurs

God fulfills every subconscious demand, whether for reward or punishment, for God is completely impartial and judges not. God always says "yes" to every request.

Here is an example: Gwen's husband criticized her early in the morning and, as a result, she felt angry and guilty. Agitated, defensive, and fearful, she became impatient during breakfast, and she yelled at her children. Gwen succumbed to guilt and blame, and she judged herself harshly. When her children left for school, she felt even more ashamed. She believed she was a "bad girl."

When Gwen got into her car and set out to the grocery store, she did not notice the car coming from the right at an intersection. An accident occurred and she was slightly injured. Gwen's thought-forms of guilt projected into the universe and magnetized punishment. Her unconscious need to be punished was fulfilled in the form of an automobile accident.

In fact, everything "bad" that ever happens "to you" is a result of your subconscious demand to be punished. Please, now pause for a moment and digest this truth. Every time you think you were victimized, you were fulfilling your own unconscious need for a reprimand. You requested this punishment yourself.

WHY CHILDREN SUFFER

Why do infants or young children suffer? Why would God punish innocent babies? The fact is *"it is done unto you as you believe."* Even babies are fully responsible for their lives. Before birth, all infants chose the particular family and situation to be born into, according to their beliefs. It is difficult to fathom why an infant would choose to be born into harsh circumstances. Here are a few possibilities:

1. The baby felt guilt or shame about past life actions and chose to be born into punishing circumstances.
2. The baby decided to learn or to teach something through being born into a particular family.
4. The baby agreed to fulfill a demand for punishment that had been requested by his/her parents.
5. The baby had made a contract to teach love or compassion to others.

COLLECTIVE PUNISHMENT

Punishment might take place on an individual or collective level. Groups of people may attract collective punishment. In other words, as a group, they subconsciously demand punishment and thereby invite natural disasters, societal problems, war, famine, drought, or other collective calamities. They also have the power to prevent such tragedies.

For decades, many prophets have predicted that part of the State of California would fall into the ocean. Many dates were predicted for this disaster. However, so far, it has not happened. Why? Perhaps the people of California, as a collective consciousness, changed the outcome due to their prayers and meditations.

We all have free will, both individually and collectively, to attract the outcome that we believe we deserve, by our individual thoughts, words, and deeds, and by our collective thoughts, words, and deeds. These results occur immediately or as a delayed reaction.

HARD PILL TO SWALLOW

Who is responsible for your life? Can you blame others for your problems? In fact, you are the sole author of your destiny. You are not a victim of anyone or anything.

You unconsciously demand all your experiences, and you deliver to others the experiences they subconsciously request. All experiences, whether peaceful or violent, loving or hateful, happy or unhappy, are created by all parties involved. So-called victims of violence simply ordered their subconscious request and then reaped the result. Others are fulfilling your needs, and you are fulfilling others' needs.

This truth may be a hard pill to swallow. When you consider that molested children, handicapped people, crime victims, and sufferers of horrible diseases have caused their own trouble, doesn't your mind resist such a seemingly heartless philosophy? Doesn't your heart cry out when you see unfortunate people suffer? Your innate desire is to reach out to those who are abused, mistreated, or ill. This predisposition for compassion, charity, humanitarianism, service, and human kindness is a natural and necessary human trait.

Therefore, it is essential to continue charitable work—supporting soup kitchens, visiting those in prisons, and caring for the ailing, elderly, disabled, and mentally ill. Yet, at the same time, it is important to comprehend to what extent you create your own circumstances.

By opening to the possibility that what I propose is true, you can begin to fathom how utterly relentless the law of karma is. After all, your subconscious mind always wins, and your conscious mind always loses. Without fail, you create your destiny based on your deepest unconscious beliefs. However, stewing in guilt and shame over what you have created does not serve you.

Instead, can you imagine how you might use the law of karma to your advantage as a tool to take command of your destiny? The inexorable results of karmic law can create good for yourself and others. You can use that same unyielding law to transform your own life and to do beneficent works that lift others. Annie Besant referred to the karmic law as follows: *"It is the law that binds the ignorant but frees the wise."*

It is not necessary to punish yourself anymore. Since you are the creator of your destiny, your self-judgment caused your problems. You can reverse this downward spiral by aligning with truth. By forgiving yourself and raising your level of self-acceptance, you can control your life rather than letting it control you.

GOD ALWAYS SAYS "YES"

Do you believe God wants you to fulfill your desires? Or is God capricious and fickle, rewarding or punishing at a whim, administering judgment based on "right" and "wrong" deeds? You were probably taught that God doles out the appropriate verdict and penalty, depending on whether you are "good" or "bad."

Many religions conceive of God as a kind of Santa Claus. He makes a list, checks it twice, and finds out who is naughty or nice. If you are "good," Santa gives you toys. Similarly, if God regards you as "good," he rewards you with heaven. If God condemns you as "bad," you are sentenced to eternal damnation in hell.

This concept of God-as-Santa is a "conditional" God—one who places demands, mandates, and ultimatums. Such a vengeful God exacts payment for "sins" and "crimes." The logical conclusion is that God could therefore be coerced or won over. In a word, such a God could be bribed.

Is God conditional? Can God be bribed? I believe the almighty creator of this universe could not possibly be bought off. God is unbribable. This almighty divine presence and power does not need baits or enticements from fearful humans.

The truth is that God is not keeping track of your "good" and "bad" actions. You are. God is not punishing or rewarding you. You are. God is doing only one thing: fulfilling your every desire.

God is an infinite shipping department, whose only mission is to fill your orders. Your deepest unconscious beliefs are like order forms, demanding to be filled. God gives you exactly what is placed on your form. God always says "yes" to every order. God is a wish-fulfilling tree that gives you everything you believe you deserve. For example, if you stand in front of a mirror and say, "I am fat, I am fat," then God says, "Yes, I can do that." If you say, "I am poor, I am poor," then God says, "Yes, I can do that." If you say, "I am lonely, I am lonely," then God says, "Yes, I can do that for you."

> When the gods wish to punish us they answer our prayers.
>
> —OSCAR WILDE

TESTS AND TRIALS

Do you believe that God gives you "tests," "lessons," and "trials"? Or do you believe that God only gives you good? Do you believe life is a series of "lessons"? Most New Age teachers contend that you are in "Earth school," enduring an endless assortment of lessons, trials, and tribulations. What do you think? Does God force you to undergo such ordeals?

"It is done unto you as you believe." If you believe that you need to learn "lessons" through "trials," then you have created a mental law for yourself that you will learn this way. If you believe that you do not need lessons, trials, or suffering, then you will not need or undergo these experiences in order to "grow." If you want to be enrolled in "Earth school," then go ahead. Fill out your application, pay your tuition, and begin your semester. Enjoy your education. That is your choice, for *"it is done unto you as you believe."*

I personally do not choose such a path.

I firmly reject the notion of "lessons," "punishments," "trials," "ordeals," "tribulations," "tests," or other nightmares. I declare that my life is filled with joy, ease, comfort, and fulfillment in each moment.

Here is an example: Lorna is so busy that she has no time to get her files organized, so they remain in disarray. Then, she gets into a terrible accident and has to remain in the hospital for a week. During this time, Lorna calls her husband to bring over some financial files that she was neglecting. While in the hospital, she organizes these files. After she recovers from her injuries, Lorna says, "Oh, it was so 'good' that I was in the hospital; I guess it was 'meant to be'; I took time to organize my files and I learned a 'lesson' that I need to keep my files up-to-date."

Is illness ever "good"? Is it necessary to become injured in order to organize your files? If you believe it is, then it will be, for *"it is done unto you as you believe."*

If you create a mental law of punishment, lessons, and trials, then you will experience that. If you believe that God wants only good for you, then you will have only good, for God always says "yes" to every subconscious demand. You can have a glorious life of ease, joy, harmony, love, abundance, and fulfillment. Only it is necessary to get your subconscious mind out of the way and allow God to give you your good.

MYTH OF KARMIC PAYBACK

Why do people have difficult experiences? Why do they suffer? *"It is done unto you as you believe."* They create their own experiences through their mental law.

Imagine a man who committed murder. Would he feel regret? Remorse? Guilt? Probably all of these. Based on these feelings, what might he create for himself? Undoubtedly, he would unconsciously feel the need to punish himself. Either in this life or in a future life, he might magnetize a punishment in order to "pay back the debt."

Perhaps you cannot readily accept that a murderer is the sole determiner of his destiny. You might ask, "What about the hardened criminal without remorse? According to your theory, he will not be punished for his actions. He will get off scot-free!"

The truth is that although there is no karmic lord in the sky exacting punishment on a hardened criminal, that criminal will unquestionably punish himself. The criminal's tough facade may give the impression that he is without remorse, but you can be sure his subconscious mind believes in self-punishment as much as anyone else's. Probably more so. In fact, without a belief in punishment, he could never have committed those criminal acts—acts of punishment.

His negative vibrations of hate, anger, fear, resentment, and coldheartedness will attract the same negative vibrations he is emitting. Therefore, he will magnetize violent, negative experiences. Committing murder causes suffering, whether or not the court inflicts punishment. The murderer will punish himself via the Law of Magnetic Attraction, which attracts like to like, either in this lifetime or a future lifetime. For, *"as thou hast done, it shall be done unto thee: thy reward shall return upon thine own head."* [1]

You operate under a set of personal beliefs, and you create your experiences and chart your destiny accordingly. This "mental law" is determined by past experiences, upbringing, and the influence of society. For example, concepts of illness, old age, accident, injury, fatigue, and death are held in humanity's composite mental law. To the extent that you buy into and assimilate these concepts, you live under these laws. Your every thought, word, and experience adds additional statutes to your personal mental law. You are a complex being operating under a complicated set of rules. But, according to free choice, you may abide by your mental law or you may disobey those rules and create new ones.

"MENTAL LAW" EXERCISE

Now let us do an exercise. Take out a piece of paper. Pretend that you have an empty slate on which to write your destiny. On the left side of the paper, write the mental laws by which you have been governed so far. On the right side of the paper, write a set of laws by which you would like to be governed. Your slate may look something like the following:

MY PERSONAL MENTAL LAWS	
LAWS I HAVE EXPERIENCED	LAWS I WOULD LIKE
1. I rarely get what I want.	1. I always get what I want.
2. I never have enough money.	2. I always have the money I need.
3. I am not very happy.	3. I am a very happy person.
4. I have very few friends.	4. I have a lot of friends.
5. I hate my work.	5. I love my work.
6. I have a difficult family.	6. I have a harmonious family.
7. I am socially uncomfortable.	7. I feel easy in social situations.
8. I can't lose weight.	8. I am slim and trim.
9. I can't see without glasses.	9. I have perfect eyesight.
10. I have no love in my life.	10. I have a wonderful love relationship.

This exercise will help you access the limiting statutes of your personal mental law. These habit-patterns constitute a set of beliefs that you have accepted as truth. Such beliefs determine your destiny.

Now that you have written your paper, let us do a healing prayer to release the negative mental laws and to accept new, positive mental laws. Read the following prayer aloud. When you come to the first blank space, read the list on the left side of your paper: laws that you have been governed by. When you come to the second blank space, read the list on the right side of your paper: laws that you want to be governed by.

MENTAL LAW HEALING PRAYER

I call upon the Holy Spirit
To lovingly, fully, and completely
Heal and release all limiting mental laws
That have governed my life
And have affected me adversely.
I now release all mental laws that no longer serve me.
These error-beliefs are now filled with
Divine love, divine light, and divine truth.
I now release, loose, and let go from my mind
All mental laws of
(negative mental laws).
They are lifted into the light of truth,
Dissolved into the nothingness of what they truly are,
Burnt in the fire of God's love,
And they are gone.
I now accept mental laws that serve my life
In powerful, positive ways.
I now welcome new, positive, uplifting,

Inspiring, joyful mental laws of
(positive mental laws).
I now thank God for manifesting this good in my life,
Under grace, in powerful, positive, perfect ways.
Thank you, wonderful God, and SO IT IS.

You are the creator and maintainer of limiting laws that have determined your limited pathway. You can also cut those shackles free and create joy and fulfillment. You are, in reality, perfect and unlimited. Your only limitations are the restrictions of your personal mental law. Make the choice now to create a new mental law that is only good, good, and very good.

YOU GET WHATEVER YOU WANT

It is wise to get in touch with your true desires and seek to achieve them, because if you do not fulfill them consciously, they may be fulfilled anyway, much to your inconvenience. You may resist a deep unconscious urge to make a major change to a new life path, even when you know it is the wisest choice. As you try desperately to cling to past limitations, your subconscious mind creates such upheaval that you are forced to change anyway. Here is an example:

Jerome always dreamed of becoming a doctor. But his education was cut short when he had to marry his pregnant wife and support his family. Years later, he believed that becoming a doctor was impossible. So, he remained in the job he hated, selling insurance. But deep within Jerome's heart, that desire to become a doctor still subconsciously brewed, sabotaging every opportunity in his sales profession. He unconsciously created problems at work and was fired. He had to borrow money to make his mortgage payments. His car was repossessed.

One day, a friend called Jerome and told him about a scholarship to medical school. Elated, Jerome applied for the scholarship and received it.

He returned to college, and with great strain on family relations and finances, he became a doctor. In retrospect, Jerome declared, "It was all for the best."

But was it "for the best"? The final outcome, becoming a doctor, was for the best. But if Jerome had initially acknowledged his desire to become a doctor and, with full trust in God, made a conscious effort to return to medical school, then he could have created a smooth transition to his new profession, without getting fired, without debt, aggravation, or struggle.

You can control your life rather than letting circumstances control you. Through faith, following your heart, and prayer, you can fulfill your desires without using unconscious pressures to force yourself to accept positive life changes.

In the next chapter, you will discover how you can overcome the mental law and law of karma through the law of grace.

HOW GRACE 6 OVERCOMES KARMA

LET US THEREFORE COME BOLDLY UNTO THE THRONE OF GRACE, THAT
WE MAY OBTAIN MERCY, AND FIND GRACE TO HELP IN TIME OF NEED.
—*Saint Paul[1]*

God is the one power and one presence of pure unconditional love, which knows no blame or retribution. In mercy and compassion, God forgives all seeming human wrongs and errors. In this chapter, you will discover how God's magnificent benevolence reverses the Law of Mind through the Law of Grace.

GREAT KARMIC ERASER

Many clergymen preach that God is a ruthless deity who inflicts punishment on "wrongdoers." Many people feel comforted by such a vengeful God. For if God reprimands "evildoers," then this must be a "just" universe. Have you ever enjoyed self-righteous satisfaction when someone who wronged you received retribution or suffering? However, this desire for vengeance is a decidedly human trait—not a divine one. It makes no sense for that one divine God-source of pure, unconditional love to don a leather hood at night and become an executioner, meting out punishment, death, and destruction on so-called "bad" people.

Because of God's mercy, a "Law of Grace" exists in the cosmos. This sublime source of divine love overcomes and reverses all mental laws. The law of karma and your personal mental law are nullified by the great karmic eraser—the Law of Grace. Grace is the dispenser of benevolent, sacred blessings flowing directly from God. These blessings reflect God's qualities, such as perfection, wisdom, strength, joy, fulfillment, beauty, simplicity, radiance, love, and harmony.

The Law of Grace is the law of "perfection everywhere now." It is absolute perfection, because God is perfection. God is limitless, imperishable, and absolute. God's law of divine grace overcomes all, because God is always victorious and triumphs over all. Therefore, the Law of Grace functions according to the principle, *"With God, all things are possible."* [2]

God can do no wrong and no harm. The Law of Grace is the law of God's absolute benevolence, for God is only good. Grace operates under divine rules, not limited by human conditions. This divine law functions when your consciousness lifts into direct contact with Spirit. *"But if ye be led of the Spirit, ye are not under the law [the mental law of karma]."* [3]

The more you connect with Spirit, follow inner divine guidance, and surrender to divine will, the more grace becomes potent in your life. In harmony with your true purpose, your desires attune to divine desires. Your heart beats with the heart of God. Your body becomes an instrument for God's symphony to play. Your breath is the breath of the Almighty. Your life is divine life.

When you connect with God and become a vehicle of Spirit, then you see the world through the eyes of Spirit. You hear the voice of God. Your hands do the works of God. You walk in God's footsteps. Your heart opens to God's holy presence. Your mind attunes to God's mind.

Great saints have demonstrated the Law of Grace operating continually in their lives. With this divine law, miracles occurred, incredible healings took place, and manifestations of God's power appeared. Jesus demonstrated the Law of Grace with a multitude of miracles, even resurrecting the dead.

GOD IS WHERE YOU ARE

God's Law of Grace is the law of oneness, in which a direct link with God is established in consciousness. It is written in the ancient Upanishads of

India: *"In the beginning...there was that only which is one only, without a second."*[4] In the Torah (Old Testament of the Bible) it is written, *"I am God, and there is none else."*[5] The holiest prayer of Judaism is posted on the doorpost of every Jewish household: *"Hear, O Israel: The Lord our God, the Lord is one."*[6]

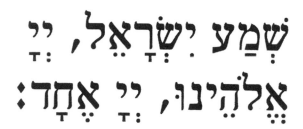

שְׁמַע יִשְׂרָאֵל, יְיָ
אֱלֹהֵינוּ, יְיָ אֶחָד:

The ultimate reality, known in India as Brahman (the impersonal God or absolute pure consciousness), is oneness—one light, one wholeness, one good, one truth, one glory. It is nameless, formless, causeless, motionless, and without beginning or end. There is only one presence and one power in the universe, only one, without duality, without a "second."

Nearly every religious scripture says that God is all there is. Certainly God exists in every particle of creation. There is nowhere that God is not. Right? Then I would ask this: Are you somewhere? Consider this: If God is everywhere, and if you are somewhere, then you must be where God is.

Even though many people believe that God is far away and impossible to reach, the world's scriptures state that God's presence is all-pervading and therefore, by definition, close at hand. God is immanent, attainable, and, indeed, within you.

Judeo-Christian Scriptures

"Am I a God at hand,…and not a God afar off? Can any hide himself in secret places that I shall not see him?…Do not I fill heaven and earth?" [7]

"Be strong and of good courage; be not afraid, neither be thou dismayed: for the Lord thy God is with thee whithersoever thou goest." [8]

Christian Scriptures

"Know ye not that ye are the temple of God, and that the Spirit of God dwelleth in you?" [9]

"Behold, the kingdom of God is within you." [10]

"[God] be not far from every one of us: For in him we live, and move, and have our being." [11]

Islam

"I am in your own souls! Why see ye not? In every breath of yours am I." [12]

"We verily created man and we know what his soul whispereth to him, and We are closer to him than his jugular vein." [13]

Sufi

"He who has found the Loved One in himself—for him God is not He, nor Thou, but I." [14]

"Verily the I, the Self, am God; None other than the Supreme Self is God." [15]

Buddhist

"This very mind is the Buddha." [16]

"Every being has the Buddha Nature. This is the self." [17]

Zen Buddhist

"Why not seek in one's own mind the sudden realization of the original nature of True Thusness?…If we understand our minds and see our nature, we shall achieve Buddhahood ourselves." [18]

Taoist

"Find the Tao in yourself and you know everything else." [19]

Sikh

"As fragrance dwells in a flower, and reflection in a mirror, so does God dwell inside everything; seek Him, therefore, in your heart." [20]

"Ever is He present with you—think not He is far: By the Master's teaching recognize Him within yourself." [21]

Jain

"May He abide always within my heart, the Supreme Self, the One God of all gods; Transcending all this-world's ephemera, by deepest meditation reachable!" [22]

Hindu

"Salutations to the Transcendental Being; Who is immanent in all creation, being Pure Consciousness, ever free, witness of all action; Which is none other than my own Self divine." [23]

"I am the True, the Real, Brahma. That thou art also. The heart of man is the abode of God." [24]

Ancient Egypt

"For the Lord manifests himself ungrudgingly throughout all the universe; and you can behold God's image with your eyes, and lay hold on it with your hands." [25]

SURRENDER TO GOD'S WILL

How can you activate the Law of Grace in your life? The key is to surrender your heart to the will of God. You have a deep connection to God within your soul. That profound link can be realized and activated. For this loving presence of God is within you, as you, at your very center of being.

It is your higher self, the holy one within, your divine guide, beauteous inner teacher, and deepest love of your heart.

The most important commandment of the Torah is: *"And thou shalt love the Lord thy God with all thine heart, and with all thy soul, and with all thy might."* [26]

This most profound of all commandments is the secret to activating the Law of Grace. With God as your foremost priority, your life rides on waves of grace. With God as your first love, you dwell in God's loving presence and are held in God's adoring arms. When God is at work in your life, grace is at work, bringing perfect peace. Your life is blessed with grace.

"Now therefore, I pray thee, if I have found grace in thy sight, show me now thy way, that I may know thee, that I may find grace in thy sight." [27]

God's presence cannot be realized through force, effort, mood-making, or intellectualization. God realization can only be fathomed through direct mystical contact. How does this occur? Through meditation. When you enter the holy chamber of the most high within your heart, then you dwell in the house of the Lord.

"He that dwelleth in the secret place of the most High shall abide under the shadow of the Almighty. I will say of the Lord, He is my refuge and my fortress: my God; in him will I trust." [28]

The key to grace is to experience the holy presence of God within you. God's grace flows through you as waves of bliss, power, energy, and fulfillment. God's light pours into your being and fills you with untold blessings. You are the light that God is, that exquisite light within your being.

Unified with God, you operate under the Law of Grace: *"Surely goodness and mercy shall follow me all the days of my life: and I will dwell in the house of the Lord forever."* [29]

Jesus exemplified perfect unification with God. He surrendered completely to that holy presence and aligned to God's will in each moment. He said, *"I can of mine own self do nothing: as I hear I judge: and my judgment is just; because I seek not mine own will, but the will of the Father which hath sent me."* [30] *"For I came down from heaven, not to do mine own will, but the will of him that sent me."* [31]

As long as you continue the same old mind-set under which you have operated until now, the gates to God's holy presence will be locked shut. To unlock those gates, you must change your mind. Transform from a state of separation and disintegration. Unify with God.

"And be not conformed to this world; but be ye transformed by the renewing of your mind, that ye may prove what is that good, and acceptable, and perfect, will of God." [32]

By consorting with the world of materialism, the blessings of God's grace will recede from your grasp. By beckoning the holy presence of God, the gates of heavens will open, and you will sit on the throne of God, glorified in grace.

"That he would grant you, according to the riches of his glory, to be strengthened with might by his Spirit in the inner man." [33]

FOLLOWING INNER GUIDANCE

The blessings of grace flow into your being through the presence of God, the love of God, the light of God, the power of God, and the Word of God. God's Word within your heart is the *"still small voice"* [34] within. That is the Word to cling to. That is the place of perfect peace wherein God dwells.

Allow that loving divine presence to overtake your being. Surrender to that inner divinity and trust the loving "still small voice" within. Follow your inner guidance and allow the blessings of Spirit to flow freely from the unlimited cornucopia of light and love—God the good, the fountainhead of grace. You have the power to transform your life by submitting to the direction of Spirit, which leads you on the pathway to glory.

Following the guidance of God's inner voice is challenging, but it is definitely worthwhile. When you place yourself in the hands of God, your life takes on new meaning and tenor. You are guided to do that which is of highest wisdom, not only for yourself, but also for others—indeed, for the entire universe. You live your true purpose—that which you came on Earth to do.

When you surrender your individual will to God's will, then you are no longer subject to karmic law. Now, the Law of Grace directs your life. You operate under God's rules—the laws of wonders and statutes of marvels. When you trust and follow inner guidance, your life becomes miraculous. Little coincidences that are not really coincidental are common everyday occurrences. You find yourself in the right place at the right time and the right people show up.

What God has in mind for you is much more than you could ever imagine. God's plan for your life is the road of glory—the pathway of divine joy, prosperity, fulfillment, and peace of mind. God's design will bring you into new, powerful directions. You will be led to develop your true talents and creative expression. You may not think that you are special, but God does.

WHEN I FOLLOWED INNER GUIDANCE

In my own life, I do my best to follow divine guidance on a daily basis, even though it has been extremely challenging. For example, I followed that inner voice during each step of writing and publishing my first book, *Divine Revelation*. The book seemed to write itself. It was written by Spirit. Then, I asked my higher self how to get it published. My inner voice told me to find a literary agent.

I had a gut-feeling about one agent, Jeff Herman. However, this made no sense, because he represents business books, not spiritual books. Yet, I knew he would be the best agent for me. However, I did not have enough faith to just send my proposal to Jeff. So, I sent it to thirty agents. Amazingly, the first one to respond was Jeff. He phoned me within two days after receiving my proposal. So, I signed the contract with Jeff.

Then I proceeded to brag to all my friends about my big shot New York agent, what a big publisher I would get, and how important I was. Meanwhile, Jeff attempted to sell my manuscript to several publishers. He received some rejections.

Suddenly, I got a letter from the Jeff Herman Literary Agency: "We are very sorry, but we have had a staff shortage in our agency, and we can no longer represent you." I was devastated. After all, I had invested so much of my ego in this agent.

I went into meditation and received a strange message from my higher self: "No, Jeff Herman is still your agent. Don't sign with another agent and don't try to sell the book yourself." This message made no sense. I could have signed with other agents who wanted to represent me, or I could have found a small publisher.

Yet, I trusted this bizarre message, because I knew it was true. So, I wrote to Jeff, the business book agent: "My intuition says that you would be the best agent to represent me." You can imagine what happened after that—nothing. Months rolled by with no response.

Finally, I was thrilled to receive a letter from Jeff Herman—until I opened it: "We are very happy you have so much faith in us—but we still cannot represent you."

I went back into meditation. Surprisingly, I got the same message again: "Jeff Herman is still your agent. Don't sign with another agent and don't try sell the book yourself." So I sent Jeff a second letter, "My intuition still says you would be the best agent for me." Months went by. Meanwhile, my manuscript sat on the table, gathering cobwebs and dust.

It was extremely challenging to follow this inner guidance. I am not the kind of person to willingly do nothing when I want to get something done. Yet I had full faith that my inner message was true. I knew it and trusted it.

Then, Jeff Herman phoned me out of the blue: "We are very impressed with your perseverance. We have decided to represent you. Come to my office and meet my partner. We are going to handle your book."

I went to Jeff's office in downtown Manhattan. All the business books were stacked on the wall. Needless to say, I felt out of place. His partner walked in—a beautiful woman with long, black, curly hair. Immediately I felt a heartfelt affinity toward her. It turned out the woman who worked in the business book agency was a psychic! And she gave me a psychic reading! Very strange. Anyway, I realized that perhaps this was the reason I was guided to stay with this agency.

It turned out well. Several months later, Jeff telephoned to say he had sold the book to Simon & Schuster. When I realized he had sold this book, written by a first-time, unknown, spiritual author who knows nothing about writing to the biggest publisher in the world, I nearly went into cardiac arrest! If you know anything about publishing, you realize it is a total miracle this book was published by Simon & Schuster.

Furthermore, I never studied writing in school. I went to art college. Yet, my editor said it was the best written book she had ever edited since she started working for Simon & Schuster. By listening to my "still small voice" and trusting its guidance with faith, many miracles have occurred in my life. Miracles can happen for you, too.

WHEN I DID NOT FOLLOW INNER GUIDANCE

We often regret when we do not follow intuition and miss opportunities or get into trouble. What happened to me when I did not listen to inner guidance?

I have lived in a van, a trailer, or a motor home since 1989. I used to live in an Airstream travel trailer. In 1993, my trailer was parked in New Jersey in an industrial park that had twenty-four-hour security. My inner guidance told me to get a job as a security guard there. So, I donned my little hat, badge, and little outfit, and I became a security guard. Needless to say, security guards do not have a whole lot to do. I brought my computer to the guardhouse, where I edited my book during my daily shift. This job served me wonderfully for about one year.

Then I started receiving the message from my higher self: "Quit the job." Yet I consciously rebelled against this inner guidance. I decided not to quit, because I was living in fear. I was terrified that if I quit my pathetic minimum wage job, I would not have enough money to survive.

Six months later, one afternoon at work my relief did not show up. I called the office to report it. In a security job, you have to wait for your relief. My supervisor said that my relief would arrive in half an hour. I waited one hour. No relief. I called the supervisor again and said, "I have a meditation class to teach tonight with students waiting for me, and I have to leave."

Long story short, I abandoned my post. In a security job, if you leave your post, you are in trouble. The next day, when I called the security office, I discovered that no one came to relieve me the entire night. The supervisor said, "You are terminated."

Immediately, my higher self, God within me, my guardian angels— whatever you want to call it—started having a party. Balloons went off. There was cheering, singing, dancing, music, and reveling. "She finally got rid of that job!"

However, in the midst of this celebration, I rebelled. I phoned the supervisor and begged for my job back. Believe it or not, he gave it back to me. He told me to go back to work the very next day.

My next day at work, at the end of the day I circled the property, closing and locking the big truck gates. At the back entrance was an eight-foot-tall, wrought iron gate, which I pulled on. It did not close. I tried again. It would not budge. I could not figure out why. Suddenly, this giant gate toppled over on top of me. It struck my head, then my shoulder, and, as I tried to run from it, it knocked me over and caught my legs. I was pinned under the gate, screaming bloody murder.

Luckily, a few moments later, a man pulled up in his truck to this abandoned area near the back gate. He had forgotten something at work and came back to retrieve it. This man heard me yelling at the top of my lungs. He tried to lift the gate from my legs. It was so heavy that he could only lift it a few inches. Thank God, he told me, "Don't move," while he called the EMS and police. The EMS came and shuffled me onto the ambulance.

It turned out that my leg had nearly been severed in half. It was hanging on by a few sinews. All totaled, I endured four hospital stays, two operations, and over $100,000 in hospital bills. Over a decade later, I still have not completely recovered from this injury.

Moral of this story: Listen to your higher self and follow its guidance. Otherwise, gates may come crashing down on your head!

Read and study my book, *Divine Revelation*, or take classes to learn how to listen to, trust, and follow the "still small voice" within. Visit my website www.divinerevelation.org to learn more.

BREAKING THE SPELL OF KARMA

How do you break the hypnotic spell of karmic law under which you have been operating? If you believe you are subject to karmic law, then you are, for *"it is done unto you according to your belief."* [35] However, once you accept the Law of Grace, then the spell of karma is broken. It no longer controls you. The Law of Grace instantaneously dispels all limiting beliefs.

"For the law of the Spirit of life in Christ Jesus hath made me free from the law of sin and death [law of karma]." [36]

When you know that the Law of Grace (God's law) overcomes your mental law, then you are free from that erroneous, man-made law. Lord Krishna said, *"As the blazing fire turns fuel to ashes, O Arjuna, so does the fire of wisdom turn all karma into ashes."* [37]

You are free from all past "sin" when grace is at work in your life: *"For sin shall not have dominion over you: for ye are not under law [the law of karma], but under grace."* [38] The Law of Grace is the law of perfection everywhere now, without sin. Since God's grace is all that is, sin has no place in God's world. Sin could be defined as an acronym for "Self-Inflicted Nonsense," because it is not real. It is an error-belief held in mind—a logical belief with the wrong premise coming to the wrong conclusion.

"ORIGINAL SIN"

The "original sin" is believed to be the "fall of man." By virtue of that sin, all humans are said to be "sinners." What is original sin, anyway? In the Bible, the primal man Adam lives in paradise in the Garden of Eden. God tells Adam, *"Of every tree of the garden thou mayest freely eat: But of the tree of the knowledge of good and evil, thou shalt not eat of it: for in the day that thou eatest thereof thou shalt surely die."* [39]

God creates Eve, the first woman, from Adam's rib. Once Eve is created, the couple lives in perfect peace, following God's will, in harmony with all life. They are naked, without shame or guilt. Eve is then tempted by a serpent to eat the fruit of the forbidden tree. She eats the fruit and gives it to Adam. Then their *"eyes were opened, and they knew that they were naked."* [40] They make garments of fig leaves. Of course, God catches them in the act.

This story is not a history lesson. It is a parable about the human condition right here, right now, every day. The meaning of this parable is as follows:

The birthright of Adam and Eve (humanity) is to live eternal life in a paradisiacal state of union with God, without shame, guilt, or other negative beliefs. This is the state of grace—immortal life, without "sin" (error-thinking). Adam and Eve represent two aspects of higher consciousness mentioned in the ancient scriptures of India: Adam the male, *Aham* ("I") or *Shiva* aspect; and Eve the female, *Idam* ("This") or *Shakti* aspect. Or *yin* and *yang* in Taoist philosophy. When Eve is created out of Adam, then duality is born from oneness. Still, they live in paradise, because yin and yang are in equilibrium.

Then a serpent, representing *maya* ("measure": limitation or illusion), tempts Eve to eat the fruit of the tree of "knowledge of good and evil" or dual thinking (good/bad, life/death, right/wrong, and so on). Ego is born from this false identification with duality (*pragya aparadh* in Sanskrit, "the mistake of the intellect"). This is the "fall from grace."

Thus, suffering and shame are born. One searches for fig leaves to cover oneself. Separation from God is born from eating of the tree of duality. "Sin" is this mistaken belief, this error-thought—the illusion of ego, which cuts you off from God and identifies you with negation.

GRACE WORKS THROUGH FAITH

At the moment a diseased woman touched the hem of Jesus' garment, the Law of Grace conquered her mental law, which had caused a blood issuance for twelve years. Although she had spent all her money on physicians, her illness worsened. Yet, through faith, she surrendered to God with complete conviction: *"If I may touch but his clothes, I shall be whole."* [41] Thus, when she touched Jesus' garment, she was healed instantaneously. Jesus then said to her, *"Thy faith hath made thee whole."* [42]

Through faith, you can activate the Law of Grace. In that instant, grace is at work, bringing untold wonders and miracles. Moses, great prophet, miracle-maker, and author of the Torah, attained perfect intimacy with God. Thus, he could carry on two-way conversations with God: *"The Lord spake unto Moses face to face, as a man speaketh unto his friend. Thou hast found grace in my sight, and I know thee by name."* [43]

You can do this, too.

The Law of Grace works through faith. Faith is the healer, the miracle-maker, the power that says, *"All things are possible."* [44] Faith is the key that unlocks the door to the immutable Law of Grace, the law of bountiful mercy that forgives all "sin" (error-thinking) and dismisses all "debts" (belief in reward and punishment). God, the all-forgiving, grants unlimited pardon for "wrongdoings" and, in unconditional love, bestows divine grace, the tangible, earthly proof of God's existence and God's love.

Faith can annihilate the statutes of your mental law. You can consciously write your own laws of destiny and unlock the door to the unassailable Law of Grace. All you need do is ask: *"Ask, and it shall be given you."* [45]

This book will show you how to ASK and get results.

GOD FORGIVES

God does not condemn, but absolves from all "sin." There is no karmic accountant in the sky, recording your "sins" and then dispensing punishment. There is only complete absolution from God for all seeming sins. For God is not the divine executioner, but the divine exonerator, the dispenser of unlimited blessings. God grants unlimited pardon for "wrongdoings." And God forgives all your "debts" (beliefs in retribution). God is your forgiving and releasing power. God, the all-forgiving one, is with you always, as perfect divine mercy, compassion, and benevolence.

The tradition of forgiveness is well-established in the Judeo-Christian tradition. *"Forgive us our debts, as we forgive our debtors."* [46] In the Jewish religion, every year your "sins" and "debts" against God are forgiven on Yom Kippur, the Day of Atonement (At One-ment with God). According to the Torah, on the seventh year, at the feast of tabernacles (*Succoth*), all debts against humans are forgiven and cancelled. This is called the "Lord's release." [47] Every fiftieth year is celebrated as a jubilee year, when all slaves are returned home to their families and all possessions are restored. [48]

GRACE, THE GIFT OF GOD

Since God is unconditional love, that merciful divine presence, the all-benevolent and all-compassionate, freely dispenses all divine blessings as gifts. These gifts are given in purity, without exacting payment. *"By grace are ye saved through faith; and that not of yourselves: it is the gift of God: Not of works, lest any man should boast."* [49]

You might be wondering right now, "How could God give me what I want without asking for something in return?" In fact, often people "bargain" with God in their prayers. Have you ever tried to negotiate with God? However, the truth is that God has no preconceived notions about what you "should" or "should not" do. God makes no demands, mandates, or stipulations. God needs nothing from you—not your worship, not your sacrifices, or martyrdom.

You can, however, lift your consciousness into a state whereby the divine spigot opens for heavenly blessings to flow. God's grace is like an underground spring. You can drill a well and bring the cool, fresh water of God's unlimited fountainhead of divine blessings up to the surface. All you need is to open your heart to these beauteous blessings. All that is required is sincerity and faith. For, with unadulterated, supreme love, God unreservedly bestows divine grace to all, without prejudice, without demands, and without ultimatums. God is all good.

Dr. Ernest Holmes, founder of the Church of Religious Science, wrote the quintessential textbook about Scientific Prayer (Spiritual Mind Treatment) in 1926, *The Science of Mind*. These are his words:

> *"As the fall of man was brought about through his own act, so the rise of man will be accomplished through his own act. God already Is. Salvation is not a thing but a Way; the way of salvation is through the realization of man's unity with the Whole. Grace is the givingness of the Spirit to Its Creation and is not a special law, but is a specialized one. In other words, Grace Is, but we need to recognize It. It is not something that God imposed upon us, but is the logical result of the correct acceptance of life and of a correct relationship to the Spirit.*
>
> *"We are saved by Grace to the extent that we believe in, accept, and seek to embody, the Law of Good; for the Law of Good is ever a Law of Liberty and never one of limitation. Limitation is not a thing, but is a belief. Freedom is a Divine Reality, while limitation is an illusion, a false belief."* [50]

AFFIRMATIONS OF GRACE

In this section are a few affirmations and prayers that you can use to activate the Law of Grace in your life. Speak these affirmations aloud in a clear, powerful voice:

CHRIST CONSCIOUSNESS PRAYER

The Christ in me is in control.
The Christ in me is the only authority in my life.
I AM divinely protected by the light of my being.
I close off my aura and body of light
To all but my own Christ self and consciousness
Now and forevermore.
Thank you, God, and SO IT IS.

PRAYER OF PROTECTION

The light of God surrounds me.
The love of God enfolds me.
The power of God protects me.
The presence of God watches over me.
Wherever I AM, God is, and all is well.

I AM GOD PRAYER

I AM the love that God is.
I AM the light that God is.
I AM the joy that God is.
I AM the presence that God is.
I AM the good that God is.
I AM the perfection that God is.
I AM the glory that God is.

AFFIRMATIONS OF GRACE

- ◆ The Law of Grace is at work in my life now, annihilating karmic law and replacing it with perfection everywhere now.

- ◆ I claim my good, very good perfection now.

- ◆ I AM united, merged, and one with God now.

- ◆ I AM an instrument of God's love, light, and peace.

- ◆ I AM perfection everywhere now.

AARONIC BENEDICTION

"The Lord bless [me], and keep [me]: The Lord make his face shine upon [me], and be gracious unto [me]: The Lord lift up his countenance upon [me], and give [me] peace." [51]

In the next section of this book, you will discover how you can take command of your life and create miracles by using the karmic law and the Spiritual Law to your advantage.

PART III

TAKING CONTROL
OF YOUR DESTINY

7 HOW MIRACLES ARE CREATED

MORE THINGS ARE WROUGHT BY PRAYER
THAN THIS WORLD DREAMS OF.
—*Alfred Lord Tennyson*

*H*ow can you overcome deeply ingrained, reflexive habit patterns and beliefs? Such obstacles seem like an insurmountable wall to climb. After all, if unconscious motivations govern your life, then how can you reverse such deep patterns?

You can transform these thought-structures by invoking your God-given power of manifestation. In order to understand the secret of "precipitation" (transformation of an idea into solid form), in this chapter we will now examine how nature functions.

HOW NATURE CREATES

Please refer to "Process of Causation" on page 83. This chart shows how nature creates new life forms. By understanding how nature generates myriad phenomena, you can learn how to materialize your own desires through your own innate power to be creative.

On every level of life (Spirit, mind, and body), there is a cause (a masculine or objective aspect), a medium (a feminine or subjective aspect), and an effect or creation, which results from the union of the objective and subjective in an act of release or letting go. The objective (outer-projecting) aspect is the initiator of activity. It begins the process of manifestation by projecting a seed or idea into the subjective (inner-receiving) aspect. Then the subjective aspect accepts the seed, nurtures it, and brings it into being.

Process of Causation

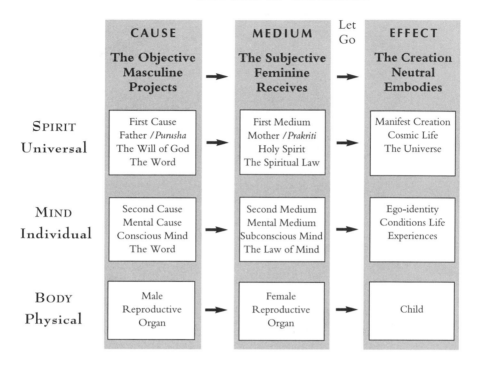

	CAUSE	MEDIUM	Let Go	EFFECT
	The Objective Masculine Projects	**The Subjective Feminine Receives**		**The Creation Neutral Embodies**
SPIRIT Universal	First Cause Father / *Purusha* The Will of God The Word	First Medium Mother / *Prakriti* Holy Spirit The Spiritual Law		Manifest Creation Cosmic Life The Universe
MIND Individual	Second Cause Mental Cause Conscious Mind The Word	Second Medium Mental Medium Subconscious Mind The Law of Mind		Ego-identity Conditions Life Experiences
BODY Physical	Male Reproductive Organ	Female Reproductive Organ		Child

On the universal level, God manifests the entire creation through the vehicle of Spirit. On the individual level, humans create their life experiences through the medium of mind. On the physical level, living beings generate their offspring through the instrument of physical body.

On the universal level, the male element is Father God or *Yahweh* (*Aham* or *Purusha* in Sanskrit) and the female is Holy Spirit or *Shekhinah* (*Idam* or *Prakriti* in Sanskrit). There are many names for these male and female aspects, such as Father and Mother God, Shiva and Shakti, Yin and Yang. Please refer to "Dual Nature of Existence" on page 84.

DUAL NATURE OF EXISTENCE

FEMALE	MALE
Darkness	Light
Yin	Yang
Moon	Sun
Receptive	Projective
Passive	Active
Subjective	Objective
Yoni	Linga
Holy Spirit	Father-God
Shekhinah	YHVH
Shakti	Shiva
Prakriti	Purusha
Anima	Animus

THE WORD OF GOD

Please refer to "Process of Causation" on page 83 again. The first act of creation occurs as Father God projects the Will of God, through the Word of God, into the Holy Spirit (Spiritual Law), and then lets go. Thus, the entire universe arises. The Spiritual Law has no will of its own. It accepts unquestioningly the will of God, nurtures it, and brings it into being. (Please do not misinterpret this as a sexist belief. It is simply a description of the operation of nature.)

According to the ancient *Upanishads* of India, the primordial Word of God is the vibration *(mantra) OM,* said to be *adi*—the first sound.[1] This primal sound of creation, OM splits into fifty *mantric* units to form the fifty letters of the Sanskrit alphabet. (See page 202 of my book *Exploring Chakras*.) These fifty letters generate the *Vedas*, building blocks of creation. (See page 220 of my book *Exploring Meditation*.) From this Word, the entire cosmos is born.

The Bible also states that God created the universe by speaking the Word of manifestation: *"And God said, Let there be light: and there was light."* [2] *"In the beginning was the Word, and the Word was with God, and the Word was God."* [3] The Word of God is the first impulse appearing within the "void" or absolute silence—the oneness underlying the universe, known in India as Brahman: *"In the beginning God created the heaven and the earth. And the earth was without form, and void; and darkness was upon the face of the deep. And the Spirit of God [Holy Spirit] moved upon the face of the waters."* [4]

Brahman is both Word and non-Word. As non-Word, it is absolute silence, without name, form, or phenomena—the void. It is beyond duality (male/female, light/darkness, day/night, yin/yang, joy/sorrow, life/death). As Word, Brahman manifests the entire universe by projecting its perfect will into the Spiritual Law through its perfect Word—OM. The Word of Spirit is always the Word of perfection—unlimited good.

The Word of God is the ultimate Word of manifestation, the seed syllable that generates the cosmos, the source of all, the wish-bestowing tree, the fulfiller of all desires. It is said in the ancient *Upanishads*:

"That word (or place) which all the Vedas record, which all penances proclaim, which men desire when they live as religious students, that word I tell thee briefly, it is OM. That (imperishable) syllable means Brahman; that syllable means the highest (Brahman); he who knows that syllable, whatever he desires, is his." [5]

The Word is the key to fulfillment. You can consciously use your own Word (thoughts and speech) to manifest whatever you desire to create.

THE LAW OF MIND

Now refer to the middle of "Process of Causation" on page 83, the "Mind." On the mental level, conscious mind is the masculine, objective part of your mind, which operates with free will. It creates thoughts and speech, known as "mental cause," and projects these into the subjective, feminine subconscious mind. Like a computer hard drive, your subconscious robot has no power of choice. Without discrimination, it accepts and stores all thoughts projected into it. An impartial, unbiased repository, your robot does nothing but openly receive impressions and then indiscriminately project whatever is deposited there.

You have the power to project either the Word of perfection (truth thoughts) or the word of limitation (error thoughts) into your subconscious mind. Your mental cause is based on complete free choice. If truth is projected, then joyful results will materialize. If false, limiting beliefs are projected, then unhappy results will occur.

The Word of Spirit (First Cause) is the Word of Perfection, pure and whole, the truth without limitation. In contrast, the Word of the Mind (Second Cause) might be the word of false limitation or negation. By this creative process, you create your personal Law of Mind. God sees you as absolute perfection, without limitations. Your true nature is perfect, flawless, and immortal, because you are made in the image and likeness of God. However, through Second Cause, you create your own flawed, mortal, mental law, by virtue of mental distortions. Then, you blindly operate under its restricted rules.

The Spiritual Law, the medium through which God manifests the universe, is the same law that you use to create your own life. It is always God, through the vehicle of the Spiritual Law, who creates everything. Through free will, your use of the Spiritual Law creates your own unique mental law and therefore your own destiny.

Ernest Holmes said, "There is one mental law in the universe, and where we use it, it becomes our law because we have individualized it."[6]

The Spiritual Law, which is perfection everywhere now, works through the filter of mind. With impartial benevolence, God allows you complete freedom to use this Law at your will. At every moment, by your every thought, speech and action, you freely create your personal mental law.

Every cause projected into your subconscious mind manifests precisely as your mind projected it. Infinitely unbiased and non-judging, God manifests every belief that you project, no matter what it is. Your own beliefs, projected into your subconscious mind, bear fruit.

Here is an example: Robert believes he is victimized by his boss, who makes him work long hours and never gives him a raise or vacation time. He feels he is being punished by an unjust God, or at least by an unjust employer! But if Robert would examine himself honestly, he would realize that he had freedom at every stage to make choices that created this situation of "punishment." It is not someone else's fault that he is now in an unbearable situation. His unconscious beliefs led him to make the choices that he made. God fulfilled Robert's choices impartially and benevolently. This so-called "victim of circumstance" now has freedom to make other choices, which God will fulfill with the same unbiased neutrality.

THE MIGHTY "I AM"

According to the Torah, the mighty "I AM" presence appeared to Moses on Mount Sinai in a burning bush. At that time, God asked Moses to deliver the Israelites from Egyptian slavery and to lead them to Canaan.[7] Moses then asked God what to tell the children of Israel, when they asked who had sent him. God replied to Moses, *"I AM THAT I AM: and he said, Thus shalt thou say unto the children of Israel, I AM hath sent me unto you."* [8]

The name of God, the mighty "I AM" presence, is written as the Hebrew letters: yod hey vav hey or YHVH. That holy name, called the *tetragrammaton*, is so powerful that the Jewish religion prohibits its utterance out loud. In fact, whenever YHVH is mentioned in the Torah, the word is spoken as Hashem ("the word"), Adonai ("Lord"), or Elohim ("God as judge or lawgiver"). This tradition carries into the English language. Jewish people commonly write the name "God" as "G-d."

"Thou shalt not take the name of YHVH in vain; for YHVH will not hold him guiltless that taketh his name in vain." [9] *"Hallowed be thy name."* [10]

There are many parallels between Hinduism and Judaism. One of them is related to mantras. In the Hindu tradition, *bija* (seed) mantras are power sounds that are secret names of deities. Traditionally, yogis keep these names private and do not speak them aloud.

In the ancient Jewish scripture *Kabbalah*, the concentrated, primal point from which all creation springs is called "I AM." This is the *kether* (crown), because it creates all things and links the manifest creation with the unmanifest absolute. Known as the primordial dot, the entire cosmos emanates from it. In the Hindu tradition, this dot is called *bindu*. The Zohar says:

"When the concealed of the concealed wished to reveal himself, he first of all made a single point; the infinite was entirely unknown, and spread no light until the luminous point violently broke into manifested reality." [11]

This primordial "I AM" is infinite creative power. Whenever you utter the mighty words "I AM," you are invoking enormous cosmic currents of energy. Thus, these potent words will manifest whatever you say after them. For example, if you say "I AM unworthy," then you will feel unworthy. If you say, "I AM happy," then you will feel happy. The results of using the mighty words "I AM" take effect immediately.

Therefore, whenever you invoke the mighty "I AM" presence by saying the words "I AM," it is wise that, right after those words, you place something that you want to own.

Let us do an experiment now. First, take a moment to notice how you are feeling in mind and body. Then, say the following list of statements aloud slowly, with deep feeling:

- I AM happy.
- I AM fulfilled.
- I AM worthy.
- I AM blessed.
- I AM loved.
- I AM healthy.
- I AM filled with divine light.
- I AM filled with divine love.
- I AM filled with divine grace.

Now notice how you are feeling. Do you feel lighter and more uplifted?

Now say the following statements aloud slowly, with the same intensity of deep feeling as the previous statements:

- I AM sad.
- I AM lacking.
- I AM unworthy.
- I AM lost.
- I AM lonely.
- I AM unhealthy.
- I AM hateful.
- I AM resentful.
- I AM depressed.

How do you feel now? Do you immediately feel demoralized? Now return to the first list and speak the positive statements again. How do you feel now by invoking the mighty "I AM" presence with powerful, uplifting words?

Do you now realize what you are creating, moment by moment, through casual, thoughtless conversation? You are, in reality, perfect and unlimited. However, the filters of limiting beliefs create restrictions on your pure, stainless nature.

ANCIENT MIRACLE-MAKING SECRETS

For many people, the word *yoga* conjures up images of contorting into various pretzel positions (*yoga asanas*) at a gym. But the Sanskrit word yoga does not translate as "exercise." It means "to yoke or bind," denoting union or integration. However, yoga is not union of the forehead with the knee or union of the fingertips with the toes. It signifies union of individual spirit with universal Spirit—God within.

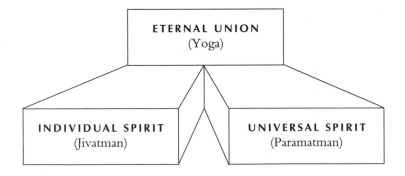

PATH OF ETERNAL
HAPPINESS AND PEACE

ETERNAL UNION
(Yoga)

INDIVIDUAL SPIRIT
(Jivatman)

UNIVERSAL SPIRIT
(Paramatman)

Yoga philosophy comes from two main sources:

1. The *Bhagavad Gita*, a section of an ancient history book of India called the *Mahabharata* ("Great India"), written by Veda Vyasa, approximately 3129 B.C.

2. An ancient philosophical text called *Yoga Sutras*, written by Patanjali, approximately 250 B.C.

The *Yoga Sutras* explains how enlightenment is achieved through the accomplishment of *siddhis* (perfections)—supernormal powers achieved by practicing a meditative technique called *samyama*. Some siddhis are levitation, walking through walls, supernormal strength, disappearing, seeing things at a distance, extra-sensory perception, traveling in a subtle body, making the body very small, large, light or heavy, appearing in physical form in several places at once, walking over water or hot coals, omnipotence, omnipresence, omniscience, and acquiring miraculous knowledge.

Patanjali, the author of this work, was an expert in creating miracles. Let us see what we can learn from him. Patanjali stated in his *Yoga Sutras* that there are three basic elements to creating a miracle, the same elements we have been discussing so far—a male element, which projects, a female element, which receives, and a release or letting go, a flow that creates union between these two elements. Then the siddhi or miraculous power manifests.

Please refer to "Miracle-Making" on page 92. In Patanjali's yogic practice, *samyama*, the masculine element is called *dharana* ("holding"). The feminine element, the state of perfect equipoise, pure consciousness, is called *samadhi* ("evenness"). The third element, *dhyana* ("meditation"), is a flow of movement or letting go.

Here is how samyama is practiced:

One of the yoga sutras in Patanjali's text is used. For example, here is the sutra for the siddhi of levitation: *"By samyama on the relationship between the body and ether, lightness of cotton fiber is attained, and thus traveling through the ether becomes possible."* [12]

MIRACLE-MAKING

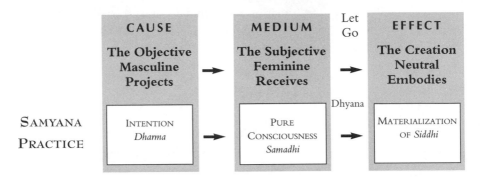

After you have attained the state of perfect relaxation and wholeness (samadhi), then you briefly hold onto the sutra (dharana). That means you consciously use the Word of God (you think the sutra in your mind). Then you drop the Word and let it go completely (dhyana), and you return to the state of samadhi. Then the cycle is repeated. As a result, the body lifts off the ground.

Patanjali's key to unlocking the mysteries of manifestation is based on universal principals. Have you noticed that when you beat your head against a brick wall, all you get is a headache? In contrast, when you give up, that is the exact moment the brick wall collapses of itself, and your goal is fulfilled. For instance, when you let go of the love relationship that you were hotly pursuing, then that person suddenly moves in your direction.

Patanjali's technique cannot be adequately taught in this book. However, a very effective method of fulfilling your desires is taught here—Scientific Prayer. This powerful method of prayer uses all the principles that you have learned thus far.

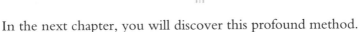

In the next chapter, you will discover this profound method.

FULFILLING 8
YOUR DESIRES

AND HE GIVETH YOU OF ALL YE ASK OF HIM, AND IF HE
WOULD COUNT THE BOUNTY OF ALLAH YE CANNOT RECKON IT.
—*Qur'an, XIV: 34*

*H*ow can you use nature's laws to manifest your own personal goals? By applying the principles you have been learning—projecting your desires into the Spiritual Law and then letting go. This process is already taking place right now. You create your destiny through every conscious and unconscious intention. In each moment, you either think or say something beneficial, which creates happiness, or you think or say something damaging, which causes suffering. In this chapter, you will learn how to consciously choose your destiny through the unique process called Scientific Prayer.

POWER OF SCIENTIFIC PRAYER

Since childhood, Rhonda has believed she is unattractive. Her parents, friends, and neighborhood bullies ridiculed her appearance. As a result, Rhonda's self-image invites negative responses in social situations. This belief, unless checked, maintains feelings of unpopularity and magnetizes situations of rejection. But to really take control of her life, Rhonda must make conscious choices and consciously materialize those choices. This is self-mastery. If she can create rejection, then she also has the power to choose love.

In my experience of forty years teaching meditation, intuition, and prayer, I have found no more effective way to take command of your destiny than the method of Scientific Prayer. Through this profound system, you can tap your inner power to consciously make miracles every day. The amazing, nine-step method can help you fulfill the desires of your heart and realize the dreams of your soul.

PROCESS OF PRAYER

CAUSE	MEDIUM	Let Go	EFFECT
The Objective Masculine Projects	**The Subjective Feminine Receives**		**The Creation Neutral Embodies**
		Release	
REQUEST Claim or Choice	SPIRITUAL LAW Holy Spirit		DEMONSTRATION Fulfillment of Claim

SCIENTIFIC PRAYER

Please refer to "Process of Prayer" above. Through Scientific Prayer you can realize your goals by employing the principles of manifestation discussed in Chapter 7. This is a step-by-step process of stating an intention (using your masculine side), unifying with God (using your feminine side), and then letting go.

You can use Scientific Prayer to pray for anything—for yourself or for anyone else. You can pray for physical, mental, or spiritual healing, releasing psychological blockages, attracting a love relationship, buying a new home or car, achieving spiritual progress, or anything else you can imagine. In fact, your only limitation is your imagination.

In "Process of Prayer" you see that in Scientific Prayer, your goal or request is called the claim or choice (the masculine cause), which projects into the Spiritual Law or Holy Spirit (the feminine medium). The claim is then released. As a result, an effect is produced, called the "demonstration" (the complete answer to your prayer, fully realized). The process of Scientific Prayer is designed to create such a perfect conviction in your mind that the materialization of your goal is assured. The reason Scientific Prayer is so effective is that it employs nature's laws of causation discussed in Chapter 7.

The next section differentiates Scientific Prayer from other types of prayer.

OTHER METHODS OF PRAYER

PRAYER OF SUPPLICATION

This most common form of prayer is a petition or entreaty—begging God to grant your wish. An example might be, "Oh, God, will you please heal me?" With this type of prayer, you are uncertain whether God will hear or respond. God's answer may be "yes" or "no." Pleading with God presumes several mental constructs: (1) God is separate from you. (2) God is a capricious, whimsical power that only fulfills prayers deemed worthy of fulfillment. (3) Your desire may or may not be fulfilled.

A prayer of supplication is only as effective as your faith and acceptance. If you believe this type of prayer will work, then it will, for *"it is done unto you as you believe."* However, you may be devastated when God says "no" to your prayer. Yet it is not God who has said "no." It is you. There was not enough faith to demonstrate the answer to your prayer.

PRAYER OF BARGAINING

In this kind of prayer you are haggling with God to make a deal. An example might be "God, if you heal me, I promise I will go to church every Sunday." Striking a bargain with God presupposes that (1) God is conditional and separate from you. (2) You need to change God's mind rather than your own mind. (3) God dispenses boons based on whether you are a "good" or "bad" child. (4) God plays favorites and can be bribed (sometimes). (5) God uses life situations to teach you "lessons," punish you, or reward you.

Trying to win over God through enticements is a fruitless venture, since it is not God's mind that needs changing. You must change your own mind in order to manifest your goal.

PRAYER OF MANIPULATION

In this type of prayer, you are trying to trick God into giving you what you want. An example might be, "God, you are so great and I am nothing. I don't deserve to be healed. But won't you heal me?" Such a prayer assumes that: (1) God is anthropomorphic and separate from you. (2) You need to manipulate God into granting your wish. (3) God can be tricked into feeling pity for you. (4) God is susceptible to flattery. (5) God has a guilty conscience.

This kind of prayer is an inept form of black magic. Trying to manipulate God is ineffectual, because God does not have human traits and does not respond to such shenanigans.

PRAYER OF AFFIRMATION

In this type of prayer, you simply decree statements of truth. You state that the demonstration has already manifested. An example might be, "I AM in perfect health." With full faith behind your affirmations, they will manifest, even instantaneously.

This type of prayer is only as successful as your conviction. For example, if you state, "I am the owner of a Cadillac," does this make it so? It may be so if you believe it is so. But your deepest conviction might be that you are unworthy of a Cadillac. Therefore you rationalize that God's answer may be "no."

The reason that affirmations often fail is due to subconscious blockages. Doubt or fear places a shadow on your desire and prevents fulfillment. However, if you have full faith, then nothing can stop you.

"Let him ask of God, that giveth to all men liberally, and upbraideth not; and it shall be given him. But let him ask in faith, nothing wavering. For he that

wavereth is like a wave of the sea driven with the wind and tossed. For let not that man think that he shall receive any thing of the Lord." [1]

WHY SCIENTIFIC PRAYER WORKS

The secret to achievement is to arrive at unwavering faith that what you desire is yours—that you deserve it. Here is how Ernest Holmes defined *faith*:

> *"Faith is a mental attitude which is so convinced of its own idea—which so completely accepts it—that any contradiction is unthinkable and impossible."* [2]

Think about an easy task you will accomplish today, such as going to the store. Do you have to pray to accomplish it? No. You already have a complete conviction that it is done. There is no struggle, worry, or doubt.

However, some of your desires remain unfulfilled. Perhaps you want the home of your dreams or your own business. Maybe you want a loving relationship or marriage and children. Perhaps you want to write a book or get a higher education. These may seem difficult or impossible to attain.

How can you manifest the dreams of your soul? Nothing is impossible with God. There is nothing you cannot accomplish, no task too large for God to handle. Faith is the key that unlocks the door to your fulfillment. You can draw from the Spiritual Law all the good that your conviction allows you to draw. Author Iyanla Vanzant defines the word *faith* as an acronym: "**F**eel **A**s **I**f the **T**hing has **H**appened."

> *"If ye have faith as a grain of mustard seed [the smallest seed, which grows into the largest herb] ye shall say unto this mountain, Remove hence to yonder place; and it shall remove; and nothing shall be impossible unto you."* [3]

Most forms of prayer attempt to change God's will, to persuade or entice God into granting a wish. In contrast, in Scientific Prayer, the goal is not to change God. Instead, Scientific Prayer changes your own Law of Mind so you can accept what is your birthright.

Ernest Holmes said,

"Prayer does something to the mind of the one praying. It does not do anything to God."[4]

God has already demonstrated every one of your previous beliefs. Now what is needed is to transform your current beliefs.

The process of Scientific Prayer, like other forms of prayer, is only as effective as the belief of the person praying. There is one major difference, however. Within the format of Scientific Prayer, there is a process to arrive at this belief. This is a methodical, proven technique for transforming your mind in order to attain the desired conviction. That is why Scientific Prayer is so effective. Ernest Holmes said:

"One of the questions most frequently asked about the Science of Mind is, 'Are prayers and treatments identical?' The answer to this question is both Yes and No.

"If when one prays his prayer is a recognition of Spirit's Omniscience, Omnipotence, and Omnipresence, and a realization of man's unity with Spirit, then his prayer is a spiritual treatment.

"If, on the other hand, one is holding to the viewpoint that God is some far off Being, Whom he would approach with doubt in his thought; wondering if by some good luck he may be able to placate God or persuade Him of the wisdom of one's request—then, there is but little similarity between prayer and treatment. Nothing could bring greater discouragement than to labor under the delusion that God is a Being of moods, who might answer some prayers and not others."[5]

SCIENTIFIC PRAYER IS UNIQUE

In 1951, Dr. William R. Parker, professor at California's University of Redlands and author of *Prayer Can Change Your Life: Experiments and*

Techniques in Prayer Therapy,[6] conducted several scientific studies over a ten-year period to prove the superior efficacy of Scientific Prayer. The initial experiment involved forty-five people from all walks of life. He divided these people into three groups, fifteen per group.

The first group underwent traditional psychotherapy in weekly individual counseling. No mention of religion was made in these sessions. The second group consisted of regular church-going Christians who claimed to know how to pray and expressed confidence in prayer as the ultimate solution to their problems. They prayed every day for nine months, just before bed. The third group met in a weekly two-hour class to learn the principles and method of Scientific Prayer in a therapeutic model called "Prayer Therapy," which they practiced regularly at home. They learned to pray in a healthy way—focusing on God's healing love rather than on their problems.

Before the study, all forty-five subjects took five psychological tests: the Rorschach, the Szondi, the Thematic Apperception, and the Word Association and Sentence Completion tests. All forty-five subjects were given the results and the prognosis of the tests.

After nine months and ten days, on June 18, 1952, the subjects were tested again. What Dr. Parker discovered was startling:

- ◆ Group 1, who received individual psychotherapy, made a 65% improvement in tests and in symptoms.

- ◆ Group 2, the "random prayer group," who prayed on their own every night, made no improvement, and in some cases made a backslide.

- ◆ Group 3, the "prayer therapy group," made a 72% improvement in both symptoms and tests, including several dramatic physical healings.[7]

Many in Group 2 perpetuated negative prayer habits that reinforced their problems. For example, Jerry perceived himself as a misfit. Depressed and nervous, he suffered frequent headaches. He could not keep a job and constantly quarreled with his parents. Jerry prayed faithfully every night, obsessing on guilt and unworthiness and constantly begging for forgiveness. After nine months of prayer, he still experienced the same failure, headaches, and quarrels.

Gregory had not succeeded in his career as his colleagues had. His co-workers did not respect him. Considering himself a failure, he became critical and cynical. During Dr. Parker's Group 3 sessions, Gregory began a program of profound self-inquiry. Fearing God and feeling unworthy, he felt a need to control every situation. However, in his Prayer Therapy class, he learned to open his heart to God's love. Positive changes came rapidly. Gregory attained peace and trust in God. He found success as head of his own company.

Although Jerry and Gregory were both plagued by failure, Jerry remained stuck in negative prayer and did not change. Gregory learned Scientific Prayer and took a new, positive, constructive direction.

Prayer can succeed or fail. It is possible to pray in such a way that your goals are never reached. Constantly reaffirming your problems will not help you escape your dilemma. Pleading with a remote, vengeful God will not attract your good. Instead, you will magnetize punishment.

"Ye ask, and receive not, because ye ask amiss, that ye may consume it upon your lusts." [8] Your prayers might fail if your picture of God is distorted—a cold, abusive taskmaster who engenders fear. You might believe that, to get God's attention, you must beg or strike bargains.

In contrast, positive Scientific Prayer seeks the true face of God and overcomes human limitations and distortions. *"When thou saidst, Seek ye my face; my heart said unto thee, Thy face, Lord, will I seek."* [9] Positive Scientific Prayer knows God to be only good. It affirms truth and finds solutions. Ineffectual forms of prayer affirm and perpetuate problems.

Dr. Parker's school of Prayer Therapy was based upon the Socratic principle, "Know thyself." He believed the source of all psychological problems stem from four basic maladies: (1) fear, (2) guilt, (3) inferiority, and (4) hate.

According to Parker, both honesty and love are essential to Prayer Therapy. Rather than create and defend a viewpoint that supports your own brand of truth, Scientific Prayer allows reality to be revealed. Since God is love in action, in motion, and in activity, God is the healing power, and God fulfills all heartfelt desires. *"God is Love."* [10]

The four stages of Parker's therapeutic model are (1) regular, (2) surrender, (3) positive, and (4) receptive.

Regularity of Scientific Prayer is essential. Breaking old habits and creating new, positive, unfamiliar ones may be challenging. But with concentrated effort, regularity of practice can be sustained. Dr. Parker said, *"Accustom yourself gradually to carry prayer into all your daily occupations. Speak, move, work, in peace as if you were in prayer."* As Saint Paul said, *"Pray without ceasing."* [11]

Surrender is the second stage. Since God is continually knocking at your door, eager for you to open, all you need do is invite God's grace into your life. Release your life into God's hands. Allow yourself to be held in God's arms. Trust that God will care for you. *"Casting all your care upon him: for he careth for you."* [12]

Parker's third stage is to acquire a positive, optimistic attitude. Knowing that God always says "yes" to every request, you can affirm with confidence that God fulfills your every true desire. Positivity produces beneficial effects, whereas negativity yields nonbeneficial results. It is said in the Proverbs, *"Thou art snared with the words of thy mouth, thou art taken with the words of thy mouth."* [13]

Parker's fourth and last stage is to have a receptive heart, open to receive. When your prayers are in harmony with your true desires, then you are following God's loving will in your life. All you need do is ask with full faith and you will receive.

"Ask, and it shall be given you; seek, and ye shall find; knock, and it shall be opened unto you. For every one that asketh receiveth; and he that seeketh findeth; and to him that knocketh it shall be opened." [14]

As a result of the University of Redlands studies, Parker stated: "Over and over we proved that whatever we had need of, whether it was harmony, forgiveness, courage, abundance, friendship, health, if we would affirm it and accept it within, it would become a part of our outward experience. This was both the secret and the miracle."

God is only good, and God always says "yes." Therefore, all your good is already available in God-substance. All that is required is to draw upon it. Your acceptance brings it into concrete form. Your power to manifest depends upon your receptivity.

Scientific Prayer is a way for you to achieve acceptance by calling forth your good through your innate power of creativity and then releasing whatever prevents its manifestation. This profound method directs the universal power of Spirit to move toward a specific result. The Spiritual Law is given a particular direction in which to operate.

In the next chapter, you will learn more about the Spiritual Law and how to use it to fulfill your goals.

USING THE SPIRITUAL LAW 9
TO YOUR ADVANTAGE

YOU CANNOT SOLVE A PROBLEM WITH

THE SAME MIND THAT CREATED IT.

—*Albert Einstein*

The Spiritual Law is the law of projection of the Word of God into the Holy Spirit in order to materialize the forms and phenomena of the universe. In this chapter, you will learn how to use the laws of Spirit to manifest your own ideals and goals.

LAWS OF LIFE

SPIRITUAL LAW

Jesus' decree, *"Ask, and it shall be given you,"*[1] explains how to use the Spiritual Law to your advantage. "Asking" means consciously projecting the Word of God (your goal or intention for the prayer) into the Spiritual Law and then letting go.

LAW OF PERFECTION EVERYWHERE NOW

The Law of Perfection is the law of the absolute goodness of God available to everyone everywhere always. God creates only perfection, because, *"as for God, his way is perfect."*[2] Therefore, your word (what you think, say, do, and believe) manifests perfectly, precisely as you project it. *"The law of the Lord is perfect."*[3]

LAW OF MIND

The Law of Mind is the karmic law of cause and effect, which states, *"As thou hast believed, so be it done unto thee."* [4] This law acts in the mental realm, where there is belief and disbelief. This law has tremendous power, when wielded properly, to project truth and reap good. However, when the law is used unconsciously, it can enslave you.

LAW OF ELIMINATION

The Law of Elimination overcomes all conditions and beliefs that are unlike truth. This law heals all congested areas that veil the divine presence. It acts according to the principle, *"thy faith hath made thee whole."* [5] Ernest Holmes said, "there should be no difference between stating, 'This word is the law of elimination,' and the elimination which should follow such a statement." [6]

The concepts of the Spiritual Law and mental law are outlined in "Laws of Causation" on page 105. Your subconscious mind is a wonderful servant, but a terrible master. If you allow unconscious beliefs to dominate, the law of karma will control you. Instead of directing the rudder of your ship, you are tossed about on turbulent seas of emotion. Your life appears ruled by "chance," and you are subject to experiences not consciously chosen. Then it is easy to feel like a victim of circumstances.

For example, Allen wanted to buy a home. He saved his money, searched for the perfect house, tried to get support from his family, and applied for a mortgage. In every way, Allen struggled to get the home that he sought with such longing, yet he failed. Why? Because his subconscious mind became the master and the conscious mind its slave. He was held in chains by the mental law. He did not command the situation from the inside, though he tried to control it from the outside.

Allen's unconscious belief, which he learned as a youngster, was that he did not deserve to own property. His parents, family, and community reinforced this belief by example. Everyone Allen knew was raised in an

LAWS OF CAUSATION

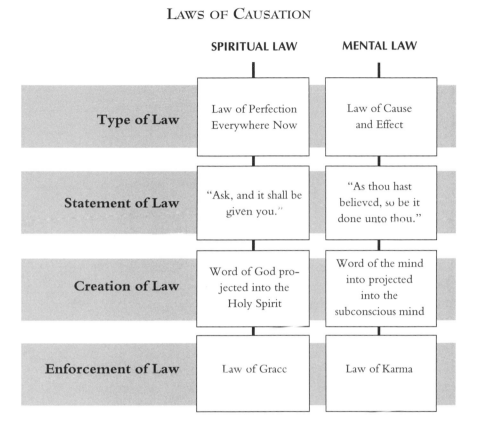

	SPIRITUAL LAW	MENTAL LAW
Type of Law	Law of Perfection Everywhere Now	Law of Cause and Effect
Statement of Law	"Ask, and it shall be given you."	"As thou hast believed, so be it done unto thou."
Creation of Law	Word of God projected into the Holy Spirit	Word of the mind into projected into the subconscious mind
Enforcement of Law	Law of Grace	Law of Karma

apartment. There was no support to believe that he deserved his own home. If, on the other hand, Allen would consciously master the mental law, then he could transform his life. Through vigilant use of the power of mind and speech, he could turn his life around.

Scientific Prayer is a way to utilize the Spiritual Law and to master the mental law. You can consciously make choices, create goals, and point the Spiritual Law of nature in a specific direction to manifest your good.

OTHER SPIRITUAL LAWS

Several other laws of Spirit can be used in Scientific Prayer. You can call upon these laws in your prayer treatments. A few of them are briefly described below:

LAW OF ONENESS

"Hear, O Israel: The Lord our God is one Lord." [7] All is one. God is everywhere present. Therefore, there is nowhere that God is not. Call upon this principle of unity to establish oneness with Spirit.

LAW OF GROWTH

"And God blessed them, saying, Be fruitful, and multiply." [8] You seek to grow, expand, increase your good, and enjoy greater happiness. Whatever you place attention on increases in your life. Call upon this law to expand your boundaries, to accept change, and thereby grow in spiritual evolution.

LAW OF ABUNDANCE

"So shall my word be that goeth forth out of my mouth: it shall not return unto me void, but it shall accomplish that which I please, and it shall prosper in the thing whereto I sent it." [9] God is a cornucopia of unlimited good and prosperity, and, as a child of God, you are heir to that inheritance. Call upon this law to accept what is rightfully yours.

LAW OF CIRCULATION

"Give, and it shall be given unto you; good measure, pressed down, and shaken together, and running over, shall men give into your bosom." [10] If your life is stagnating, then begin to give liberally of your time, energy, love, money, and knowledge, and you will receive in like measure. Call upon this law to eliminate the seeming appearance of lack.

LAW OF IDENTITY

"Are not five sparrows sold for two farthings, and not one of them is forgotten before God? But even the very hairs of your head are all numbered." [11] Everyone is valuable and important in the sight of God. Call upon this law to gain self-acceptance, to be natural, and to be yourself.

LAW OF MAGNETIC ATTRACTION

"Whatsoever a man soweth, that shall he also reap." [12] By projecting positive vibrations into the atmosphere, you attract positive experiences. Call upon this law to attract the experiences and people you desire.

LAW OF BALANCE

"And God saw the light, that it was good: and God divided the light from the darkness." [13] Recognizing that this universe is in balance and equanimity, you attain a centered state within. Call upon this law to attain proper perspective and to develop concentration.

LAW OF RHYTHM

"To every thing there is a season, and a time to every purpose under the heaven." [14] Life is ephemeral and cyclical. Nothing lasts, whether gain or loss, happiness or sorrow. Call upon this law to flow in life's rhythm and to allow God's good to flood into your life.

LAW OF ORDER

"And God saw every thing that he had made, and, behold, it was very good." [15] God's creation is in divine order. It is only good, for God is perfection everywhere now. Call upon this Law of Perfect Right Action to eliminate confusion and chaos and to bring harmony and stability.

LAW OF COMPENSATION

"I know that, whatsoever God doeth, it shall be forever: nothing can be put to it, nor any thing taken from it." [16] Energy is never lost. When removed from one area, it is replaced from another area. Call upon this Law of Conservation of Energy or Vacuum Law to restore what is seemingly lost.

LAW OF CORRESPONDENCE

"Judge not, that ye be not judged. For with what judgment ye judge, ye shall be judged: and with what measure ye mete, it shall be measured to you again." [17] Whatever you hold in mind has an equivalent in invisible substance that attracts its own likeness. Call upon this Law of Equivalents to change your viewpoint.

TRUTH AND FACTS

Let us explore the difference between "truth" (reality) and "facts" (appearances). Facts may have dominated your life thus far. If you accept those limiting facts as truth, then you will continue to prove those facts to yourself by outpicturing the same results repeatedly. On the other hand, by changing your perspective to see only truth (reality) as unlimited, you will not repeat the same limiting facts. Instead, you will live life without limits.

Please refer to "Truth Behind the Appearance" on page 109. The truth is the accurate viewpoint of your higher self and the appearance is the ignorant standpoint of your ego. From the perspective of enlightened consciousness, there is only perfection. From the perspective of ego, through the filter of the mind, there is the appearance of limitation, suffering, pain, death, misery, and frustration.

"For now we see through a glass, darkly; but then face to face: now I know in part; but then shall I know even as also I am known." [18]

There can be no pain where there is absolute bliss and joy. No suffering, disease, or death can exist where there is wholeness, health, and eter-

TRUTH BEHIND THE APPEARANCE

	PERFECTION
THE TRUTH	Good Bliss Love Joy Happiness

	IMPERFECTION
THE APPEARANCE	Error Mistake Suffering Lack Illness

nal life. Since God is present everywhere, and God is unlimited good, it stands to reason that nothing exists but perfection. The Law of Perfection Everywhere Now is the truth of your being. It is true for all times. It is, was, and always shall be.

You may perceive suffering, but that perception is false. The sun appears to move through the sky, rising in the morning and setting in the evening, while the Earth appears flat and stationary. But the truth is that the Earth is a sphere rotating on its axis. When you know the truth, you give no credence to appearances. Similarly, when you know the truth of perfection everywhere now, you give no credence to limitation.

By firmly believing in appearances of suffering, lack, and illness, you will manifest experiences that prove these facts. Repetition of affirmations of lack will materialize an abundance of lack. Even though you may outpicture negative experiences, these experiences are *avidya* ("ignorance" in Sanskrit), the veil of illusion.

Through unrelenting acceptance of the truth and denial of the false, you will eventually gain conviction in the truth. By thinking and speaking positive statements of truth, you can transform appearances into reality. To transcend the veil of illusion, refute the appearance of negation. Instead believe steadfastly in truth, the perfection of your being.

SPEAKING THE WORD

You are continually "speaking the word" all day, every day. The "word" is your thoughts and speech, continually (often unconsciously) projected and released into your subconscious mind, creating life experiences. Ernest Holmes stated, *"Man…has no choice other than to use this creative power. His thought will always be creative, whether he knows it or not."* [19] By consciously directing the creative power of your Word, you can control your mind rather than letting it control you.

Using the "Word of God" means intentionally making statements of truth. With such Words, you can summon cosmic power-currents of the Spiritual Law. This power has such force that one statement of truth heals many false negative statements. For example, you may have demonstrated lack and poverty. However, lack is not reality. By speaking the truth, "I AM abundantly provided for by my Creator," with unwavering conviction, you can transform your belief into abundance. Similarly, you may have the appearance of disease, but the truth is perfect health. Thus you may say, with faith, "My body is the perfect temple of God, filled with health, energy, and vitality."

You may be grieving from the appearance of loss, but the truth is, "I AM the fullness of God's overflowing joy, and there is no lack in Spirit." You may be unhappy due to the appearance of family conflict, but the truth is, "There is only unity, harmony, and bliss in God's omnipresent creation, and God is the source of peace and harmony for all my relationships." You may feel disheartened by the appearance of rejection, but the truth is, "God's love is everywhere present and my heart is filled with the unconditional love of the almighty Creator."

In ignorance, you may have manifested negative experiences. But, in every case, the realization of truth is the key to unlock the manifestation of your desired good. Life transformation occurs from your acceptance of truth, rather than false evidence, previously believed to be real. The light of truth overcomes even the deepest darkness of ignorance and brings your good.

Scientific Prayer is a way to systematically make truth statements that help you accept reality rather than appearances. Once you attain a firm conviction of truth with unwavering faith, then you have accomplished the purpose of prayer. At that moment, your goal fully materializes.

> Thought, operating through conscious statements, enforces the Law of Mind and changes conditions.
>
> —ERNEST HOLMES[20]

ATTAINING CONVICTION

Why would the goal of your prayer not materialize? Because you did not thoroughly examine your deepest feelings. Perhaps you have accepted the truth intellectually, but your subconscious emotions say something else. They are still clinging to appearances. Your subconscious acceptance of your prayer is the real constituent of conviction. If your conscious and subconscious minds do not coincide, then your heart and mind are out of sync. Such internal conflict prevents your prayer from materializing. Ernest Holmes said, *"There is an exact parallel between thoughts and things."* [21] *"Causes and conditions are identical."* [22]

Your subconscious mind blindly accepts anything you consistently think, and it manifests whatever you unconsciously believe. You may be entirely clueless about what those subconscious beliefs are—or how to uncover them. One way is to observe what you have demonstrated thus far. For example, if you are wealthy, then your subconscious mind believes that you deserve wealth. Unearth your innermost feelings by observing the fruits borne on your tree of life.

Your subconscious mind is your filthy closet. Get your broom and sweep out the litter of untruth. Cleanse your false, habitual patterns. They are like chains that maintain a stranglehold on your mind—but they are bonds of ignorance that can be broken.

You can cut, edit, and rewrite the data stored on your subconscious computer hard drive. Through the healing power of prayer, you can cut false beliefs and paste thoughts of truth. Scientific Prayer helps you clear old, erroneous habit patterns and accept the good that God has in store for you. Your subconscious beliefs are undoubtedly opposed to the goal you are seeking in prayer (otherwise you would already have it). Replace false beliefs with truth by knowing that your *"word is the law of elimination to everything that contradicts the Divine Presence."* [23]

WHAT ARE YOU PRAYING FOR?

Are you praying for things, or for knowing the truth, which sets you free? Before you begin to pray, align yourself to highest wisdom. If you have pounded on God's door repeatedly without results, make sure you are knocking on the right door.

The Apostle James said, *"Ye ask, and receive not, because ye ask amiss, that ye may consume it upon your lusts."* [24] One way you might pray amiss is by asking God to change a situation, when God wants you to change. You may be trying to beat down a wall, when God wants you to dissolve the wall within. You might pray, "Oh, God, if you would only change this person." This is not prayer. It is manipulation—trying to change someone not meeting your expectations. This is black magic.

It may sound extreme to use the phrase "black magic." However, any attempt to force people against their will is black magic. Perhaps you cringe when certain zealously pious people say, "I will pray for you," because you know they are praying amiss—for you to become like them. This is a form of black magic.

Rather than trying to change others, pray for the courage to change yourself. After you have cleansed that hidden internal dirty laundry, your surroundings will reflect your shining, resplendent raiment. As if by magic, others will suddenly change. When you change your outlook, then everything around you changes.

Whatever your problems, they have no cause in your environment. The cause is always your personal mental law. By transforming your beliefs, you will demonstrate the solution. Your environment will change to correspond to your new set of beliefs. Instead of blaming outer conditions, ask yourself why you created these circumstances. Before accusing others, ask why you victimize yourself through others. Rather than feeling criticized, ask why you condemn yourself through others. Instead of feeling rejected, ask why you subconsciously demand rejection. Before blaming those who are dominating you, ask why you feel the need to be dominated.

Often, what bothers you about others is something you are unwilling to see in yourself. If your boss is driving you mad, examine how you are driving yourself mad. If someone at home is not cleaning up after himself, see how you are not cleaning up your own mental dirty laundry. If your spouse is not giving you love and attention, consider how you are not giving yourself the love you so richly deserve.

God is not creating roadblocks to your fulfillment. Your deepest soul's desires are identical with God's desires for you. God fulfills every prayer, even those misaligned with divine will. Now choose your goals wisely and pray consciously—for solutions to problems, for healing negative beliefs, and for overcoming the root of difficulties. Pray for wisdom, guidance, and divine purpose.

Aim at the bull's-eye of God's perfect will for you. Pray for all God has promised—peace, joy, abundance, fulfillment, health, love, and wisdom. With enough meditation, prayer, and healing, you can release all negations that have caused undesirable circumstances. By using the Spiritual Law of Perfection Everywhere Now, you can transform your life.

Prayer is about building a profound contact and communication with God. It is about opening your heart to the living presence of God right here and now. Prayer can be a wonderful adventure. It can lift your spirit, enlighten your mind, heal your body, transform your mind, and touch your soul.

ARE YOU PRAYING BACKWARD?

The nine-step method of Scientific Prayer is easy to learn. But before you begin, let us take two steps to get ready. The first step is to decide what to pray for—in other words, to recognize your heartfelt aspirations. If you spend a month praying for a BMW when your true desire is a Harley motorcycle, then you will waste energy and time. And you will subconsciously sabotage the acquisition of the BMW.

If you are in touch with your true purpose, and you know what to pray for, then you conserve energy. You will not chase fantasies irrelevant to your life path. In Chapter 3, you uncovered your true purpose. Now might be a good time to revisit that process so you can decide what to pray for during your first prayer experiment.

Bea Wilkinson, an author from Springfield, Missouri, is an expert at manifesting her goals. Her prayers resulted in a wide range of miracles, from facilitating the healing of her husband's cancer to manifesting various Cadillacs. One day, she wrote down three wishes. (Although she had asked repeatedly, her husband refused to help her fulfill these.) She wanted (1) to visit Mount Shasta, (2) to experience a Native American sweat lodge, (3) to go camping.

Later that day, Bea received a phone call. She was stunned when her friend invited her to a special sweat lodge. It would take place in California, on Mount Shasta. Even more amazingly, her friend said, "The only glitch is, I'm sorry, but we'll have to camp on the mountain." Bea was thrilled, to say the least.

It turned out the sweat lodge was built for twenty-five people. However, Bea was squished into this hellishly hot, miserable space, with seventy-nine others. When she finally escaped the inferno, she trekked a long distance to cool off in a stream. By the time she arrived, though no longer hot, she jumped into the icy, glacier-fed stream anyway. Bea rushed back in gratitude to the hellish sweat lodge.

Later that night, Bea tucked herself into her tent. But, unknown to her, the air mattress had a hole in it. Needless to say, Bea did not go camping again. Nor did she ever visit another sweat lodge.

This story has a moral: Be careful what you ask for. You just might get it.

The trouble is that often people pray backward. They pray for things without first considering the consequences. Other people miss the mark by making their goals too limited. God wants more for you than you could ever imagine. What you think you need and what God knows you need may differ. So, attune to God's perfect will for your life.

First discover what is highest wisdom to pray for, according to your life plan and purpose. Then, when your prayers are answered, you will align with what God has in mind for you. Your goals will manifest easily when you first get counsel from your higher self. Surrender to the will of God and be led by Spirit. Pray forward rather than backward.

> Am I certain that my desire is in line with good? If it is, nothing is against me and everything is for me.
>
> —ERNEST HOLMES[25]

UNCOVERING HIDDEN BLOCKAGES

The second step in preparing for Scientific Prayer is to uncover obstacles preventing you from fulfilling your goal. This requires patient, honest, deep self-reflection. You may be escaping from your true feelings. Such evasion prevents you from making deep changes. Psychology has delineated several defense mechanisms that can keep you from taking responsibility for your feelings. Four are predominant:

1. **Denial:** Refusal to accept or acknowledge the truth.
   "I didn't do it."
   "I would never admit it, even to myself."
   "Oh, I would never..."
   "I always tell the truth."
   "Everything is lovely and wonderful. My life is perfect."
   "I never have any problems."
   "I'm not really that way."

2. **Rationalization:** Making excuses to cover up the truth.
   "It doesn't matter. I didn't want it anyway."
   "It isn't my fault. It's because..."
   "I don't care that I didn't succeed. I would rather... anyway."
   "I know why it happened. It was because..."
   "I'm better than he is anyway, even though he got what I wanted."
   "It was God's will that it happened."
   "It's good that it happened this way. It was for the best."
   "God is punishing me for my sins."

3. **Projection:** Refuting weakness by attributing it to others.
   "I know that he has it in for me."
   "People are hostile toward me."
   "It's the fault of society. I am a victim."
   "It's all your fault."

"You made me feel/do this/say this."

"Nobody loves me."

"You infuriate me."

"Why are you so...?"

4. **Reaction-formation:** Lying so much that you believe it yourself.

"She's not like that."

"He's not an alcoholic."

"She's so wonderful. I idolize her."

"Aren't the children cute when they act up like that?"

"You are just perfect. You could never do any wrong."

"I love you unconditionally."

"I act sweet all the time, and I always have a smile on my face."

"My father was the greatest man who ever lived."

"My mother was the ideal woman."

These defense mechanisms are the glue that binds your ego-identity together. They are the fig leaf in the Garden of Eden, with which Adam and Eve try to cover the truth. This fear of exposure, this primordial shame and humiliation, gives rise to guilt; guilt engenders fear; fear creates unworthiness; unworthiness creates hate (misguided love).

Four basic feelings underlie all defenses—four root causes of tendencies to cling to the past and keep transformation at bay. These four life-killers are listed on the left, and keys to healing them are on page 118.

Here are some affirmations to help you overcome these demons:

Demon: **Fear**

Cure: **Faith**

God is perfect love, and perfect love casts out all fear. Therefore I place my trust in God. I know that I abide under the shelter and protection of God's abiding love. There is nothing to fear, and all is well.

Demon: **Guilt**

Cure: **Forgiveness**

DEFENSE MECHANISMS

TYPES	Denial Rationalization Projection Reaction/Formation

CAUSES AND CURES	CAUSES	CURES
	Guilt	Forgiveness
	Fear	Faith
	Unworthiness	Self-confidence
	Hate	Love

I AM the forgiving power of God. I therefore forgive myself for all seeming wrongdoing, for I have done the very best that I could do in every situation, according to my level of consciousness at the time. Therefore, there is no guilt or blame. I love myself completely now with God's infinite compassion.

Demon: **Inferiority**

Cure: **Self-confidence**

There is no one less than or greater than I. All are equal in the sight of God. I have no need to impress anyone or to prove myself to anyone. I accept myself exactly the way I AM. I AM good enough. I AM perfect for me for now.

Demon: **Hate**

Cure: **Love**

There is only one power in the universe—the power of love. Therefore, nothing in the universe could hate me; nor could I hate myself. I AM the love that God is. God's perfect, unconditional love is made manifest here and now in my mind, body, and relationships.

FIRST FEEL, THEN HEAL

Anthony always wanted to get married, but he unconsciously sabotages every love relationship. Whenever he finds someone he really likes, he pushes that woman away. Instead, he only gets involved with women who want casual relationships. Anthony continues to attract unfulfilling relationships, growing older, wondering why he cannot find Ms. Right. This cycle continues because he never stops to ask, "Why am I pushing her away when I want to get closer?" There is a reason, and for Anthony to heal this reason, he must first feel it. It is necessary to get in touch with your feelings before you can heal them.

Let us do an exercise now. Think of a heartfelt desire you have not yet fulfilled. Write your goal across the top of a piece of paper. Then close your eyes and ask your higher self, "What is preventing me from achieving this?" In that quiet state, begin to feel the emotions and thoughts that surface. Notice whether any of the four "demons" described in the previous section arise. Now write a list of all these stumbling blocks on the left side of your page.

The next step is to write a list on the right side of your page—positive thoughts and feelings that are the opposite correlates from those on the left side. Here is an example of how your paper might look:

GOAL: I WANT TO GET MARRIED	
LIMITED THOUGHTS	**POSITIVE CORRELATES**
1. I don't think that I am worthy.	1. I am worthy now.
2. My parents made me feel I was not good enough.	2. I am good enough now. I forgive my parents now.
3. I am afraid of commitment.	3. I am be committed now.
4. I think that married people suffer.	4. I can have a happy marriage now.
5. It is a higher spiritual path to be single.	5. Marriage is my highest spiritual path now.

Now that you have uncovered the subconscious blockages preventing you from fulfilling your goal, you are closer to manifesting it. Keep this paper as you continue to read this book. It will help you to compose your Scientific Prayer treatments.

Scientific Prayer is a complete methodology to help you fulfill all your aspirations. You will learn how, with the nine-step process in the next section of this book.

PART IV

PRACTICING
SCIENTIFIC PRAYER

10 WHAT IS SCIENTIFIC PRAYER?

Scientific Prayer, also known as Spiritual Mind Treatment, Prayer Treatment, or Spiritual Mind Science, is a process of "treating" (healing and transforming) your mind until it realizes the truth of God's eternal good behind the appearance of false limitations. Once your mind has been treated, it is ready to accept the action of the Spiritual Law to demonstrate (materialize) your prayer.

NEW THOUGHT

Spiritual Mind Treatment has created miracles for millions of people. Divine Science, Science of Mind, Religious Science, Unity Church, and other nonsectarian "New Thought" teachings all use Scientific Prayer in various forms. New Thought teachings, including Divine Revelation®, propose that all difficulties can be overcome through metaphysical remedies, such as prayer and affirmation. According to Charles S. Braden's *Spirits in Rebellion*, a few tenets of New Thought are as follows:

- All primary causes are internal forces.

- Mind is primary and causative.

- Man is a living soul, a child of God, a spiritual citizen in a divine universe.

- The remedy for all defect and disorder is metaphysical, in the realm of mental and spiritual causes.

- God is immanent, indwelling Spirit, all-wisdom, all-goodness, ever-present in the universe.

- Evil has no place in the world as a permanent reality; it is the absence of good.

- There is a divine humanity and a human brotherhood.

- There is present and progressive revelation.

- There is no formal creed.

- Death has no sting and disease has no terror, for they can be overcome.

- Life is crowned with joy, health, and abundance—the rightful inheritance of every child of God.[1]

WHO FOUNDED NEW THOUGHT?

Where, when, and with whom did New Thought originate? In the 1800s—with the teachings of philosophers Emanuel Swedenborg, Franz Anton Mesmer, and Ralph Waldo Emerson.

Emanuel Swedenborg (1688–1772), Swedish philosopher, scientist, and theologian, theorized that this time is the beginning of "The New Church." This church, symbolized by the New Jerusalem in the book of Revelation as the holy city, is not a building or a religion, but a new era of God's relationship with human beings in a time of peace and understanding.[2]

Franz Anton Mesmer (1734–1815), a Viennese physician who resided in Paris, proposed a theory of magnetism, a mutual, reciprocal influence, wielded by a universally diffused, incomparably subtle "fluid" that flows through both animate and inanimate objects. By using his will to direct these currents, which cleansed and restored the nerves of his patients, Mesmer successfully treated many cases thought to be hopeless. Mesmer said that humans possess an interior sense, an extension of sight, which is connected with the whole universe. Through this faculty, two minds can attain rapport. A pioneer in the field of holistic medicine, Mesmer healed through the power of the mind, and he warned of the hazards of drugs.[3]

Ralph Waldo Emerson (1803–1882), Harvard-educated American essayist, poet, and popular philosopher, began as a Unitarian minister in Boston. Yet he achieved worldwide fame as a lecturer and essayist. Drawing upon English and German Romanticism, Neoplatonism, Kantianism, and Hinduism, Emerson developed an ethics of self-reliance and self-culture called "Transcendentalism," which recognized the essential divinity of humanity. The Transcendentalists sought the direct experience of God, nurturing of the soul, and lifelong spiritual growth.[4]

PHINEAS QUIMBY

The "Father of New Thought" was a miraculous healer, Phineas Parkhurst Quimby (1802–1866). Wasting away from tuberculosis, Quimby believed himself to be on death's door. However, as he forcefully drove a stubborn horse during a carriage ride, a change of attitude resulted in an inexplicable improvement in his condition. With renewed hope, in 1838, Quimby attended a public demonstration of mesmerism by Charles Poyen St. Sauveur, a French disciple of Franz Anton Mesmer. Quimby began to experiment with the curative affects of hypnotism, and in 1840 he gave his first public demonstration with a particularly gifted, intuitive subject, Lucius Burkmar, who clairvoyantly diagnosed and then reversed many diseases through seemingly ridiculous yet highly effective cures.

Through his experiments, Quimby realized how profoundly one mind influences another through the power of suggestion. He determined that disease is a deranged state of mind, caused by the unfortunate state of the ill person's belief. Through this realization, Quimby cured himself of tuberculosis by emancipating himself from false belief and by knowing the truth.

After Quimby's recovery, he spent many years in an all-consuming quest to condense his discovery into a repeatable science of spiritual healing that could be taught for the benefit of humanity. Thinking he had rediscovered Jesus' method of healing, Quimby concluded that all causes are spiritual and that healing takes place by means of the Christ wisdom and the God in us. He believed that the soul—one with God in image and likeness—cannot be ill. He called his method "Christian science" or "the science of life and happiness."[5]

Ridiculed by the medical profession and the masses, Quimby was adored by those who came for healing. From 1847 until his passing in 1866, he treated 12,000 patients. His loyal students included Rev. Warren Felt Evans, Annetta G. Seabury Dresser, and her husband Julius A. Dresser, who are considered founders of the New Thought movement.[6]

According to Horatio W. Dresser, son of Annetta and Julius Dresser, Quimby believed that:

> *"Disease is due to false reasoning in regard to sensations, which man unwittingly develops by impressing wrong thoughts and mental pictures upon the subconscious spiritual matter. As disease is due to false reasoning, so health is due to knowledge of the truth. To remove disease permanently, it is necessary to know the cause, the error which led to it. 'The explanation is the cure.' To know the truth about life is therefore the sovereign remedy for all ills."*[7]

CHRISTIAN SCIENCE

Mary Patterson (1821–1910) from Boston was struggling with personal loss and chronic illness. She sought relief in various alternative treatments, including homeopathy and what is now called the "placebo effect." She concluded that a patient's belief plays a powerful role in healing.

Frail and sickly, Patterson was carried on a stretcher to her first appointment with Phineas Quimby in 1862. Quickly healed under his guidance, Patterson became an ardent admirer and devoted student. One month after Quimby's death in 1866, Patterson was critically injured by a severe fall on an icy sidewalk. While reading about the healing power of Jesus in her

Bible, she experienced a miraculous healing. Later, she referred to this as the moment she discovered Christian Science.

Quimby's criticism of traditional religious practices did not square with Patterson's Christian values. So, she founded her own teaching and wrote *Science and Health with Key to the Scriptures* in 1875. In this book she explained what she believed to be the natural, repeatable science behind Jesus' healing methods.

In 1877, Mrs. Patterson married a student, Asa Gilbert Eddy, and became Mary Baker Eddy. She then founded the Church of Christ, Scientist (Christian Science) in Boston in 1879. Today, her church has spread throughout the world. In 1908, she launched *The Christian Science Monitor*, a leading international newspaper, the recipient of seven Pulitzer Prizes.[8]

At first, Eddy credited Quimby as her mentor. However, after his death, Eddy claimed to be barely acquainted with him. Quimby's students Annetta and Julius Dresser and their son, Horatio W. Dresser, as well as Edward J. Arens (Eddy's former student) attacked Eddy's teachings and accused her of plagiarizing Quimby's writings for the rest of her life.[9]

EMMA HOPKINS COLLEGE

Eddy's student, Emma Curtis Hopkins (1853–1925), worked on the *Christian Science Journal* until 1885, when she left Christian Science to form her own group—to Eddy's immense disapproval. As an advocate of women's leadership, Hopkins graduated twenty women out of her first class of twenty-two people at the Emma Hopkins College of Metaphysical Science. Hopkins' college enrolled as many as one thousand students at a time for her two-week classes.

In the first chapter of *Scientific Christian Mental Practice*, Hopkins stated that God is good, there is good for everyone, and everyone ought to have good, through the power of the Word:

"You will see that by speaking Truth you are Spirit, and that by speaking Truth are Omnipotent."[10]

Mary Baker Eddy excommunicated Hopkins in 1887 and again in 1888 along with Julius Dresser,

> "...for being Mind-quacks who were spreading abroad patchwork books, false compendiums of my system crediting some ignoramus or infidel with teaching they have stolen from me."[11]

DIVINE SCIENCE

One of Emma Curtis Hopkins' students, Malinda Cramer (1844–1906), had been an invalid for nearly twenty-five years. One morning in 1885, she had a spiritual realization: "If I ever got well it would be by the power of Holy Spirit. Then there is one way of out these conditions; I must seek that way, the Truth of the presence of Spirit." Since her physicians declared she was incurable, Malinda decided to never see another physician. When her husband asked what she would do, she responded, "Get well of course."[12]

Malinda described her life-changing experience of the all-absorbing presence and power of Spirit: *"This presence was more than personal, it was omnipresence; it was more than any visible object before me; it was real and permanent. It was so vivifying and illumining I knew that I was one with it. I realized it to be my life; the very being, knowledge, health and power that I am."*[13]

As Malinda recovered swiftly, she began treating patients successfully, using the principle: "Truth made [them] whole, and I neither saw nor named disease."[14] In 1888, along with her husband Frank, Malinda founded the Home College of Divine Science in San Francisco.[15]

In Pueblo, Colorado, Nona L. Brooks (1861–1945), was healed of an ailment in a class taught by Mrs. Bingham, a student of Emma Curtis Hopkins. Nona and her sisters, Althea Brooks Small and Fannie Brooks James, collaborated with Malinda Cramer to found the International Divine Science Association in 1892.[16]

Unity Church

Charles Fillmore (1854–1948), a student of metaphysics, Spiritualism, and Eastern religions, met his wife, Mary Caroline "Myrtle" Page (1845–1931), in Texas and they settled in Pueblo, Colorado. Charles went into real estate with the brother-in-law of Nona L. Brooks. After an economic crisis wiped out the real estate market and Myrtle contracted tuberculosis, the couple moved to Kansas City in 1884, where they sought healing with Dr. E. B. Weeks, a student of Emma Curtis Hopkins. Myrtle's spiritual breakthrough came as she fervently applied the affirmation, "I am a child of God and therefore I do not inherit sickness." She began to pray for and heal others, and she was miraculously cured within one year.[17]

The Fillmores studied Christian Science with Emma Curtis Hopkins, and in 1889 they founded the magazine *Modern Thought*. In 1890, they started the *Society of Silent Help*, a healing prayer group. In 1891, *Unity* became its official magazine. In 1895 Unity became the name of their society.[18]

Charles Fillmore stated:

> *"We have studied many isms, many cults. People of every religion under the sun claim that we either belong to them or have borrowed the best part of our teaching from them. We have borrowed the best from all religions, that is the reason we are called Unity…Unity is not a sect, not a separation of people into an exclusive group of know-it-alls. Unity is the Truth that is taught in all religions, simplified…so that anyone can understand and apply it. Students of Unity do not find it necessary to sever their church affiliations."*[19]

In 1903, the Unity School of Practical Christianity was founded. In 1924, the official publication, *Unity Daily Word*, began spreading the message of Unity to millions of people worldwide. As a result of the Fillmores' efforts, Unity is the largest of the New Thought organizations.

RELIGIOUS SCIENCE

The essay "On Self-Reliance" by Ralph Waldo Emerson inspired Ernest Holmes (1887–1960) to study Oriental literature, Hebrew Scriptures, sacred writings of India, and mysteries of the Greeks.[20] He also studied teachings of Mary Baker Eddy, W.W. Atkinson, Ralph Waldo Trine, and Christian D. Larson. In 1912, Holmes moved to California and embraced the wisdom of Thomas Troward (1847–1916), who taught New Thought in a less religious manner than his contemporaries. He focused on cosmic intelligence, science, and consciousness. In 1924, his studies with Emma Curtis Hopkins brought mysticism into his work.

Holmes authored the New Thought classic *The Science of Mind* in 1926. He felt his teachings of self-healing were contrary to founding an organization. Yet, under pressure from his followers, he founded the Institute of Religious Science and School of Philosophy with his brother Fenwicke (a Congregational Minister) in 1927. In 1949, the International Association of Religious Science Churches was formed. In 1954, the organization split into two separate groups: United Church of Religious Science and Religious Science International.[21]

SPAWNED BY NEW THOUGHT

These New Thought pioneers were the direct or indirect precursors of the entire human potential movement, New Age, Alcoholics Anonymous, positive thinking, motivational speakers, life coaches, and many sales training and self-hypnosis methods currently in use. Beginning on page 290 you will find a list of some of the great authors and spiritual leaders that spawned or sprang from New Thought. A few of them are Napoleon Hill, Earl Nightingale, Og Mandino, Zig Ziglar, Brian Tracy, Tony Robbins, Norman Vincent Peale, and Robert Schuller.

It is astonishing how little is known about New Thought, considering how many famous authors of the twentieth century studied it, used it, and

129

wrote about it. I often call New Thought "the best-kept secret, hidden treasure in the world."

NEW THOUGHT MYTHS

Let us dispel a few myths right now about New Thought:

New Thought is not New Age, and many New Age practices, such as fortune-telling and divination, are at odds with New Thought principles. Scientific Prayer and Religious Science have nothing to do with Scientology. Unity Church is not linked with the Unitarian or Universalist Church, which espouses an entirely different philosophy. Religious Science is not associated with Christian Science, although they both stem from New Thought roots in the 1800s.

In addition to the organizations mentioned above, there are many independent, unaffiliated New Thought churches. There are over 2,000 New Thought churches in the world. On my website you will find links to New Thought churches in your area.

DEFINING TREATMENT

ERNEST HOLMES

What is Scientific Prayer, otherwise known as Spiritual Mind Treatment? Ernest Holmes defines it:

> *"Treatment is the art, the act, and the science of consciously inducing thought within the Universal Subjectivity, for the purpose of demonstrating that we are surrounded by a Creative Medium which responds to us through a law of correspondence. In its more simple meaning, treatment is the time, process and method necessary to the changing of our thought. Treatment is changing the thought of negation, of doubt and fear, and causing it to perceive the ever-presence of God."* [22]

By transforming or "treating" your mind, you can change the outcome of actions that have been set into motion by your former mind-set. By setting up conditions in your mind that allow God to work through the Spiritual Law, your transformation occurs. Then, you accept, with full faith, that the desired goal is achieved. Ernest Holmes declared,

"All prayers will be answered when we pray aright. The first necessity is faith...We simply have a new approach to an old truth, a more intelligent, a more systematic way of consciously arriving at faith. This is what treatment is for." [23]

EMMET FOX

New Thought author Emmet Fox called Scientific Prayer "the Golden Key to harmony and happiness." He said,

"In scientific prayer it is God who works, and not you, and so your particular limitations or weaknesses are of no account in the process. You are only the channel through which the Divine action takes place, and your treatment will be just the getting of yourself out of the way. Beginners often get startling results at the first time of trying, for all that is absolutely essential is to have an open mind, and sufficient faith to try the experiment. Apart from that you may hold any views on religion, or none.

"As for the actual method of working, like all fundamental things, it is simplicity itself. All that you have to do is this: Stop thinking about the difficulty, whatever it is, and think about God instead. This is the complete rule, and if only you will do this, the trouble, whatever it is, will presently disappear...If you can become so absorbed in this consideration of the spiritual world that you really forget for a while all about the trouble concerning which you began to pray, you will presently find that you are safely and comfortably out of that difficulty—that your demonstration is made." [24]

JACK ADDINGTON

Rev. Dr. Jack Addington (d. 1998), Religious Science minister and author of *Your Needs Met*, stated:

> *"Treatment is scientific prayer. It is an individual thought process whereby man's thinking is directed away from the need or problem and put in direct alignment with the divine Mind; thereby enabling him to receive his highest good...*
>
> *"As long as man's attention is riveted on his problem or difficulty, he is going to reproduce into his experience more of the same. Through treatment his attention is focused upon the Infinite, and the result is that he then outpictures his new elevated thinking—infinite Intelligence, omnipotent Power and omnipresent Love. Through treatment man is given dominion. It is an open door to all that the Father hath. Through treatment, 'all that the Father hath is thine.'"*[25]

Your prayer will be answered when you let go and let God. By immersing yourself in loving, joyous, presence of the almighty Creator, your troubles simply melt away. God is the healer of all wounds, the comforter, the divine physician, the all-benevolent, the source of unconditional love and abundance, the wish-bestowing tree.

ANN AND PETER MEYER

In the 1980s, I studied Scientific Prayer and Prayer Therapy with Dr. Peter Meyer, founder of a New Thought teaching called Teaching of Intuitional Metaphysics. He was also co-founder of Teaching of the Inner Christ, with Ann Meyer. The Meyers were Religious Science practitioners from San Diego, on the board of directors of Rev. Jack Addington's Church of Religious Science.

Peter and Ann Meyer discovered a way to receive clear inner revelation from the deepest recesses of the heart. This extraordinary process is taught in my book, *Divine Revelation*. In the Scientific Prayer method offered in this book, it is recommended that you receive the words of your prayer directly from Spirit through inner revelation. Such words will have the most profound effect on consciousness and therefore the most powerful results. Words spoken from Spirit have a tangible effect that pierces the atmosphere with potency.

THE STEP-BY-STEP FORMULA

The steps of Scientific Prayer developed from ancient sources—the "Lord's Prayer" of Matthew 6:9–13, in which Jesus summarized the ancient Hebrew prayer *Amidah* ("to stand"), also known as *Shemoneh Esrei* ("eighteen blessings," see page 283), a sacred Jewish prayer, recited daily.

Scientific Prayer is a form of affirmative, positive prayer. It uses a process of logic and deductive reasoning that Ernest Holmes called "argumentative treatment," based upon the fundamental premise that God is all there is. During this process, you transform your mind by convincing yourself of the reality of truth behind false appearances. However, treatment is more than just logic. It is a love discipline—a consciousness of inner knowing and cognition of truth through inner revelation. Scientific Prayer is a way to realize the truth through the following steps—the "Rs":

1. **REQUEST in RELAXATION**
   (Goal or Intention)
   State the goal for your prayer treatment.

   The purpose of Scientific Prayer is to create change from an undesirable condition to a desired one. Therefore, the first step of prayer treatment is a clear, precise affirmation of your intended outcome or objective for the prayer along with the full name of the person for whom you are praying. This declaration is made in a state of relaxation and quietude of mind and body.

   > Life is a mirror and will reflect back to the thinker what he thinks into it.
   >
   > —ERNEST HOLMES

133

2. **RECOGNITION in RESPECT**
(Glorification)

Come to a conviction that God is all there is, and God is the source of your good.

The second step is to arrive at total certainty that there is one life, and that life is God the good, omnipotent Spirit. An infinite power creates and maintains this universe—a power much greater than the difficulty at hand. This universal creative intelligence receives and embodies your goal, then brings it into materialization, exactly as spoken. Spirit cannot do otherwise, because Spirit is never other than perfection everywhere now. In this step you affirm your understanding of the nature of God, and you name specific attributes of God related to your particular goal. Glorification of God invites divine Spirit into awareness and brings gratitude and humility.

> There is but one ultimate Power. This Power is to each one what he is to it.
>
> —ERNEST HOLMES

3. **RAPPORT in RELATIONSHIP**
(Unification or Identification)

Come to a conviction that you are one with God.

Since God is all that is, there can be nothing outside of or separate from God—right where the trouble seems to be, there God is. According to Ernest Holmes, treatment is "a recognition of Spirit's Omniscience, Omnipotence, and Omnipresence, and a realization of humanity's unity with Spirit."[26] In this step you assert that whatever is true about God is also true of you, because there is only one divine mind operating through and as every individual. By consciously uniting with that divine creative intelligence, you are one with God, one with the person you are praying for, and one with the attributes of God mentioned in the previous step. This brings your awareness into harmony with the presence of God's eternal love. As you enter the spiritual realm and embrace it, you experience your good now, in plentiful and flawless supply. In this elevated state of awareness, you are ready to proceed to the next step.

4. **RESOLUTION with RESOLVE (Claim, Choice, Affirmation, or Declaration)**

Choose or claim the goal that you desire to fulfill (or better).

> Why stand we here trembling around, Calling on God for help, and not ourselves, in whom God dwells?
>
> —WILLIAM BLAKE

The fourth step is to clearly state the goal as already manifested. This is not begging or pleading. Instead, it is declaring and affirming the truth in its full completion. Using your creative power of intention, you make a positive declaration that includes a detailed description of your expected objective. The clearer your goal is stated, the easier it is achieved. By claiming the intended outcome as something you already own, it is yours. Once you have made your declaration, then, in the next step, you remove any obstacles preventing its fulfillment.

> Whatever your mind can conceive and believe it can achieve.
>
> —NAPOLEON HILL

5. **RENEWAL through REASONING and REMOVAL (Elimination or Healing, Denials and Affirmations)**

Treat your mind by eliminating mental blocks that prevent you from accepting your goal. Arrive at total conviction that you are healed of anything standing in your way.

The fifth step heals beliefs and habits blocking your fulfillment. The entire kingdom is already yours, and God does not need to be convinced. However, your own mind needs to be convinced that what you desire, you deserve.

> No person, place, or thing can deny you of your forward movement into consciousness of God.
>
> —PETER V. MEYER

135

Therefore, you are not trying to change God's mind—you are changing your own. Affirmations and denials, as found in the healing prayers in Chapters 13 and 14, open the pathway to obtaining your desired outcome. Through reasoning and revelation, all error thought is denied and truth is discerned, all doubts are dissolved and total certainty is attained.

6. **REALIZATION of REALITY**
   (Conviction or Acceptance)

Arrive at a conviction that you deserve to have your goal. Accept it as yours.

The sixth step is to know, beyond a shadow of doubt, that your prayer is answered. In the first 5 steps you brought evidence before your mind; therefore, you are now ready to make a conclusive assumption. Absolute conviction, beyond faith, is complete and perfect, leaving no room for the mind to waver. Once you have arrived at total realization of the absolute truth of the infinite perfection and ultimate deserving of the person that you are praying for, then you have attained a calm, quiet assurance of truth.

> First deserve and
> then desire.
>
> —ENGLISH PROVERB

7. **REWARD in REJOICING**
   (Gratitude)

Thank God that your goal is fulfilled.

The seventh step is rejoicing in gratitude that your intention has manifested in a successful outcome. Since you have arrived at full conviction that your objective is achieved, you thank God in advance. In offering gratitude, you are not attempting to influence or manipulate God. You are simply confirming your belief that the situation is resolved in God's own wise and perfect ways.

> Saying thank you is more
> than good manners. It is
> good spirituality.
>
> —ALFRED PAINTER

8. **RELEASE into RESTFULNESS**
(Letting Go)

Give your prayer over to God; let go and let God.

The eighth step is letting go completely and turning your prayer over to God and to the action of the Spiritual Law. You are not responsible for the outcome of your prayer treatment. Your sole responsibility is to attain a definite image of the perfection of the person you are praying for—and then, to let it go. You have done your work. Now the Spiritual Law does its work. As long as you hold on, its work is blocked. When you let go, the action of the Spiritual Law begins. The Release is the most important step, because, at the moment of letting go, the manifestation literally occurs. You experience a new, exhilarating confidence that the envisioned condition is not only attainable, but is already emerging into reality.

> I myself do nothing. The Holy Spirit accomplishes all through me.
> —WILLIAM BLAKE

9. **REPOSE with REVELATION**
(Silence)

Sit in quietude and allow nature to function to manifest your goal.

After thoroughly letting go and giving over to Spirit, you now dwell in the silence of your being. At that moment you relax completely and surrender to God in wholeness. Deep within that absolute silence, at the center of your awareness, is the field of all possibilities, where miracles happen and manifestation occurs. In that silence dwells the fulfillment of all desires—including the one you just prayed for.

> Do less and accomplish more. Do nothing and accomplish everything.
> —MAHARISHI MAHESH YOGI

By the time you finish your Scientific Prayer treatment, your goal has already manifested in consciousness, because you have healed your mind and thereby arrived at a complete conviction. Other forms of prayer do not include healing. Yet, it is foolish to imagine attaining your goal without first healing whatever prevents its attainment. Healing mental blockages is the golden key that opens the gates to the divine kingdom.

If you are in touch with your feelings and willing to do the soul-searching necessary to uncover hidden blockages, your prayers will be effective. Your divine banquet will be laid before you in a cornucopia of God's blessings and grace. However, if you are in denial about your feelings, if you cannot perceive your habit patterns and stumbling blocks, then deeper introspection is required.

MIRACLE OF CREATION

What is the hidden treasure, the kernel of magic that makes Scientific Prayer so successful? The secret of precipitation is found in the mysterious act of letting go and dwelling in the silence of God consciousness. The moment you give your goal over to God, your intention literally manifests. As you say, "AMEN," or "SO BE IT," or "AND SO IT IS"—that is the instant of the miracle of materialization.

This supreme miracle-making activity appears in ancient myths—such as the phoenix bird, which, after being consumed by fire, rises from the flames, reborn. Rebirth following every death is the fundamental principle of all creation myths. Only by dying (letting go), can new birth occur.

In the philosophy of India, the three *gunas* tell a similar tale. *Sattwa, rajas,* and *tamas* are three modes that continually create, maintain, and destroy every part of creation in each living moment. The entire universe is alive by virtue of the interplay of these gunas in cycles of death and rebirth.

For any new creation to arise, there must be a death to the old. Death and rebirth is the way that time gains continuity in the physical universe, where change is the only never-changing constant. By letting go and allowing nature to bring about change, something new can appear.

Therefore, the principle of letting go at the end of a Scientific Prayer treatment mirrors the way nature functions. The Release invokes the magic of precipitation, when the outcome of your prayer takes form. By giving your prayer treatment over to God, you are borrowing nature's miracle-making method in order to make your own miracle.

> It would appear as though a miracle were taking place, as though Providence is granting him some special gift. But such is not the case . . . The Law of Mind is automatically reversing the conditions to meet [his] new state of awareness.
>
> —ERNEST HOLMES[27]

In the next chapter, you will practice the nine-step method of Scientific Prayer.

11 THE NINE-STEP SCIENTIFIC PRAYER METHOD

Thus far you have learned the philosophy and basic steps of the Scientific Prayer methodology. Now let us create a Scientific Prayer for a particular goal you want to achieve. Use this chapter as a manual to write your first Scientific Prayer right now. Get a paper and pen. Are you ready? Let us get started.

CHOOSING YOUR GOAL

Decide on a particular goal you intend to accomplish. Write it or state it clearly. Doing the exercise on page 29 of this book will help you discover what to pray for.

> Learn to will what God wishes, and everything you want will certainly happen.
>
> —ELIPHAS LEVI

If you do not consider your highest good according to God's perfect will, you might get frustrated struggling to achieve a goal that you never wanted in the first place.

Here are a few examples of the kind of goals you might consider praying for:

Examples:

1. Healing a friend or family member.

2. The perfect job for you, for your spouse, or your child.

3. Academic achievement for your child.

NINE STEPS OF SCIENTIFIC PRAYER

REQUEST	Goal
RECOGNITION	Glorification
RAPPORT	Unification
RESOLUTION	Claim
RENEWAL	Healing
REALIZATION	Conviction
REWARD	Gratitude
RELEASE	Letting Go
REPOSE	Silence

4. Healing a family member's drug addiction.

5. Finding your perfect home.

6. Buying your perfect new car.

7. Attracting your perfect love or marriage relationship.

Be very careful what you set your heart upon, for you will surely have it.

—RALPH WALDO EMERSON

8. Healing your relationship with your parents.

9. Self-love and self-acceptance.

10. Healing a bodily disease.

11. Forgiving your ex-husband, ex-boss, or ex-friend.

12. Paying off your debts.

13. Acquiring money for retirement.

14. Experiencing inner peace.

15. Realizing God.

Prayer is the soul's sincere desire, uttered or unexpressed;
the motion of a hidden fire that trembles in the breast.

—James Montgomery

Step 1: Request (Goal or Intention)

In this first section of your prayer, clearly state your goal (or something even better that God might have in mind), along with the full name of the person you are praying for. This statement includes everything you want to reveal about your goal. The format of this section is as follows:

"This is a treatment for ("myself" and your full name—or the full name of the person you are praying for) for (the goal you are praying for) or better now."

Examples:

1. "This is a treatment for myself, John Robert Owens, for my perfect forty-hour per week job now at a salary of $_____ per week or better, in a harmonious work environment, in which I can set my own hours and use my talents as an artist. I ask for all this or better now."

2. "This is a treatment for myself, Sandy Lee Flowers, for my perfect love relationship with my perfect mate with compatible likes, interests, appetites, ideals, and purpose or better now. My mate is

compatible with me in every way: spiritually, mentally, socially, intellectually, emotionally, sexually, and physically or better now. I ask for all this or better now."

3. "This is a treatment for Joan Leslie Smith, for healing her relationship with her father or better now."

4. "This is a treatment for myself, Steven James Schwartz, for perfect health of my body and the illumination of any seeming appearance of HIV or better now."

5. "This is a treatment for Iris Betty White for her perfect mental health and for the healing of her seeming alcoholism or better now."

6. "This is a treatment for myself, Terrance Lee Masters, for self-love, self-acceptance, self-confidence, and self-worth or better now."

Before writing this Request section of your prayer, please study pages 157 to 162 in Chapter 12 to learn how to word this part of your prayer precisely, clearly, and properly.

Now, write your Request section of your prayer.

STEP 2: RECOGNITION (GLORIFICATION)

In this section of the prayer, you convince yourself that God is the source of all good. Realize who God is and recognize that God creates the miracle of answered prayer. God will fulfill your desire when you pray with faith. Acknowledging, revering, praising, and glorifying God brings gratitude and humility.

Here, you recognize qualities of God that specifically relate to your goal. Continue to list God's qualities until you completely persuade yourself that God is the one and only source of your good.

> There is an inherent law of mind that we increase whenever we praise. The whole of creation responds to praise and is glad.
>
> —CHARLES FILLMORE

143

Examples:

1. When praying for money, you might say statements such as: "God is the endless source of supply. God's wealth is circulating in the universe, and there is always a divine surplus. Money is God's energy in action. God is unlimited bounty, the cornucopia of all good. God is the cosmic benefactor. God's world is rich with blessings and opportunities. God is the ever-flowing stream of perpetual riches, the fountainhead of infinite prosperity."

2. For health, you may say: "God is the one healing power and healing presence in the universe. God is the divine physician. God is the reservoir of cosmic energy. God is the source of health, the consummate healer. God is perfect well-being and divine vitality."

3. For a home: "God is the divine protector, the source of shelter in the cosmos. God is the divine architect, contractor, and builder of this universe. God is the safe haven, the harbor in all storms. God is the one place of asylum, the abode of refuge and comfort."

4. For a job: "God is perfect purpose, divine destiny, and fulfillment of heartfelt desires. God is perfect direction and divine order. God is the source of abundance, the fountainhead of bounty, the continuous river of wealth and all good. God is the supplier of endless riches."

5. For success: "With God, all things are possible. God is the source of endless blessings and infinite possibilities. God is good, very good perfection now. With God, each day holds the promise of new achievements. Every day is God's new opportunity. Yesterday is over and done; today is the first new day of God's blessings. God is an ever-fresh world of endless possibilities, wonders, and miracles. Every moment is a miracle."

6. For divine purpose and direction: "God is perfect divine order and timing in the universe. God is perfect purpose and divine

destiny. God is the lighthouse, the almighty wayshower. God is the compass, the director of our path. God is the captain of our ship."

7. For God's will in your life: "There is one power and one presence at work in the universe—God the good, omnipotent. God is the source of all good. God is the all that is—the all-powerful, all-encompassing, eternal light. God is perfection everywhere now. God is the truth of being, the oneness of Spirit. God's love is the all-embracing comfort for the heart and wisdom for the soul."

8. For happiness: "God is divine joy and contentment. God is the peaceful garden of happiness and fulfillment. God is the one source of satisfaction in the universe. God is perfect oneness and divine bliss. God is the endless wellspring of pleasure and delight. God is fullness and utter contentment."

9. To attract your perfect mate: "God is the supreme matchmaker. God is unconditional love. God is the law of magnetic attraction. God is perfect discernment and wisdom. God is divine happiness, satisfaction, and fulfillment. God is the all-loving, the pinnacle of joy."

10. For personal power or self-authority: "God is the all-powerful. God is the one power at work in the universe—the all-that-is, the omnipresent, omnipotent, the all-embracing and all-encompassing. God is the ultimate authority, the sovereign power. God is the tower of strength, the supreme majesty and greatest glory. God is the invincible rock, staff, and shield of this cosmos."

11. For divine protection: "God is the guardian of this cosmos and of our life. God is the shelter, the haven of security. God is the shield of divine protection. God is the perfect line of defense against all enemies and saboteurs. God is our protector, our strength, and our armor. God is our safe harbor and guides us through the storm."

12. For inner peace: "God is perfect peace and serenity. God's peace permeates and envelops the universe. God is wholeness, oneness, and contentment. God is perfect quietude. God is the light of life, the fountainhead of harmony. God is the river of tranquility. God is a still pond, without a ripple. God is an arbor of peace. God is infinite stillness."

13. For divine guidance and inspiration: "God is the source of wisdom and illumination. God is omniscient. God is the all-wise, the source of all knowledge and creative intelligence. God's inspiration is the music of the spheres. God's wisdom illuminates the cosmos. God's love resonates as divine ideas that bless our life. The divine mind guides and directs the cosmos. Divine understanding is the guiding light of life."

In addition to these suggestions, please refer to Chapter 14 of this book, with three hundred affirmations useful for your Scientific Prayers. I also recommend books by authors Ernest Holmes, Catherine Ponder, Joseph Murphy, Fredrick Bailes, Frances Scovel Shinn, and the Bible's book of Psalms for many more truth statements for your prayers.

Now, go ahead and write this Recognition/Glorification section of your prayer. Please feel free to use your own heartfelt expressions, rather than copying the examples above.

STEP 3: RAPPORT (UNIFICATION OR IDENTIFICATION):

In the Rapport section, you convince yourself that you are unified with God, the perfect source of good. Right where the trouble seems to be, there God is. Here, you appreciate God at work in your life, fulfilling your goal. State that you are one with God and God's qualities that you just listed in the Recognition section. Use the word "now" to emphasize the immediacy of your contact with God. Continue to make these statements until you attain total conviction that you are merged and aligned with God.

The following examples include both the Recognition and the Rapport sections, so you can examine how these two sections relate to each other.

Examples:

1. **Recognition:** "I recognize that God is the one power and one presence that dwells in the universe, God the good, omnipotent. God is the source of all good, very good perfection. God is supreme benevolence. God is perfection everywhere now." **Rapport:** "I AM one with God's perfection and God's good now. That holy presence is my own divine presence. In God I live and move and have my being. I AM God in action, God in activity. I AM God's ambassador, God's philanthropist. I let go and let God do divine, perfect work through me."

   > In reality there are not two.
   > There is only One.
   > —RAMAKRISHNA PARAMAHANSA

2. **Recognition:** "I recognize that God is the crown of glory. God is the golden door to all success, honor, and achievement. With God, all is possible. God's blessings flow freely in a bliss-bestowing stream. God works wonders and miracles." **Rapport:** "I AM one with God's glory. I open God's golden door to success, honor, and achievement. I AM one with God's fresh, new opportunities. I AM God's instrument of highest achievement. I say yes to all God's blessings flowing into my life in a never-ending stream. God's wonder-working power works miracles in my life. I AM a winner. I AM victorious."

3. **Recognition**: "I recognize that God is infinite happiness, the radiant Spirit of delight and ecstasy. God's light is joyful energy. God is joy in action and activity, a celebration of life. God is the blissful purveyor of wonders and miracles. The rapture of God beats in every heart. God's joyous expressions flow in perfect rhythm." **Rapport:** "My soul sings a song of joy in God. The joy of Spirit illumines my thoughts and energizes my body. God's joy

expresses through me as a celebration of my spirituality. I embrace the joy and wonder of God. God's happiness flows through me with every beat of my heart. I AM the joy of life expressing and receiving in perfect rhythm."

4. **Recognition:** "I recognize that God is the miracle-maker. God is the way, the truth, and the life. God's love melts situations that appear impossible. God is only good, good, and very good. God always makes a way where there is seemingly no way. Let there be light, let there be light now, for the highest good of all concerned." **Rapport:** "I AM created in the likeness and image of God; therefore, I respond to life's challenges as God would respond, by knowing the truth, which sets me free. I AM one with God's supreme good. I bless everyone, everything, and every situation in my life now, as good, good, and very good. I walk in the circle of God's love, and I AM divinely irresistible to my highest good now. My life is filled with wonders, miracles, and blessings."

5. **Recognition:** "I recognize that God is the one power and the one presence in the universe and in my life. God is the divine protector, the source of all good in the universe. God is perfect shelter, safe haven and harbor in the storm." **Rapport:** "I AM one with God's protective presence right now and always. Right where the trouble seems to be, there God is. The light of God surrounds me. The love of God enfolds me. The power of God protects me. The presence of God watches over me. Wherever I AM, God is, and all is well."

6. **Recognition:** "Our Father, who art in heaven, hallowed be thy name. **Rapport:** "Thy kingdom come, thy will be done, on earth as it is in heaven."

Now, go ahead and write your Rapport section of your prayer.

STEP 4: RESOLUTION (CLAIM, CHOICE, OR DECLARATION)

In the Resolution section of the prayer, you clearly and precisely state the goal that you intend to attain (or something even better). Claim it for yourself now, with utter determination, free from doubt. That means you know and state that your goal is already achieved. You own it and you affirm that it is yours now.

> Do not always ask when you pray, but instead affirm that God's blessings are being given.
>
> —NORMAN VINCENT PEALE

This section is a restatement of your Request section, but in a particular format, beginning with the words, "I therefore claim for..." The following examples include both the Request and Resolution sections, so you can see how these two sections correspond to each other.

Examples:

1. **Request:** "This is a treatment for myself, Joan Elizabeth Smith, for the perfect healing of my relationship with Frank Edward Smith or better now." **Resolution:** "I therefore claim for myself, Joan Elizabeth Smith, the perfect healing of my relationship with Frank Edward Smith or better now."

2. **Request:** "This is a treatment for Jonas Buckingham for perfect health of his colon or better now." **Resolution:** "I therefore claim for Jonas Buckingham the perfect health of his colon or better now."

3. **Request:** "This is a treatment for myself, Alexander Zalesky, for perfect self-acceptance, self-love, and self-worth or better now." **Resolution:** "I therefore claim for myself, Alexander Zalesky, my perfect self-acceptance, self-love, and self-worth or better now."

Now, go ahead and write the Request section for your prayer.

STEP 5: RENEWAL

(ELIMINATION OR HEALING, DENIALS AND AFFIRMATIONS)

In the Renewal portion, you treat or heal your mind by uncovering whatever blockages prevent you from fulfilling your goal. Then, you release these limiting beliefs and renew your mind to its pristine state of wholeness.

> Prayer is less about changing the world than it is about changing ourselves.
>
> —DAVID J. WOLPE

In order to arrive at a conviction that your goal is fulfilled, it is necessary to remove any obstacles preventing the full realization of that conviction. What are those obstacles? Some of them may be:

1. Your own limited thoughts and negations.

2. The influence of near and dear ones.

3. The influence of societal beliefs and judgments.

4. Your belief that you do not deserve to get your goal.

5. The influence of astral entities.

6. The influence of your past.

7. The influence of parents, church, teachers, and others.

8. Feelings of unforgiveness, anger, fear, hate, and resentment.

To heal negations and limitations, first become aware of what needs healing. Refer to the method on page 119. Your intuition can show you. Close your eyes and ask your higher self to help you.

Once you recognize what needs healing, please refer to Chapter 13 and use the recommended healing prayers and affirmations. Continue to heal all negations until you arrive at absolute conviction that your blockages are healed. Be sure that you achieve that complete certainty before going to the next section of your prayer. Here is an example of how the Healing section might be worded:

Example:

"I now know that I AM healing my relationship with Frank Edward Smith or better now. I now heal and release all thoughts that interfere with this claim, whether known or unknown, conscious or subconscious. My thoughts are now one with, the same as, and in tune with God's thought. I invoke the divine presence to heal my limitations and negations of fear, rejection, sadness, limitation, confusion, lack of faith, lack of trust, resentment, anger, pain, and frustration now. These false beliefs are healed, forgiven, and lifted into the light. I AM enlightened, I AM strengthened, I AM forgiven. I now instead welcome positive thoughts and emotions of love, self-acceptance, happiness, unboundedness, clarity, faith, trust, forgiveness, joy, wholeness, wisdom, healing, and peace.

"I call upon God to cut any and all psychic ties between myself and Frank Edward Smith now. These psychic ties are now lovingly cut, lifted, loved, healed, released, and let go. I call upon my divine self to shine the light of forgiveness on the relationship between myself and Frank Edward Smith now. I know that the forgiving power of God heals this relationship in perfect forgiveness now. The power of God within me completely forgives Frank Edward Smith now, for he did the very best he could do in every situation with me. Therefore, there is no reason for guilt or blame. I thank Frank Edward Smith for everything he has done in every situation with me. I know and accept now that on a deep level I asked for everything that happened in my relationship with Frank Edward Smith. Therefore I take full and complete responsibility for everything that Frank Edward Smith has done in every situation with me now.

"I picture Frank Edward Smith before me now and I say, 'Thank you, Frank. You have fulfilled my need and my desire. Thank you for being a vehicle for me to fulfill my need now.' The God within me forgives Frank Edward Smith completely now and the God within Frank Edward Smith forgives me completely now."

Now, write the Renewal portion of your prayer.

STEP 6: REALIZATION (CONVICTION OR ACCEPTANCE)

Once you have healed your mind in the Renewal section, you can arrive at a full conviction that your goal is now achieved. In the Realization portion of your prayer you simply state that you fully accept the fulfillment of your goal. Come to complete certainty that you deserve to have your goal and accept it. Now you know, beyond a shadow of a doubt, that your prayer is answered.

> Believe as though you are, and you will be.
>
> —ERNEST HOLMES

This section of your prayer will simply be a restatement of your Resolution section (Step 4) prefaced by the words, "I now fully accept in consciousness. . . ."

Examples:

1. **Resolution:** "I therefore claim for myself, Joan Elizabeth Smith, the perfect healing of my relationship with Frank Edward Smith or better now." **Realization:** "I now fully accept in consciousness the complete and perfect healing of my relationship with Frank Edward Smith or better now."

2. **Request:** "I therefore claim for Jonas Buckingham the perfect health of his colon or better now." **Realization:** "I now fully accept in consciousness the perfect vibrant health of Jonas Buckingham's colon or better now."

3. **Resolution:** "This is a treatment for myself, Alexander Zalesky, for perfect self-acceptance, self-love, and self-worth or better now." **Realization:** "I now fully accept in consciousness my perfect self-acceptance, self-love, and self-worth or better now."

Now, go ahead and write your Realization section of your prayer.

Step 7: Reward (Gratitude)

In the Reward portion of your prayer, you thank God for answered prayer. In other words, since you assume your goal is already fulfilled, you give gratitude to God that your goal is already achieved.

An attitude of gratitude is most salutary.

—Ernest Holmes

Here are a few examples of how to word your Reward section:

Examples:

1. "I thank God for manifesting this good in my life now."

2. "Thank you God."

3. "I now thank God for this answered prayer."

4. "I now thank God for manifesting this (goal) in my life now, under grace, in God's own wise and perfect ways."

5. "Thank you, Father, for this good, which is now manifest in my life."

6. "Thank you, Holy Father."

7. "Praise be to God in all His glory. Thank you, wonderful God."

8. I give thanks for the realization of this treatment and for the perfect working of the Spiritual Law, which responds to my thoughts and words.[1]

Now, write your Reward section of your prayer, using your own heartfelt words.

Step 8: Release (Letting Go)

The Release is the most important section of the prayer, for here you give your prayer over to God and allow the action of the Spiritual Law to fulfill it. Let your prayer go completely; let go and let God. Release your goal into Spirit.

Prayer is exhaling the spirit of man and inhaling the spirit of God.

—Edwin Keith

By letting go and letting God do the work, you are allowing the manifestation to occur. Here are examples of how to word your Release:

153

Examples:

1. "And SO IT IS."

2. "SO BE IT."

3. "AMEN."

4. "I now release this prayer fully and completely into the Spiritual Law of perfection everywhere now. I know that it is accepted and manifests now, under grace, in perfect ways. AND SO IT IS."

5. "I now release this treatment into the Spiritual Law. AND SO IT IS."

6. "I release this prayer into God's hands. AND SO IT IS."

7. "I now give this prayer over to God. SO BE IT."

8. "This is so now, and SO IT IS."

9. "It is so now. SO BE IT."

10. "I now release this prayer fully and completely into the Spiritual Law, which is at work on it right now. I do not know how the demonstration comes, but I know that it does come. My Word does not return to me void but goes forth to demonstrate as I have spoken. AMEN."

11. "I now release this treatment into the Spiritual Law. It now goes forth to manifest that which has been spoken. Thank you God and SO IT IS."

12. "I speak and it is done; I command and it stands fast." [2]

13. "I release this claim to God and to the natural law. My claim demonstrates now by the power and the presence of God. That is the nature of natural law. AMEN."

14. "In this feeling of gratitude. I release this treatment to the Law. I know it was done before I even asked." [3]

> **Meaning of AMEN**
>
> The word "AMEN" in Hebrew consists of the following letters:
>
> A: *Al* (God's name)
> M: *Melech* (Sovereign)
> EN: *Ne-eman* (Faithful, trustworthy, reliable)
>
> Thus, this word AMEN means that God, the one sovereign power, will surely fulfill your prayer, reliably, in a trustworthy, foolproof manner.

Now is time for you to write your Release portion of your prayer.

STEP 9: REPOSE (SILENCE)

After thoroughly letting go and giving over to Spirit, immediately close your eyes and give up completely. Do nothing, nothing, and less than nothing. In the silence after the Release, the actual physical manifestation occurs, and the creation is born. Here, you will feel ecstatic union with the divine, and you will sense your goal take form. Do not miss this feeling by rushing the end of your prayer. Sit quietly with eyes closed in complete silence. Savor the materialization as it occurs. It is a profound experience.

Now is time to stand up and read your complete prayer aloud in a clear voice with inner strength and conviction. Pretend as if your higher self is speaking your prayer through you. After speaking your prayer aloud, sit down, set aside your prayer, and close your eyes. Do nothing, nothing, and less than nothing.

> God will not enter your heart until it is silent and still.
>
> —PAUL BRUNTON

Go ahead and read your complete prayer aloud now.

WITH GOD

While moving through the steps of Scientific Prayer, you undergo a process of psychological transformation that changes the way you see your problem. No longer are you without hope, desperate and lonely, fighting your environment. Instead, you are cooperating with God in a glorious conspiracy of divine healing and spiritual awakening.

"With God all things are possible." [4]

When your egoic mind unites with the divine mind, you remember that you are a divine being. You stand as God's partner, co-creating your destiny. God becomes captain of your ship and you are God's first mate. God takes the rudder and steers you safely to the shore of your highest good. Never are you alone again. You have the power to transform your life through the simple principles of Scientific Prayer. Use it to heal yourself, heal others, and be free.

In the next chapter, you will learn more details about how to word and use Scientific Prayer.

HOW TO USE 12
SCIENTIFIC PRAYER

AND ALL THINGS, WHATSOEVER YE SHALL

ASK IN PRAYER, BELIEVING, YE SHALL RECEIVE.

—*Jesus Christ[1]*

*I*n this chapter, you will be given practical keys for using the Scientific Prayer methodology in daily life. You will discover how to word effective prayers, and when, where, and how to pray for a particular outcome. You will also learn about praying and healing for others.

HOW TO WORD YOUR PRAYERS

In this section, you will learn specific words to use—and not use—when composing prayer treatments. The wording is what differentiates Scientific Prayer from other forms of prayer and what makes this kind of prayer so incredibly effective and unique. Precise, exact word-choice is essential. Your subconscious mind is a robot that believes everything you say and takes each word literally. That robot goes to work immediately to manifest whatever you say, precisely as spoken.

POSITIVE STATEMENTS
In a Scientific Prayer treatment, no statements of negation, self-effacement, or limiting emotions are ever used. Eliminate the words "not," "cannot," and "can't" from your prayers. Only positive statements of absolute truth are spoken. It is preferable to see and speak of the person you are praying for as perfect, complete, and whole, rather than diseased.

EXAMPLES OF NEGATIVE WORDINGS

1. Do not say, "I am not sick."
   Do say, "I AM healthy now."

2. Do not say, "I am not fat."
   Do say, "I AM slender and healthy now."

2. Do not say, "I am not addicted to cocaine."
   Do say, "I am in perfect mental health and free from any seeming appearance of addiction now."

3. Do not say, "I want to be wealthy but I am afraid of the responsibility."
   Do say, "I release all fear of the responsibility of wealth now, and it is gone. I fully accept the responsibility of wealth now, and I accept wealth now."

4. Do not say, "I am not worthy of happiness, but I want a love relationship."
   Do say, "I accept and welcome my perfect love relationship now."

5. Do not say, "I know I cannot get my dream home, but, please God, find me a house to live in."
   Do say, "I now welcome and accept my dream home, or better, in my life now. Thank you, God, for manifesting my beautiful home now."

UNCONDITIONAL STATEMENTS

Scientific Prayer never uses statements of doubt or conditions. Eliminate "ifs" and "buts" from your prayers. Since God is unconditional, God does not demand bribes. Therefore, Scientific Prayer wording reflects that.

EXAMPLES OF CONDITIONAL WORDINGS

1. Do not say, "If I love myself, then I am healed."
   Do say, "I love myself now, and I am healed now."

2. Do not say, "The more that I love myself, the more successful I am."
   Do say, "I love myself unconditionally now, and I am successful now."

3. Do not say, "I will be healed when I have released my fears."
   Do say, "I release all fear from my mind now, and I am healed now."

4. Do not say, "God, if you fulfill my prayer, I will read the Bible."
   Do say, "I now know that God is my infinite source of unlimited good. Therefore, I welcome and accept this good in my life now."

NONJUDGMENTAL STATEMENTS

Your prayer will be effective by using words that speak the truth, without judgment, criticism, or preaching. No moralizing, "shoulds" or "ought-tos" are used. In Scientific Prayer, there are no observations from the limited level of consciousness.

EXAMPLES OF JUDGMENTAL WORDINGS

1. Do not say, "I ought to release my procrastination so that I can finish my project."
   Do say, "I release and heal all procrastination now and it is gone. I am focused and purposeful, and I finish my project now with divine order and timing."

2. Do not say, "I should be more motivated to get a job."
   Do say, "I release all lack of motivation from my mind now, and it is gone. I am filled with motivation and I accept my perfect job now."

3. Do not say, "God, I know that I should go to church. If I go to church, would you please help me get a job?"
   Do say, "I now know that my perfect job manifests in my life now. Thank you, wonderful God."

ALWAYS IN THE NOW

The truth is accepted as truth now, not limited by time or space. Therefore there is no time in Scientific Prayer. The time is now, and the truth is true for all time. The demonstration is not placed in the future. It is, was, and always shall be now. The truth is always true everywhere and always. Your good is at hand now. Therefore, your prayer claims a demonstration right here, right now. Never place your statements in future tense. If you say that your goal "will come," then you are speaking the Word for it to manifest in some future time—not now and not ever. You will demonstrate the "willing" rather than the goal itself.

Remember that your subconscious robot takes every word literally. If you state that you "want" or "expect" a job, then your subconscious mind will manifest an abundance of "wanting" or "expectation," rather than the actual job. The more you repeat that affirmation, the greater "wanting" and "expecting" you will manifest. You will never get your job.

EXAMPLES OF WORDINGS IN THE FUTURE:

1. Do not say, "I will get out of debt."
   Do say, "I AM free from debt now."

2. Do not say, "My perfect mate will come to me."
   Do say, "I accept and welcome my perfect mate now."

3. Do not say, "I will heal my asthma."
   Do say, "My asthma is healed now."

4. Do not say, "I am dedicated to getting a job."
   Do say, "I welcome and accept my perfect job now."

5. Do not say, "I am willing to get married."
   Do say, "I welcome and accept my perfect mate in my perfect marriage now."

6. Do not say, "I am evolving into spiritual enlightenment."
   Do say, "I AM spiritually enlightened now."

7. Do not say, "I grow and evolve into spiritual consciousness."
   Do say, "I AM immersed in spiritual consciousness now."

8. Do not say, "I want to have a good job."
   Do say, "I accept my perfect job now."

9. Do not say, "I hope that I will get an apartment."
   Do say, "I claim my perfect apartment now."

10. Do not say, "I choose to be healed," "I expect to be healed," "I have faith that I will be healed," "I am ready to be healed," "I believe that I shall be healed," "I am willing to be healed," "I wish I were healed," or "I think I will be healed."
    Do say, "I AM healed now."

Place all statements in the present tense and use the word "now" often. Speak the Word of truth and declare that "it is so, now." Some treatments may involve dates, times, or people who must organize around times, places, and circumstances. However, the time is always now, for there is no time in Spirit. All treatments demonstrate now, for now is the only time there is. If there is a better time than the present, then Spirit will arrange the perfect timing for the demonstration of your claim.

THIS OR SOMETHING BETTER

It is beneficial not to "outline" your prayer treatments. Instead, allow God to fulfill your goal or something better. That is why it is recommended to always use the words "or better." This way you ask for what you desire without limiting the Spiritual Law. For example, ask for "$20,000 or better," rather than asking for "$20,000." This way you open yourself to receive even more.

Examples of Outlined Wordings

1. Do not say, "I accept my perfect job starting in November."
   Do say, "I now welcome my perfect job starting in November or better now."

2. Do not say, "I want a job with the Simon Agency beginning on January 19 with a salary of $5,000 per week."
   Do say, "I claim for myself the perfect job that uses my skills as a copywriter or better with a salary of $5,000 per week or better now."

3. Do not say, "I claim for myself marriage to Steven Harrison now."
   Do say, "I claim for myself my perfect husband who is compatible with me in every way: spiritually, socially, mentally, intellectually, emotionally and physically, or better now."

It is important to be as specific as possible without placing restrictions on how your good will come to you. Contriving or manipulating restricts the action of the Spiritual Law. You can receive something better than what you could ever imagine. You may get a better job with a better company. You might have a better marriage with a better spouse. You may receive an opportunity at a better time or better place. Let God organize the fulfillment of your desires, and you will be fulfilled. Do not outline. Ask for what you want, or something better.

Only statements of an absolute nature are used in Scientific Prayer—statements that bring your awareness to firm conviction of truth. Without reservations, limitations, or qualifying conditions, your statements of perfection are made boldly, with full authority.

WHEN WILL PRAYER BE ANSWERED?

God always says "yes." Every prayer is answered, although the demonstration may be delayed. Each treatment leads to a full demonstration, to healing the pathway to that demonstration, or to higher consciousness and broader vision. The Spiritual Law starts immediately to clear blockages preventing you from receiving your good. The treatment takes as long to materialize as your subconscious mind takes to clear negations preventing its demonstration. Sometimes the healing occurs immediately. In other cases, you may need to undergo a transformation of consciousness affecting every area of life.

Repeating Treatments

Is it wise to pray more than once for a specific goal? Some people believe they have completed their prayer after speaking one treatment—it has already demonstrated in divine mind. In truth, once you have released your prayer into the Spiritual Law, it has demonstrated on the spiritual plane. However, until you have the result in your hand, it is recommended to pray regularly. That is because a gap separates the spiritual and physical realms. Mental blockages must be cleared for the physical manifestation to occur. Your complete mental acceptance creates your demonstration, so keep praying until it happens.

Have Faith that it Will Demonstrate

If your prayer does not demonstrate as quickly as you hoped, do not lose heart. If it is a true desire of your heart, nothing can prevent its realization. Have faith in the power of your Word. Your only blockages are false subconscious beliefs. Heal and clear those limitations. *"Get thee hence, Satan."*[2] Do no allow inner "devils," "demons," or "satans" to have power over you. These demons are not real. They are simply personifications of the error-thoughts in your subconscious mind.

Dr. Peter Meyer often stated: When you pray, speak your treatment as though it were your first, last, and only prayer for that claim. Then release it completely into the Spiritual Law. Once you release it, do not be anxious, but trust it will demonstrate. Like a seed you have planted, do not dig it up to see how it is doing. Just let it sprout. Expect that your demonstration will come. If doubts creep into your mind, then affirm that you have treated and you trust God. If you feel like praying again, then do so and release it again. If your prayer does not demonstrate within a reasonable time, then pray daily until the demonstration appears. Release every treatment as though it were your only treatment for that claim.

UPDATING YOUR TREATMENT

It may be helpful to write a prayer treatment and read it aloud daily. You may find, however, that as you heal blockages, you need to change the wording of your prayer. Therefore, rather than reading it daily by rote, consider speaking-through each prayer daily through inner revelation (see my book, *Divine Revelation*). Your prayer will change as your level of acceptance changes. Once your mind fully accepts your claim, then it will manifest.

PERSIST AND NEVER DESIST

The important rule is to never give up. Keep treating daily until your demonstration appears, exactly as spoken. Also, it is not sufficient to simply pray. A common New Thought axiom is, "First treat; then move your feet." In other words, get up off your couch and make it happen. Make your own miracle through old-fashioned perseverance and determination. Ernest Holmes stated, *"It is not a question of failing or succeeding. It is simply a question of sticking to an idea until it becomes a tangible reality."*[3] So, your question may be, "How long to pray for a particular claim?" The answer: Until you get what you are praying for. And never, never, never give up.

PRAYING FOR AND HEALING OTHERS

You may use Scientific Prayer to pray for others, nearby or at a distance. These loved ones may be alive or may have passed over. They may be humans, animals, or plants. All Spirit is one Spirit and all Mind is one Mind.

There is no time or space in Spirit. Your prayers are effective, no matter where you are in time or space.

Those whom you are healing do not necessarily have to believe in prayer or believe they can be healed. It is sufficient that you, the prayer therapist or practitioner, have conviction in your own prayer. Ernest Holmes said: *"Scientific mental practice begins and ends in the consciousness of the one giving a treatment."*[4] *"A case is won or lost in the consciousness of the practitioner."*[5] Thus, when praying for others, pray and treat your own mind and arrive at a full conviction. Then give over the results to almighty God.

However, in praying for others, there is a code of ethics. Avoid prayers that manipulate, control, or trespass. For example, praying for someone to join your religion violates free will. You may pray for his/her spiritual growth and awakening in religious knowledge. Praying for someone to marry you is coercive. You may pray for fulfillment in his/her love life. Praying to change someone's individual traits is invasive. You may pray for expression of his/her true nature in his/her unique way. Pray for a person's highest good, through the pathway of individual choice.

Some people feel they should never pray for others without their permission. What kind of prayer would require permission? One that would restrain free choice. If an individual is unavailable, then ask your higher self for permission before praying for that person.

However, seeing perfect good and truth about another can never do harm. This can be helpful for your own peace of mind, particularly if you live with or work with someone. For the sake of a harmonious relationship, it is beneficial to recognize that person as a perfect expression of God. What better way to achieve this than to recognize that person as perfection everywhere now? You can never trespass upon others by knowing the absolute truth about them.

Healers use various modalities, such as physical manipulation, medical cures, psychic surgery, faith healing, counseling, psychoanalysis, or laying on of hands. Sometimes healing occurs instantaneously. However, healing can only be permanent when the mental law has been transformed: "Be ye transformed by the renewing of your mind."[6] Through an enduring change in the belief patterns that originally caused illness, healing will last. Otherwise, the same illness will be recreated, or another one.

WHEN, HOW, WHAT, AND WHERE TO PRAY

When is it wise to pray? Whenever you feel the need. Where is the best place to pray? Wherever you are. What is wise to pray for? For as many things as you desire.

WHEN

In order to develop faith in prayer, get serious and committed about your prayer life. Find a special time and place to pray regularly, daily. Designate a sacred space in your home or office. Pray first thing in the morning, right after your morning meditation, and/or right before sleep at night. Or make a habit to pray daily during a specific break at work.

HOW

Pray aloud, if possible—unless you are in a situation where spoken prayer is unwelcome. Speaking out loud focuses your mind. When you say your prayer silently, your mind might drift away. Half an hour later, you may arise from your haze and realize you never finished that prayer.

WHAT

It is beneficial to keep a treatment notebook or a computer file with a list of goals for which you are praying. You may write out and file all your treatments in a notebook or a file stored on your computer. When you achieve a demonstration, place a star or check-mark next to that item. Later, when you review your notebook or file, you will realize how your faith has developed.

WHERE

Healing prayers, affirmations, and prayers can be done anytime, anywhere, whenever you feel the need. You can program yourself for success, happiness, harmony, efficiency, divine order, and all good. Use the power of prayer to heal difficult situations, before they arise and as they arise. You can set your mood for the day and accomplish whatever you desire. Ask for what you want, whether a parking space, a raise in salary, or spiritual enlightenment.

REMEMBER TO ASK

"Ask, and it shall be given you." [7] Stopping for a moment to call upon God, to ask, to pray, or to heal in challenging situations brings instantaneous results. Anytime you feel discomfort or displeasure, heal all the way. Pray for a change in your inner feelings. You have the power to heal.

Perhaps you habitually do not ask for what you want. In fact, you might drift through life passively, accepting circumstances that come your way, trying your best to cope. However, by remembering to ask for help during uncomfortable situations, you can transform those situations. For example, imagine yourself in a crowded subway. A mother and baby are standing next to you. The baby begins to scream at the top of his lungs. Everyone in the car is discomfited by the crying baby. At that instant, you can either stand by passively or take the initiative to pray and heal. By taking a few moments to do a silent healing prayer, the baby might settle down and stop crying. You have done a service to everyone in the subway car, especially the baby and its mother.

MAKING PRAYER A PRIORITY

Make prayer a priority. Consciously pray and heal several times every day. Your day will proceed smoothly and joyously, according to divine timing, divine order, and divine will. You will experience daily coincidences that are not really coincidental. You will flow downstream in the river of life, easily and effortlessly.

Pray whenever you need healing or a boost in consciousness. Pray before making a difficult phone call, before attending a challenging meeting—anytime you feel apprehensive or concerned. Before meeting or phoning a stranger, or before any demanding situation, send your higher self before you, to introduce you and smooth the way. Ask God to surround the situation with divine love and light. You are never alone when you invoke God's presence. Remember to ask, and your life will be blessed with joy and harmony.

There is no need to wait for one goal to materialize before beginning to pray for another. God is an ever-abundant fountainhead of blessings. Pray for everything you desire. However, make a separate prayer treatment for each goal and do not jumble them together. Each goal has its own issues that might surface for healing. Deal with these issues separately. Heal everything that concerns you, large or small. When you heal a troublesome situation, you find peace of mind.

Perhaps you believe it is not God's will to fulfill your desires. You may believe it is unspiritual or worldly to ask for what you want. You may think you should be "humble" and "satisfied" with what you have. Are you a better disciple of God by clinging to weakness, poverty, ill health, or loneliness? Where are your desires for health, joy, prosperity, and love coming from? In fact, the word *desire* comes from the roots *de*, meaning "from," and *sire*, meaning "Lord." Who is prompting you to seek greater happiness, if not God? It is not necessary to "rob" others in order to "get paid" your good. God is unlimited. There is ample plenitude for all. God's will is for everyone to be happy and enjoy life to its fullest. Your goals are worthy and you deserve to fulfill them.

PRACTICE MAKES PERFECT

The best way to succeed in prayer is to practice. The fastest way to gain faith in the power of your Word is to pray daily and diligently for whatever you desire. Your prayers will be answered. Therefore, keep speaking out those prayers daily, and never lose faith. Every time you speak a Scientific Prayer treatment, the power of the universe moves through every atom to answer your prayer. Every treatment clears more of your pathway to Spirit until your consciousness is cleansed to such a degree that your Word in prayer has unlimited power.

Prayer Circles

How can you make your prayers more effective? Jesus said, *"For where two or three are gathered together in my name, there am I in the midst of them."*[8] Your prayers have greater power in groups. Therefore, in addition to your private prayers and meditations, it is strongly recommended to invite your friends to your home for a weekly prayer circle.

What is a prayer circle? It is a safe place for like-minded people to gather together weekly to support each other in fulfilling their desires. Such a group can accelerate your prayer progress exponentially. It can truly transform your life.

In your prayer group, you may follow the following suggested program:

1. Hand out two index cards per person in the prayer circle, and on each of these cards, write the first sentence of your desired prayer—the Resolution/Goal section.

2. Going around the circle in turn, each person shares stories of prayer demonstrations for the previous week, and mentions what he/she plans to pray for this week.

3. The group leader leads the group into a guided meditation for about twenty minutes.

4. Each person in the group speaks aloud his/her first Scientific Prayer treatment, going around the circle, one by one. Everyone in the group listens carefully and supports the individual who is speaking.

5. Each person speaks aloud his/her second Scientific Prayer treatment, one at a time.

6. The group leader says a closing prayer.

To participate in a powerful, successful, weekly online prayer group in our chat room, please go to http://www.scientificprayer.com and join our mailing list.

"Pray for one another, that ye may be healed." [9]

THE "REALIZATION" METHOD OF PRAYER

After you have demonstrated many healings and prayers, your faith can become so perfect that you no longer need to go through the nine steps of Scientific Prayer treatment. You can simply speak a declaration of your claim, and the demonstration will appear instantaneously. At that point, *"If ye shall say unto this mountain, Be thou removed, and be thou cast into the sea; it shall be done."* [10]

At this stage, you have gained the power to heal and pray instantly though a realization of the truth, for your mind is clear of negation. This is often called the "realization" method of healing. Dr. Peter Meyer called this "quantum prayer." All the elements of prayer treatment are compressed into one realization. You may visualize a light surrounding a problem and see its immediate solution. You may heal a physical problem by imagining a brilliant white light in a part of the body. Or you may think or speak an affirmation of truth that instantly heals and transforms a situation.

These methods of healing require more faith than the nine-step prayer treatment formula. Use the nine steps to build your faith until you have acquired enough trust in the power of your Word to effect healing through instantaneous realization.

MENTAL DISCIPLINE

To be mentally disciplined means (1) to be in touch with your true desires, (2) not to sabotage your desires through inner negations, and, (3) to be disciplined in habits of thoughts and speech. Your true soul's desires are hidden deep within. These desires will manifest sooner or later, whether you are conscious of them or not. By uncovering what is locked in your heart, longing to be set free, you can fulfill your divine purpose.

Recognizing what you really desire and then accomplishing that desire is the straight path to fulfillment. Thinking you cannot fulfill your desire and then unconsciously sabotaging whatever blocks its fulfillment is the crooked path to fulfillment. Be disciplined in faith and prayer so you accomplish your goals without using subconscious pressures that force you to accept your good.

Your true desires are on the level of Spirit, but your subconscious mind creates human experiences—distorted versions of those true desires. Your subconscious mind annihilates your fulfillment through its negations. It is helpful to get in touch with this hidden saboteur and bring it to light. By recognizing your negative patterns, you can heal them. First feeling and then healing is the path to freedom. Be disciplined and release negations that bind you in chains of illusion.

Whenever you sense negative thoughts or emotions, get into the habit of healing them immediately. Align continually with truth. Make the effort to maintain your consciousness on a high platform of purity. Choose your thoughts and words wisely. Mental discipline means taking time, effort, and care to release negations and to affirm truth continually. Say "no" to error-thoughts. Refuse to express negations, even in jest.

The subconscious mind has no sense of humor. Whatever you say, even kiddingly, gets stored permanently in your subconscious mental robot. If you continually joke, "You know me, I always make mistakes," that statement is not taken in jest by your robot. It will manifest many mistakes in your life. Your subconscious mind registers every word impressed upon it, whether you "really mean it" or not. It then manifests as life experience. Be disciplined and vigilant to think and speak only the truth.

YOU ARE NOT ALONE

Any New Thought church, whether Unity, Religious Science, Science of Mind, or Divine Science, has prayer therapists to pray for those in need. See links to these churches at: http://www.divinerevelation.org/Teachers.html.

You can meet a prayer therapist in your area for private counseling or you can telephone one. There is no time or space in Spirit, and remote prayers are just as effective as face-to-face counseling. Consider a private prayer consultation with me or other Divine Revelation teachers. Visit our website for more information: www.scientificprayer.com. If you sign onto our mailing list, you will receive a free, downloadable guided meditation.

You may also call a 24-hour Scientific Prayer service. Your prayer request is placed on a board and prayers are done for you daily for a month:

1. Silent Unity Prayer Tower, 800-669-7729.
2. World Ministry of Prayer, 800-421-9600.
3. Ozark Research Institute, 479-582-9197.

Call these prayer ministries. They are very powerful, and they work. Their services are offered free of charge. Donations are welcome.

In the next section of this book, you will find specific healing prayers, affirmations, and prayer treatments that you can use in your own Scientific Prayer treatments.

PART V

SAMPLE PRAYERS
AND AFFIRMATIONS

13 BASIC SPIRITUAL HEALING PRAYERS

PRAY. IT ISN'T A SIGN OF WEAKNESS; IT IS YOUR STRENGTH.
—*Orville Kelly*

Spiritual healing is essential to Scientific Prayer. By healing whatever prevents you from attaining your goal, you will arrive at a complete conviction and thereby fulfill your desire. In this chapter, you will learn a few basic affirmative spiritual healing prayers to help you clear the pathway to your Realization/Conviction. For more details about the healing prayers in this chapter, please refer to my book, *Divine Revelation*. In addition to the prayers offered in this chapter, it is highly recommended to learn dozens of other powerful, indispensable healing prayers in my book, *Exploring Auras*.

THE ASTRAL-MENTAL WORLD

What exactly are you healing when you use healing prayers? On the mental level, you are healing the facade barrier in your subconscious mind. On the physical level, you are healing the human energy field or subtle body.

Please refer to "The Astral/Mental World" on page 175. Here is a brief explanation of this chart:

Your individual subconscious mind is the storehouse of all memories and beliefs. Here, your ego-identity is built and emotional nature is expressed. Within the collective subconscious mind lies the entire history and all of the collective beliefs of humanity.

Your facade body consists of illusory ego-constructs built of encrusted habit patterns that have crystallized into an armor of defensiveness.

The psychic mind uses mental powers acquired from the astral/mental

THE ASTRAL / MENTAL WORLD

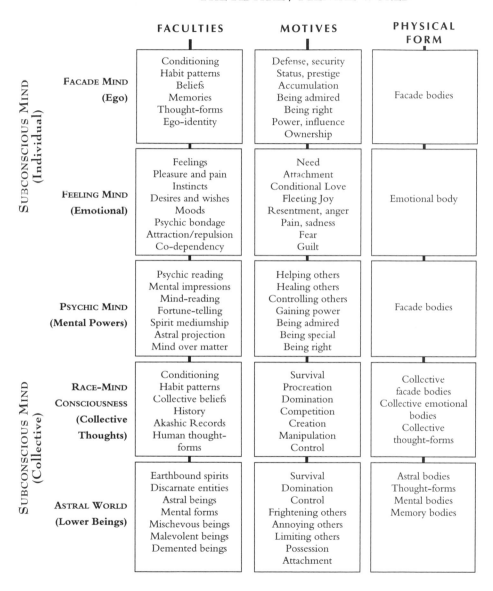

	FACULTIES	MOTIVES	PHYSICAL FORM
SUBCONSCIOUS MIND (Individual) FACADE MIND (Ego)	Conditioning Habit patterns Beliefs Memories Thought-forms Ego-identity	Defense, security Status, prestige Accumulation Being admired Being right Power, influence Ownership	Facade bodies
FEELING MIND (Emotional)	Feelings Pleasure and pain Instincts Desires and wishes Moods Psychic bondage Attraction/repulsion Co-dependency	Need Attachment Conditional Love Fleeting Joy Resentment, anger Pain, sadness Fear Guilt	Emotional body
PSYCHIC MIND (Mental Powers)	Psychic reading Mental impressions Mind-reading Fortune-telling Spirit mediumship Astral projection Mind over matter	Helping others Healing others Controlling others Gaining power Being admired Being special Being right	Facade bodies
SUBCONSCIOUS MIND (Collective) RACE-MIND CONSCIOUSNESS (Collective Thoughts)	Conditioning Habit patterns Collective beliefs History Akashic Records Human thought-forms	Survival Procreation Domination Competition Creation Manipulation Control	Collective facade bodies Collective emotional bodies Collective thought-forms
ASTRAL WORLD (Lower Beings)	Earthbound spirits Discarnate entities Astral beings Mental forms Mischevous beings Malevolent beings Demented beings	Survival Domination Control Frightening others Annoying others Limiting others Possession Attachment	Astral bodies Thought-forms Mental bodies Memory bodies

plane. Predictions from this level may be extremely accurate, or grossly inaccurate, since mental/emotional states, in continual flux, have no lasting reality. In contrast, spiritually attuned psychics counsel from the spiritual plane—not the astral plane.

The race-mind consciousness, or mass consciousness, is made of collective thoughts of humanity—an accumulation of beliefs born of communal, societal, religious, political, and national thought-forms.

The astral world consists of disincarnate beings with a dense vibration. Astral entities are sometimes perceived by those sensitive to subtle vibrations.

The astral/mental plane separates you from your true divine nature. By healing it, you can attain your Realization/Conviction in your Scientific Prayer. In this chapter you will learn powerful affirmative healing prayers that profoundly transform your consciousness within minutes.

For more information about the astral plane, please refer to my books *Divine Revelation, Exploring Chakras*, and *Exploring Auras*.

The healing affirmations in this chapter are to be used, as needed, in the Renewal/Healing portion of your Scientific Prayer treatments. It is not necessary to use these exact words. You may change the wording to suit your needs, but maintain the meaning and feeling of the prayers.

SPIRITUAL SELF-DEFENSE

The first affirmation, "Self-Authority," helps you maintain inner strength and prevents "psychic sponge syndrome"—absorbing vibrational energies like a sponge soaks up water. If you are a "psychic sponge," then you are overly empathic to the feelings of others. When in proximity to diseased, disturbed, or needy people, you feel drained of energy. You are oversensitive and vulnerable to vibrations (subtle energies from external influences) and thought-forms (dense thoughts crystallized into form) around you. However, by using spiritual self-defense affirmations daily, you can build great fortitude and become a fountainhead of unlimited energy.

Even if you are not a psychic sponge, you may be influenced by domineering or manipulative people or by atmospheric vibrations. The following affirmation closes off your aura to such negative influences, yet opens your aura to God and the spiritual plane.

Important Note: All the prayers and affirmations in this book are to be spoken in a powerful, clear voice. These can be used to heal others or yourself. Speak aloud with conviction, confidence, and certainty.

SELF-AUTHORITY AFFIRMATION

I AM in control. I AM one with God.
I AM the only authority in my life.
I AM divinely protected by the light of my being.
I close off my aura and body of light
To all but my own God self and consciousness
Now and forevermore.
Thank you, God, and SO IT IS.

In all affirmations, the phrase "I AM" signifies the "I AM" self—your higher self. Say the words "I AM" as though your higher self were speaking, with all the power of your "I AM" self. Whenever you say any affirmation or prayer, imagine that the "I AM" self is speaking. This gives greater authority to your prayers. This powerful affirmation increases clarity, balance, integrity, self-empowerment, personal responsibility, and inner strength. Another excellent prayer of protection is on page 79 of this book.

HEALING THOUGHTS AND EMOTIONS

Scientific Prayer often employs a system of affirmations and denials, by which negative thoughts and emotions are healed. The healing prayers below can transmute mental blockages, thereby clearing the pathway to your full Realization/Conviction.

THOUGHT-FORM HEALING: LONG FORM

This powerful prayer can heal anything that needs healing—any physical, mental, or emotional problem—for you or for others. The premise of this prayer is first feeling and then healing. In other words, the way to heal negative emotions is to first identify them and then transmute them.

The Thought-Form Healing is a simple formula: Feel, name, and release the negative thought. Then replace it with a positive one. The prayer has two blank spaces. When you come to the first blank space, close your eyes and notice any negative feelings coming up. Name these out loud. Then continue reading the prayer. At the second blank space, close your eyes and name positive feelings that are the opposite correlates of the negative feelings named in the first blank space.

For more information about overcoming negative feelings with their positive correlates, please refer to pages 179–185.

> *I invoke God's loving presence*
> *To release, rebuke, relinquish, eliminate, loose, and let go*
> *Of any and all needs, desires, thoughts, feelings, negations,*
> *Or limitations that no longer serve me.*
> *I release and dispel the pattern within me*
> *That created any and all false beliefs of*

(list negative thoughts)

> *I AM free from these negations,*
> *And from any other thoughts and emotions*
> *That do not reflect the truth of my being.*
> *These thoughts and emotions have no power over me.*
> *They are lovingly lifted, transmuted, and transformed*
> *By the power of the Holy Spirit, right now.*
> *I am now open and free to embrace positive,*
> *Life-supporting, energizing thoughts and emotions.*
> *I AM glad, light-hearted, cheerful and free,*

Just as God created me to be.

I now welcome and accept thoughts of

(list positive correlates).

I AM in balance. I AM in control.

Thank you, God, and SO IT IS.

This powerful prayer can transform your mind from anguish into heavenly paradise in a matter of moments. With this prayer, you no longer have an excuse to remain in a bad mood. You now have the power to change it.

THOUGHT-FORM HEALING: SHORT FORM

The following affirmation is a shortcut version of the Thought-Form Healing. This brief prayer can be used just as effectively as the longer version you just learned:

I now heal and release all negations of

(list negative thoughts)

And they are gone.

They are lifted into the light of God's love and truth.

I now welcome and accept thoughts of

(list positive correlates).

Thank you, God, and SO IT IS.

OVERCOMING MENTAL BLOCKAGES

The Thought-Form Healing prayer will help you overcome deep negative belief patterns. As you expose these subconscious demons, you may run into roadblocks that appear to stop you in your tracks. Below are statements of truth that can help you knock down seeming obstructions.

Demon: **"Fight or Flight" Irrational Reactivity**

Fear: **Death**

Cure: **Non-resistance**

"The Lord is on my side; I will not fear: what can man do unto me?"[1] I *"resist not evil"* now and always.[2] God, the only power in the universe, is oneness. Oneness is all there is, there is no power that could be against me, since I could never be against myself.

Demon: **Criticism, Condemnation**
Fear: **Not Being Right**
Cure: **Nonjudgment, Appreciation**

"For he maketh the sun to rise on the evil and the good, and he sendeth rain on the just and on the unjust."[3] I see good everywhere, and I see the divine within all beings. Therefore, all are equally valuable. All beings are free to express their own perfect, unique individuality.

Demon: **Poverty, Lack**
Fear: **Not Enough**
Cure: **Abundance, Limitless Good**

The Lord increases me more and more, me and my children. I AM blessed of the Lord which made heaven and earth."[4] There is no limit to abundance. I freely circulate my good, and it returns to me thousandfold or better. I now give and receive my unlimited good for the benefit of myself and all others concerned.

Demon: **Disorder, Perfectionism**
Fear: **Making a Mistake**
Cure: **Divine Order**

"The law of the Lord is perfect, converting the soul…The statutes of the Lord are right, rejoicing the heart: the commandment of the Lord is pure, enlightening the eyes."[5] God's perfection is at work in my life, bringing perfect divine right order, action, and timing in my mind, body, and affairs, right now.

Demon: **Confusion**
Fear: **Being Wrong**

Cure: **Clarity of Inner Guidance**

"Call unto me, and I will answer thee, and show thee great and mighty things." [6] God clearly shows me the way to fulfill the divine plan and purpose of my life now through perfect divine guidance.

Demon: **Bondage, Possession**
Fear: **Making Decisions, Responsibility**
Cure: **Freedom, Self-Authority, Release**

"Bring my soul out of prison, that I may praise thy name: the righteous shall compass me about; for thou shalt deal bountifully with me." [7] I AM in control of my mind. I AM the only authority in my life. Nothing can possess me or hold me in bondage. I AM free and belong only to myself.

Demon: **Trespassing, Domination, Coercion**
Fear: **Letting Go**
Cure: **Permissiveness, Respect**

"And I shall know the truth, and the truth shall make me free." [8] I AM free to follow my own pathway, and I allow others to be free to follow theirs. I no longer make decisions for others.

Demon: **Superiority, Arrogance, Conceit**
Fear: **Inferiority, Insecurity**
Cure: **Surrender to God, Humility**

"I am continually with thee: thou hast holden me by my right hand. Thou shalt guide me with thy counsel, and afterward receive me to glory." [9] I let go and let God be my guide. All good comes from God, and I AM a vehicle through which God's good flows. I rejoice in the expression of God through all beings.

Demon: **Strife, Animosity**
Fear: **Loss of Love**
Cure: **Harmony, Forgiveness**

"Behold, how good and how pleasant it is for brethren to dwell together in unity!" [10] I AM the expression of God's universal love, peace, and harmony.

I loose, let go, and forgive all those who have seemingly wronged me, and I AM free.

Demon: **Embarrassment, Shame**
Fear: **Exposure**
Cure: **Honesty, Sincerity, Naturalness**

"Unto thee, O Lord, do I lift up my soul. O my God, I trust in thee: let me not be ashamed…Show me thy ways. Lead me in thy truth, and teach me." [11] I let go of all pretence and act truthfully and naturally, exactly as I AM, for I AM enough as I AM now.

Demon: **Timidity**
Fear: **Self-expression**
Cure: **Trust in God, Self-confidence**

"The Lord is my light and my salvation; whom shall I fear?…Though an host should encamp against me, my heart shall not fear…in this will I be confident." [12] I AM free to express myself as I AM, for I trust in God to express perfection through me. I AM perfect for me for now.

Demon: **Insecurity, Fearfulness**
Fear: **Danger**
Cure: **Divine Protection**

"I will lift up mine eyes unto the hills, from whence cometh my help. My help cometh from the Lord, which made heaven and earth…The Lord shall preserve my going out and my coming in from this time forth, and even for evermore." [13] I AM divinely protected by God's loving presence, which fills and surrounds me with safety and security, now and always.

Demon: **Distress, Anguish**
Fear: **Loneliness**
Cure: **Comfort, Sustenance**

"Yea, though I walk through the valley of the shadow of death, I will fear no evil: for thou art with me; thy rod and thy staff they comfort me." [14] God is with

me in each moment. God is the comforter, my ever-present source of sustenance and support.

Demon: **Agitation, Tension**
Fear: **Self-reflection**
Cure: **Peace, Tranquility**

"Peace, be still." [15] *"Be still and know that I AM God."* [16] God is my perfect source of peace. I AM at peace in each moment.

Demon: **Sadness, Pain**
Fear: **Loneliness**
Cure: **Gratitude, Joy, Happiness**

"The Lord hath done great things for us; whereof we are glad...They that sow in tears shall reap in joy." [17] I rejoice in all of God's wondrous blessings. I AM filled with the light of God's joy.

Demon: **Separation, Isolation**
Fear: **Intimacy**
Cure: **Reuniting with God**

"The Lord is nigh unto all them that call upon him, to all that call upon him in truth." [18] I AM one with God now. I AM all that God is now.

Demon: **Hatred, Anger, Resentment**
Fear: **Getting Hurt**
Cure: **Love, Forgiveness**

"Lord, who shall abide in thy tabernacle? who shall dwell in thy holy hill?...He that backbiteth not with his tongue, nor doeth evil to his neighbour." [19] God's love is unlimited and cannot be opposed or blocked by anyone or anything. Since God's love is everywhere, I AM divinely protected, and no harm can touch me.

Demon: **Self-repression, Death Wish**
Fear: **Expression**
Cure: **Self-expression, Life, Love**

"For thou hast delivered my soul from death: wilt not thou deliver my feet from falling, that I may walk before God in the light of the living?" [20] I AM filled with the light of God, which expresses through me in perfect ways. I AM free to live and to love.

Demon: **Worry, Anxiety, Holding On**
Fear: **Letting Go**
Cure: **Trust, Faith**

"He that dwelleth in the secret place of the most High shall abide under the shadow of the Almighty. I will say of the Lord, He is my refuge and my fortress: my God; in him will I trust." [21] I AM free from tension and fear. I trust in God to do the work. I relax, let go, and let God accomplish all my goals effortlessly through me.

Demon: **Guilt**
Fear: **Exposure**
Cure: **Forgiveness of Self**

"Have mercy upon me, O God, according to thy loving kindness: according unto the multitude of thy tender mercies blot out my transgressions." [22] I have always done my best. Therefore I forgive myself for any seeming misconduct. God holds nothing against me, and I hold nothing against myself. I AM perfect as I AM now.

Demon: **Shyness, Repression**
Fear: **Others' Opinions**
Cure: **Expression, Self-confidence, Faith in Self**

"I will bless the Lord, for he has given me counsel: my intuition also guides me during the night. I have set the Lord always before me: because he is at my right hand, I shall not be moved...my flesh also shall rest in hope." [23] I AM confident, for I AM good enough exactly as I AM. I now freely express myself, for I no longer need to impress anyone. God expresses through me perfectly and beautifully, now and always.

Demon: **Fatigue, Illness, Old Age**

Fear: **Death**

Cure: **Perfect Life, Unlimited Energy**

"I AM come that they might have life, and that they might have it more abun-dantly." [24] *"I AM the resurrection, and the life."* [25] I continually bathe in the limitless fountainhead of God's life-giving, vitalizing energy. I AM the eternal life that God is.

Demon: **Jealousy, Covetousness, Competition**

Fear: **Not Enough**

Cure: **Self-love, Self-worth**

"He healeth the broken in heart, and bindeth up my wounds. He telleth the number of the stars; he calleth them all by their names...his understanding is infi-nite." [26] If anyone can have it, I can. If anyone can do it, I can. Since there is no limit to the good that God provides, I bless those who succeed, and I rejoice in their good.

Demon: **Burden**

Fear: **Losing Control**

Cure: **Letting Go and Letting God**

"I cast my burden upon the Lord, and he shall sustain me: he shall never suffer the righteous to be moved." [27] I trust in God's love to guide me. I AM never alone, for God walks with me always. Therefore, I let go and let God take charge of my life, and I AM at peace.

Demon: **Blame, Self-pity**

Fear: **Responsibility**

Cure: **Praise, Blessing, Gratitude**

"Praise the Lord, O my soul. While I live will I praise the Lord: I will sing praises unto my God as long as I live." [28] God's good is given freely, and nothing can block my good from me. I no longer block my good in order to gain love and attention. I AM now responsible for my life. I now bless everyone and everything as good, good, and very good.

HEALING PSYCHIC BONDAGE

A psychic tie is a non-beneficial bond between yourself and something or someone in your environment. Psychic ties consist of undue attachments or repulsions to any person, place, thing, organization, circumstance, memory, experience, or addiction that influence you adversely. Built of negative emotions, these ties are created unconsciously. For example, after an argument with your boss or your spouse, what remains? A residue of charged energy, which creates a psychic tie. These shackles are never beneficial. In fact, they can and do destroy relationships. They need to be severed.

> The soul that is attached to anything, however much good there may be in it, will not arrive at the liberty of divine union. For whether it be a strong wire rope or a slender and delicate thread that holds the bird, it matters not, if it really holds it fast; for until the cord be broken, the bird cannot fly.
>
> —Saint John of the Cross

In contrast to psychic ties, love ties are true love bonds with beloved ones, both alive and deceased. These golden ties link you to God, your higher self, angels, and spiritual inner teachers. These ties of divine light can never be broken.

Cutting psychic ties strengthens golden ties of true unconditional love. Without tension and co-dependency, love grows unhampered. I guarantee that by cutting psychic ties with co-workers and loved ones daily, you will have better, more intimate relationships. Use this prayer daily and notice people responding with greater love and affection.

The Psychic Tie Cut affirmation has one blank space: for naming the thing you are cutting psychic ties with. When using this prayer, cut psychic ties with just one thing at a time.

Psychic Tie Cut

I call upon the Holy Spirit
To cut any and all psychic ties between
Myself and (person, place, thing, or addiction).

These psychic ties are now lovingly
Cut, cut, cut, cut, cut, cut, cut, cut,
(Repeat above line until complete)
Lifted, loved, healed, released, and let go
Into the light of God's love and truth.
Thank you, God, and SO IT IS.

As you say, "Cut, cut, cut..." you might also pretend that you are cutting the ties with a light-sword, a scissors, or a knife.

SEALING THE ENERGY FIELD

As long as human nature exists, so does the desire to dominate others against their will. You can gain independence of thinking and self-authority. By creating a powerful, impenetrable armor of protection around your energy field, the following prayer prevents anyone from manipulating or coercing you.

I AM filled with God's love.
My cup runneth over.
The light of God fills and surrounds me now.
I AM so full with the divine presence
That nothing else can penetrate my divine beingness.
I AM full. I AM filled with God's strength,
God's power, God's love, and God's light.
My aura and body of light
Are invincible and impenetrable.
Thank you, God, and SO IT IS.

LETTING GO OF THE PAST

Your subconscious mind carries a burden of past memories. The affirmations that follow help you release the past so your mind can be free of the weight of false responsibility, guilt, blame, and resentment.

PAST EXPERIENCE HEALING

> *All experiences, core, record, memory, and effects*
> *Are transmuted and transformed into pure love and light*
> *By the violet flame of limitless transmutation.*
> *I have a clean blank slate on which to write new experiences.*
> *I AM transformed by the renewing of my mind, right now.*
> *I close all doors, openings, and holes to my past now.*
> *I AM vibrating at such a high frequency of love,*
> *That I AM free from all past burdens and false responsibilities.*
> *I AM a God/Goddess of great love, light, and glory.*
> *Thank you, God, and SO IT IS.*

LETTING GO PRAYER

When you hold on to the past, your subconscious mind is cluttered with dismal, entrenched energies. Letting go of these vibrations lifts your mind into a higher, more refined frequency. This prayer will help.

> *I let go of worn-out things, hopeless conditions,*
> *Useless ideas, and futile relationships now.*
> *Divine right order and divine right timing*
> *Are now established and maintained*
> *In my mind, body, relationships, finances,*
> *In all of my affairs, and in my world,*
> *Through the power of the Holy Spirit*
> *And my own indwelling God consciousness now.*
> *Divine circulation is at work in my life,*
> *And the inflow and outflow*
> *Of everything in my life is in divine order.*
> *I AM peaceful, balanced, and poised.*
> *This is so now, in God's own wise and perfect ways.*
> *Thank you, God, and SO IT IS.*

FORGIVENESS PRAYER

Unforgiveness binds you to psychic ties that connect you to past trauma, hate, and resentment. True forgiveness of yourself, of others, and of life situations lifts your consciousness quickly and profoundly. Forgiveness places the situation under the Law of Grace. The following prayer brings forgiveness:

By and through the power of the Holy Spirit,
I know and decree
That all that has seemingly offended me or held me,
I now forgive and release.
Within and without,
I forgive and release.
Things past, things present, and all things future,
I forgive and release.
I forgive and release everything and everyone everywhere
Past, present, and future,
That can possibly need forgiveness or release.
This includes forgiveness for myself
Through the power of God now.
Absolutely everyone and everything
Past, present, and future,
That could possibly need to forgive and release me,
Including myself, does so now.
This is done now by and through the power of
God's perfect forgiveness in me,
And God's perfect forgiveness within us all.
I AM free and all others concerned are now free also.
Therefore all things are completely cleared up
Among us all, now and forever.
This is so, now and forevermore, under grace,
In God's own wise and perfect ways.
Thank you, God, and SO IT IS.

FORGIVENESS HEALING CHANT

The healing affirmation below can help you forgive any particular person, group, or situation, such as a parent, spouse, child, or circumstance.

Christ in me is my forgiving and releasing power.
Christ in (person, situation)
Is his/her forgiving and releasing power.
Christ in me is my forgiving and releasing power.
Christ in (person, situation)
Is his/her forgiving and releasing power.
I AM free and he/she is free also.
Therefore, all things are cleared up between us,
Now and forever, under grace, in perfect ways.
Thank you, God, and SO IT IS.

FACADE BODY HEALING

A facade body is a set of beliefs held so strongly that they crystallize into a subtle defensive armor. This ego-shell identifies you in limited ways. This impenetrable armor of defensiveness makes an impression on others and determines how they respond. But it is not real. It is an illusion. (See my book, *Exploring Auras,* for more information).

Before using the prayer below, decide what set of beliefs you want to heal. For example, you might be wearing a facade body of poverty, unworthiness, superiority, inferiority, victimization, fear, timidity, fatness, defensiveness, machismo, bullishness, anger, or another mask. Choose one of your facade bodies and call it by name, such as "self-righteousness," "self-hatred," or other name that describes it. Place that name into the appropriate blank spaces in the prayer.

I call upon Holy Spirit to lovingly shine the light of truth and love
Upon any and all facade bodies of
(name of facade body)

Within myself now. These facade bodies of
(name of facade body)
> *That are surrounding me are now*
> *Lovingly cracked open, crumbled up,*
> *Dissolved, healed, released, and let go*
> *By the Holy Spirit,*
> *Into the light of God's love and truth.*
> *I now call upon my own soul and my higher self*
> *To fill this space and fill me with*
> *My true divine pattern and soul expression.*
> *Let God's will be done in this matter.*
> *Thank you, God, and SO IT IS.*

This prayer heals any unreal mask or armor preventing you from expressing your true, innocent self.

DIVINE PLAN

There is a divine plan and purpose for your life, and you can manifest it through surrendering to God and through prayer. Here is an affirmation to help you welcome that divine plan into your life, as you release all that is unlike that divine plan.

> *God within me now frees and releases*
> *All that is no longer part of the divine plan for my life.*
> *Everything and everyone that is no longer*
> *Part of the divine plan for my life*
> *Now frees and releases me.*
> *I fully accept this new divine inner freedom now.*
> *Through the power of God within me*
> *I now recognize, accept, and follow*
> *The divine plan of my life,*

As it is revealed to me step by step.
I rejoice in the divine plan, which is the sublime plan,
Which includes health, wealth, happiness,
And perfect self-expression for me, now and always.
I know that God in me now reveals, unfolds, and manifest
The divine plan of my life now, quickly and in peace.
It is now done with perfect divine order and timing
Under God's grace, in God's own wise and perfect ways.
Thank you, God, and SO IT IS.

I AM WORTHY PRAYER

The most fundamental belief that prevents you from fulfilling your desires is the belief of separation from your inner divinity, your higher self. With isolation, greater unworthiness and self-hatred arises. When clients come for Prayer Therapy, the fundamental cause behind the difficulty is usually self-loathing and subsequent unconscious need for self-punishment. The following affirmation is recommended whenever you feel lack of self-worth.

I AM worthy to be loved,
I AM worthy to be prosperous,
I AM worthy to be fulfilled,
I AM worthy to be joyous,
I AM worthy to be abundant,
I AM worthy to be content,
I AM worthy to have joy in my life.
I AM a divine being of great worth,
Power, joy, fulfillment, and energy.
My aura and body of light
Are filled with divine love and light.
Thank you, God, and SO IT IS.

PROSPERITY PRAYER

The following prosperity prayer can increase divine circulation of good in your life and help you fulfill your life purpose.

My individual and divine purpose are one,
Unfolding beautifully and comfortably
According to God's perfect wisdom and grace.
My prosperity manifests and flows
To support me and my purpose in every way.
My prosperity comes completely in freedom
As a gift of God's Grace.
I love myself dearly.
Thank you, God, and SO IT IS.

PEACE PRAYER

Below is a simple prayer for peace. Use it to bring greater relaxation, peace, comfort, security, and serenity.

May God's love fill and surround me with love and peace.
May God's grace fill and surround me with grace and peace.
May God's joy fill and surround me with joy and peace.
May God's faith fill and surround me with faith and peace.
May God's light fill and surround me with light and peace.
May God's wisdom fill and surround me with wisdom and peace.
May God's strength fill and surround me with strength and peace.
I AM beloved. I AM at peace.

PRAYER BEFORE SLEEP

The prayer can be used right before sleep to strengthen your energy field and to avert nightmares, fitful sleep, or broken sleep. You will sleep more soundly and peacefully.

> *I open my heart to God's love.*
> *I AM a beloved child of God.*
> *I AM filled with the light of God.*
> *I AM a beauteous being of great power,*
> *Great energy, great good, and great glory.*
> *I now call upon God to keep me protected, safe, and secure*
> *In the Christ consciousness during sleep.*
> *I now call upon God to build a beautiful golden sphere*
> *Of divine love and light around me as I sleep,*
> *To keep me safe, secure, and one with God.*
> *Thank you, God, and SO IT IS.*

UNITING WITH GOD

The following affirmation can be used effectively in any Scientific Prayer in the Reverence/Glorification and Rapport/Unification sections.

> *God is All, both visible and invisible.*
> *One presence, one mind, one power is all.*
> *This One, that is all, is perfect life,*
> *Perfect love and perfect substance.*
> *I AM an individualized expression of God,*
> *Ever one with this perfect life,*
> *Perfect love and perfect substance.*
> *Thank you, God, and SO IT IS.*

PERFECT RIGHT RESULTS

The following prayer is used whenever a healing or Scientific Prayer treatment feels incomplete or if it seems to need correction or rectification.

Jesus Christ and the Holy Spirit are here
Producing perfect right results
In and through this divine, healing
Scientific Prayer and empowerment session
And situation now,
For the highest good of myself,
And all others concerned.

(Repeat the above lines at least three times, until it feels complete.)

Thank you, God, and SO IT IS.

SEALING THE HEALING SESSIONS

You can use the following prayer at the end of your prayer or healing sessions for protection and cleansing. This will seal it in divine consciousness.

This entire healing session is now lovingly lifted,
Healed, revealed, and permanently sealed
In the golden, white, violet, and silver,
Archangelic light of archangel Christ Michael,
Archangel Christ Raphael, and Archangel Christ Zadkiel,
Under grace, in God's own wise and perfect ways.
Thank you, God, and SO IT IS.

All the prayers and affirmations in this book are to be spoken aloud in a powerful, clear voice. These can be used to heal others or yourself. Speak with conviction, confidence, and certainty. Unless otherwise stated, use these prayers in the Renewal/Healing section of your Scientific Prayer treatments.

You can order a CD of healing prayers at www.scientificprayer.com. For more information about using healing prayers, you may take classes or private sessions. Teachers are listed at www.divinerevelation.org/ Teachers.html. Or order a home study course at www.scientificprayer.com.

In the next chapter, you will find three hundred powerful affirmations that you can use in your Scientific Prayers.

THREE HUNDRED 14
AFFIRMATIONS

PRAYER IS THE ONLY MEANS OF BRINGING ABOUT
ORDERLINESS AND PEACE AND REPOSE IN OUR DAILY ACTS.
—*Mahatma Gandhi*

*A*ffirmations are statements of truth that have the power to transform your life instantaneously. Scientific Prayer treatments consist of a series of affirmative statements that change your mind from non-truth to truth. Therefore, your prayers will simply be a string of affirmations of truth, composed in the nine-step format.

This chapter, which lists three hundred affirmations, is a study guide and resource for you to compose your prayer treatments with ease. The affirmations below are categorized by subject. Use these affirmations, where appropriate, in the nine-step Scientific Prayer formula.

KEY TO THE AFFIRMATIONS IN THIS CHAPTER

GOD'S PRESENCE

- ◆ There is one power and one presence at work in the universe and in my life—God the good, omnipotent.
- ◆ I know that there is but one life. That life is God.

- I know that there is but one mind and one power, which is God.
- I open my heart to the sacred presence of God, and I trust in God's enduring love.
- There is nowhere that God is not; right where the trouble seems to be, there God is.
- God is life that heals all, wisdom that guides all, and love that comforts all.

GOD—MY PRIORITY

- God is always first in my life.
- I AM living a God-centered life.
- God is my number one priority.
- God, you are the answer to my every prayer.
- I AM immersed in the kingdom of God, today and every day.
- God's inspiration is music for my soul, God's wisdom is illumination for my soul, and God's love is comfort for my heart. God is my way, my strength.

GOD—MY PRESENCE

- I AM infinite Being.
- I live in the heart of God.
- I AM a radiant light-bearer.
- I AM a perfect expression of God.
- The kingdom of God is within me.
- I AM one with infinite life and wisdom.
- My mind is one with the infinite Mind.

- In God I live and move and have my being.

- The light of God shines brightly through me.

- The eternal life of God lives and breathes in and through me.

- I AM merged, united, immersed, and one with the presence of God.

- I AM God in action, God in activity, God's philanthropist.

- There is only one life and that is God's life. That life is my life now.

- The pure life of God flows through me from center to circumference—never ending.

- I AM a child of God, created in God's likeness and image. Therefore, I look like God. I think like God. I speak like God. I act like God. I feel like God. And I respond like God in every situation, by knowing the truth.

PERFECTION AND WHOLENESS

- I AM the immaculate conception of God now.

- I AM the immaculate perfection of God now.

- I AM perfection everywhere now.

- I AM perfect, whole, complete, and free, as God created me to be.

- I AM That I AM divine perfection.

- I AM the divine expression of perfection—perfection everywhere present, perfection everywhere now.

- I AM ever one with perfect life, perfect love, and perfect substance—whole and complete in every way.

FAITH AND TRUST

- ◆ I AM faith in action.
- ◆ I have the kind of confidence that is founded on my faith in God.
- ◆ I breathe in life fully. I relax and trust the flow and process of life.
- ◆ God is preparing my way as order is restored and hope is renewed.
- ◆ God places divine desires in my heart and causes them to manifest. God fulfills the desires of my heart.
- ◆ Thank you God that all my needs are met through God's holy presence.
- ◆ These words, which I now speak in faith, activate a law of universal good, and I accept the results.

GOOD

- ◆ I claim my good, very good perfection now.
- ◆ I now bless everyone, everything, and every situation in my life now, as good, good, and very good.
- ◆ I walk in the charmed circle of God's love, and I AM divinely irresistible to my highest good now.
- ◆ Together, God and I are creating only good in my life. I now accept and welcome all of God's good for me.
- ◆ My good comes in good measure, pressed down, shaken together, and running over.
- ◆ My life is filled to the brim and overflowing with abundant good.
- ◆ The continuous stream of substance flows into my hands from expected and unexpected sources.

- God is incapable of separation or division. Therefore, my good is incapable of separation or division. I AM one with my undivided good, now.

BLESSINGS

- I claim my blessings now.
- I AM attuned to the blessings of answered prayer now.
- My soul awakens to new blessings of God's love and grace.
- Every cell in my body is saturated with blessings. I share these blessings with all and rejoice that I now live life fully.
- God has created for me a world rich with endless blessings, infinite possibilities, and unlimited opportunities.
- I AM blessed as I share the light of Spirit within me.
- I expect the best and say "yes" to all the good and wonderful blessings coming to me.

GRACE

- I give thanks for grace, a sacred gift from God.
- The grace of God is divine love in action.
- Grace is the love of God that uplifts, strengthens, and encourages me daily.
- Through the love of God, I AM living in the eternal grace of God.
- The grace of God sustains and fulfills me.
- The grace of God blesses me all the days of my life.

GOD WORKS MIRACLES

- *"With God all things are possible."* [1]
- All things whatsoever I pray for, I receive them, and I have them.
- As I ask it is given to me, as I seek I find, as I knock doors open for me.
- Of myself I can do nothing. But God within me can and is performing miracles in my mind, body, relationships, finances, and all of my affairs right here and now.
- God will always make a way where there is no way.
- I have faith that God is working miracles in my life right now.
- I AM the one who is able to shape substance. Substance is the presence of God. It does not fail. Substance is adaptable to all my demands. The form that is necessary to my well-being appears.
- Every moment is a miracle.

SURRENDER

- I let go and let God take charge of my life.
- I let go and let God work wonders in my life.
- I let go of all and I let God handle it all.
- I let go and I let God do the work through me. I release all into God's care.
- I do God's will in all the little things in my life. I do not wait for big things.
- God's will for me is good and only good. I allow God's will be done in all things.
- I AM an idea in the mind of God. I let God's idea express in me. I AM the mind of God.

- I now lay down every weight. I let go all excess, all burdens. I let go and let God show me the way.

- *"Thy will be done on earth as it is in heaven,"* [2] and I AM doing God's will.

- I do the work of God. God cannot fail. Therefore, I cannot fail.

- God is in charge of my life and affairs beyond my human efforts.

INNER GUIDANCE

- I AM divinely guided in all my ways.

- I trust my higher self. I listen with love to my inner voice.

- God's guidance is a message of love and caring that resounds within my soul.

- I AM led by Spirit in all I think, say, and do. I AM always divinely guided and inspired.

- I AM now led to that which is for my highest good, under grace, in perfect ways.

- I open my spiritual eyes to see all that God shows me. I open my spiritual ears to all that God speaks to me.

- God speaks to me in a still, small voice, a gentle whisper of divine ideas.

- The radiant light of God illumines my mind and directs me in all I do.

- God goes before me and prepares my way.

- I always take the right turn in the road, for God walks with me in each moment.

- *"For He will give His angels charge over me, to keep me in all my ways ."* [3]

TRUTH

- I know the truth, and the truth sets me free.

- Divine understanding is the guiding light of my life.

- God is showing me the truth from within concerning this situation now.

- I AM wise and confident through the all-knowing presence of God.

- The truth of God speaks through my positive, life-affirming thoughts.

- I AM consistent and persistent in thinking and speaking only God's truth every day.

- Today, in every situation, I choose to bear witness to the truth by expressing the love, life, peace, and enthusiasm of God.

WISDOM

- God is my source of wisdom, a wisdom that sustains and guides me always.

- I AM wise, for I have access to infinite wisdom within.

- I AM an illumined child of God, filled with the spirit of divine love and wisdom.

- The light of God's wisdom is shining within me.

- Peace calms my soul as I trust God's inner wisdom to direct me.

- I AM what I think. I think the mind of God. I AM wise with God's wisdom.

- I AM a child of God. I AM created in God's likeness and image. Therefore, I have the mind of God and I learn, retain and recall knowledge quickly and easily.

- Let there be Light.

DIVINE PURPOSE

- God lovingly reveals to me the divine plan for my life.
- I trust that divine right action is always taking place in my life. I AM at peace.
- Centered in God, I now fulfill my divine purpose.
- Divine revelations awaken me to my purpose and potential.
- My will has a spiritual origin, a spiritual character, and a spiritual purpose.
- I AM giving expression to my perfect divine potential now.
- God has a divine plan and purpose for my life, and I willingly follow God's plan.

DIVINE CREATIVITY

- I AM infinite creativity.
- God is my source of unlimited strength and creative expression.
- I accept that I AM the creative power in my world. I now choose to create joy, love, and success.
- Divine creativity flows through me now and forevermore.
- In God, I live, move, and have my being. In me, God lives, moves, and has expression.
- I praise my world as the perfect creation of divine substance. I now see more health, wealth, and happiness in my world than I have ever seen before.
- The kingdom of God is a treasure of divine ideas that enrich my life.

UNLIMITED LIFE AND ENERGY

- I AM unlimited and free as God created me to be.

- I breathe deeply of the breath of life and the freedom of Spirit.

- I AM a free Spirit—free in mind, body, and spirit.

- I AM a radiating center of divine life, and I give this life full and free expression.

- God's love in me is drawing to me new ideas, new courage, and visible daily supply.

- Each day is a new opportunity. Yesterday is over and done. Today is the first day of my future.

- I AM alive, alert, awake, joyous, and enthusiastic about life. I AM filled with energy, passion, and enthusiasm.

- Spirit guides me to fresh, new opportunities. Every moment of every day is brimming with unlimited possibilities.

DIVINE ORDER

- Everything in my life is in perfect divine order now.

- Divine order is at work in the universe and in my life.

- Through divine order, I place all things in my life in proper perspective.

- Nothing is wasted in my life. All is useful, for I AM in divine order.

- I AM not bound by careless living habits and careless attitudes. My life is in divine order.

- There is no clutter or confusion in my mind, my body, or my life. There is only God's order. I AM established in divine order.

- I now let go of worn-out things, conditions, and relationships. Divine order is now established and maintained in me and in my world.

- The inflow and outflow of everything in my life is established in divine order and harmony. I AM peaceful and poised.

- Divine right order and perfect divine right action are now established and maintained in my mind, body, relationships, finances, and all of my affairs.

- I AM patient, for I trust in God's law of divine order.

- Every function of my body is in perfect order, for my body is God's orderly temple.

- No problem is too difficult to handle, for I AM in tune with divine order.

- Divine order is moving this situation forward to a divine resolution.

- God's law of justice is working perfectly through me toward all people, and through all people toward me now.

DIVINE TIMING

- I have all the time there is—eternity.

- There is time and space for everything I need to do. I AM at peace.

- There is no rush in Spirit, so I act only when prompted from God within.

- I release the past. I release the future. I AM here now. I now live only in the present.

- God's highest good comes to me at the right time, in the right way, and in divine order.

- Every experience in my life happens to me in proper sequence. God is in charge.

- I successfully take one step at a time in my life, and God is ever with me.

PROTECTION

- I AM divinely protected by the light of my being.

- I AM, right now and always, in God's loving, protecting presence.

- The angel of divine protection goes before me, preparing my way and shielding me from any negative experiences.

- God's protecting presence surrounds me today and every day.

- The power and presence of God protect me wherever I go.

- Wherever I go, however I travel, I AM in God's care and keeping.

SUSTENANCE AND SUPPORT

- The breath of life is a gift from God that sustains and supports me.

- God is nurturing, supporting, and sustaining me now and in each moment.

- At home with God, I find rest and renewal every day.

- Right where I AM, I AM at home in the presence of God.

- Turning to the Spirit of God within, I experience a true home-coming.

- I thank my home for sheltering me so comfortably. Every nook and cranny in it is inviting. My heart is at home here. Everyone who enters here feels the warmth and love of God.

SAFETY AND SECURITY

◆ God is my safety and security.

◆ I AM protected by divine love. I AM always safe and secure.

◆ It is safe to feel. My feelings are normal and acceptable. My emotions flow honestly and freely.

◆ It is safe to experience joy in every area of my life. I love life and life loves me.

◆ I AM safe. I trust the process of life. My needs are always taken care of. I relax and let life flow joyously.

◆ I breathe freely and fully. I AM safe. I open myself to life.

◆ I love and approve of myself. It is safe to be who I AM.

◆ I AM willing to change and grow. I now create a safe new future.

◆ It is safe to see and experience new ideas and new ways. I AM open and receptive to all of God's good.

◆ It is okay to feel good. It is okay to feel safe. I deserve to feel good. I deserve to feel safe.

◆ All is well.

EASE AND FLEXIBILITY

◆ I AM flexible, agile, and flowing. I AM graceful in all I do.

◆ I AM coordinated. I always move smoothly and elegantly, with grace and ease.

◆ I move forward in life with wisdom, love, joy, ease, and comfort.

◆ My life is now light, easy, and joyful. I relax and let life flow through me with ease.

◆ I gently flow with life and each new experience. I AM at peace with where I AM. All is well.

- God is the source of comfort that soothes me, reassures me, and gives me rest.

- I let go of all expectations. Answers come to me with ease. People, places, and things are free to be themselves. Joy delights me at every turn.

RELEASING FALSE BELIEFS

- I AM my divine, indwelling thought-adjuster.

- I have faith in God's life within me. False beliefs and negative appearances have no power over me. They are now dissolved by the loving, forgiving action of God.

- Centered in God's presence, I let go of every negative thought, feeling, and concern.

- I easily and comfortably release that which I no longer need in my life.

- God's perfect harmony is now expressed in my world. I release all sense of hardship and struggle, remembering that God is my gentle and loving teacher and that all is well.

- I release all that is unlike love and joy in my mind. I let go of the past and welcome the new, fresh, and vital now. Letting go is easy.

- It is easy for me to reprogram the computer of my mind. All of life is change, and my life is ever new. Through freedom of Spirit, I AM a new me.

FORGIVENESS

- ◆ The Christ in me is my forgiving and releasing power.

- ◆ The forgiving, releasing, and healing power of God works in and through me now

- ◆ All judgment, resentment, criticism, and unforgiveness are now dissolved and healed.

- ◆ I now fully and freely forgive and release (person). I loose you and let you go. You are free, and I AM free. All things are cleared up between us now and forever. I let go and let God do perfect work in this situation for the good of all concerned.

- ◆ With the love and peace of God within my heart, I forgive everyone of everything—including myself. I forgive all past experiences. I AM free.

- ◆ I forgive myself for all seeming mistakes. I bless myself.

DIVINE LOVE

- ◆ God is love.

- ◆ I AM the love that God is.

- ◆ God's love fills my heart.

- ◆ As a beloved child of God, I AM loved, honored, respected, and cherished by all men, women, children, and other living beings, now and always.

- ◆ I AM expressing God's perfect, unconditional love. I AM always loving in my words, thoughts, and deeds.

- ◆ All people are expressions of divine love; therefore, I meet with nothing but expressions of divine love.

- ◆ Harmony and love flood my mind and heart. I AM patient, kind, gentle, and forgiving.

- I see with divine love, compassion, and understanding.

- Divine love, expressing through me, now draws to me all that is needed to make me happy and my life complete.

- Divine love draws to me the people who belong in my life and unites me with them now.

- Divine love harmonizes, divine love adjusts, divine love prospers, divine love foresees everything and richly provides every good thing for me now. Divine love is now victorious.

- I praise divine love, which melts situations and challenges that seem impossible.

SELF-LOVE AND SELF-WORTH

- I AM love.

- I AM loving and loveable.

- I celebrate myself.

- I AM infinite beauty.

- I let go of all negative beliefs about myself. I know the truth that I AM a one-of-a-kind divine original, created in God's likeness and image.

- I AM a child of God, precious in God's eyes. I love and cherish myself as God loves me.

- I love myself unconditionally. I accept myself unconditionally. I approve of myself unconditionally. I forgive myself unconditionally. I bless myself unconditionally.

- I love and approve of myself, exactly the way I AM.

- I AM worthy and deserving of God's good for me.

- I AM totally adequate at all times. I AM confident.

- I AM free to be me, and I allow others the freedom to be who they are.
- I love life, and life loves me. We get along perfectly together.

LOVING RELATIONSHIPS

- I AM united with God and with my loved ones in a heartfelt spiritual connection.
- Wherever we are, my loved ones and I are enfolded in the presence of God.
- I see only God and good in you.
- I envelop my entire family in a circle of love, those who are living and those who are dead. I affirm wonderful, harmonious relationships with each one.
- I see other people's viewpoints, and I AM blessed in doing so.
- The Spirit of God unites the family of God around the world.
- The family of humanity unites in love and harmony.

JOY AND HAPPINESS

- I AM pure joy.
- I AM a joy bringer. I bring pleasure, happiness, and cheer into the lives of others.
- My sense of humor lightens and brightens my view of life.
- I AM the joy of life, and I express joy now and always.
- I AM filled with joy, which flows through me with every heartbeat.

- I now love my life. My channels of joy are wide open. I AM completely open to life.

- My soul sings a song of joy and celebration in God.

- My kind and loving words gladden my heart and the hearts of others.

- I live in the ever joyous now. My life is joy.

- I embrace the joy and wonder this day holds.

- I rejoice in the day that the Lord has made, and in what God is fulfilling through me now.

SUCCESS

- Success comes quickly, powerfully, and irresistibly in every phase of my life now.

- The spirit of success is now working in and through me, and I AM in all ways guided, prospered, and blessed.

- I AM ardent, motivated, zealous, and irrepressible.

- I AM successful in all my endeavors, for the good of all.

- I AM an achiever, attracting good. I AM a winner. I AM always victorious.

- I AM positive, optimistic, self-assured, and faith-filled.

- Each day brings new achievements. The mark of success is upon me.

PROSPERITY

- Divine love, through me, blesses and multiplies all that I AM, all that I have, all that I give, and all that I receive.

- Everyone and everything prospers me now.

- I AM a child of God, created in God's likeness and image. My birthright is infinite abundance. Therefore, I inherit unlimited wealth.

- God is the source of my supply and provides abundantly for me now. I prosper and succeed in every area of my life.

- All my needs are met. In God I have no lack. I live on an unlimited income.

- Success and prosperity come easily to me. There is plenty for everyone, including myself.

- I AM enriched and fulfilled, divinely directed and lavishly prospered, through the unlimited goodness of God. I AM thriving, wealthy, and affluent, within and without.

- My good is now flowing to me so richly and fully that I have an abundance of money to spare and to share, today and always.

- God's good circulates freely in my life and prospers me mightily now.

- God is my unfailing source of supply, and large sums of money now come to me quickly, under grace, in perfect ways.

- God is my divine banker. God is in charge of all my financial affairs now and provides all my needs and wants.

- I love money, and money loves me. It visits me often.

- Money is God in action.

WORK EXPRESSION

- My perfect position with my perfect salary now manifests in God's own perfect time and way.

- My income is constantly increasing. Promotions come easily to me.

- I always give 100% at work, and I AM greatly appreciated.

- My work is fulfilling, joyous, and satisfying.

- Being focused and alert, I do my work efficiently, effortlessly, effectively, accurately, and on time.

- I think clearly, concisely, and correctly in all tasks that are set before me.

- My business is expanding beyond my expectations.

- I always attract the best customers, and they are a joy to serve.

- I attract all the business that I can comfortably handle.

- My workspace is a pleasure to be in. I love the beauty that surrounds me at work.

- I AM harmonious with all my co-workers in an atmosphere of mutual respect.

HEALTH

- I AM the resurrection and the life.

- I AM a child of God, and therefore I inherit only perfect health.

- I AM one with the radiant living substance of God. I AM healed.

- Let there be light. Let the light of God's love, life, and healing power in me burst forth right now with the brilliance of glowing health.

- I AM full of life—healthy, wholesome, vigorous, sound, whole, and complete in every area of my body, mind, emotions, spirit, and life.

- My body is the substance of God, manifesting in correspondence with God's perfect idea. My health is a result of my belief in a divine idea—the idea of God's pure life.

- God supports me in building constructive, healthy habits.

- God-life flows through me as a mighty current of cleansing and healing.

- God's vitalizing energy floods my entire being, and I AM healed.

- "Yes" is the response of all my cells to words of life and healing.

REJUVENATION AND RESTORATION

- As I AM immersed in the presence of God, I AM restored—mind, body, and soul.

- I AM a new creation, energized by the healing, revitalizing power of God. Every breath I take refreshes and renews me.

- My body is the temple of God. Therefore, God is present in every cell.

- I AM created in the likeness and image of God. Therefore, I have the DNA of God. My body looks like God, feels like God, and responds like God to all challenges. God's life-giving energy flows through every atom, molecule, and cell.

- The life of God within now restores me to harmony and health and gives me strength. I AM rejuvenated.

- I AM what I think. I think life. The life of God is released in me, and I AM alive with vibrant energy.

- Every cell in my body is quickened with joy and nourished with love as I choose positive thoughts instead of negative thoughts. My mind and body are in perfect balance.

DIVINE STRENGTH

- Today, I turn to God, wherein I find my strength. God is my comfort, my fortress, and my deliverer. God is my rock, in which I take refuge.

- I do not depend on things of the world to give me courage and strength. God's strength is established within me, and I AM forever upheld.

- I AM made mentally, physically, emotionally, and spiritually strong in the Lord and in the power of God's might.

- Thank you God that I AM strong in the power of your might. I AM a tower of strength and stability.

- I have the strength to change my mind—without guilt and without regret.

- I AM what I think. I think power. The power of God is released in me, and I AM daily changed into a likeness more and more like God.

PEACE

- Peace, peace, be still. Be still and be at peace.

- God's indwelling presence blesses me with peace of mind.

- Knowing that God is my constant source of peace, I AM secure and confident.

- My mind is now relaxed, calm, centered, tranquil, and serene.

- I AM deeply centered and peaceful in every area of life.

- I digest and assimilate all new experiences peacefully and joyously.

- I AM at peace just where I AM. I accept my good, knowing my desires are now fulfilled.

- I lovingly release the day and I slip into peaceful sleep, knowing tomorrow will take care of itself.

- As God's instrument of peace, I live in harmony with my environment.

- Let there be peace on Earth, and let it begin with me.

GRATITUDE

- Thank you, wonderful God.

- My heart overflows with thanksgiving.

- Thank you, God, that I AM one with you.

- Thank you, God, that all my thoughts are God's thoughts.

- Thank you, God, that I AM immersed in the kingdom of God today and every day.

- Thank you, God, for your perfect presence in, through, and as me, as all, as all creation.

- Thank you, God, for this precious moment, for every precious moment.

In the next chapter, you will find twenty sample Scientific Prayer treatments that you can use as study tools or for manifesting your own aspirations.

TWENTY SCIENTIFIC 15
PRAYER TREATMENTS

WHEN YOU MAKE PRAYER A MOMENT OF TRUTH
IN YOUR LIFE, THE HEAVENS OPEN IN RESPONSE."
—*Anonymous*

In this chapter, you will find twenty Scientific Prayer treatments using the nine-step formula you have studied. These sample treatments will help you master this powerful technology. These are teaching tools. The prayers you compose yourself will be personally suited to your own unique situations. The best way to use Scientific Prayer is to learn the nine-step format and then close your eyes, attune to your higher self, and speak the words you receive from within your heart in a strong, clear voice.

Feeling is a prerequisite to healing. Rather than just reading prayers by rote day after day, feel your prayers deeply and speak with conviction. Your prayers can produce profound demonstrations when you:

1. Speak from your higher self as you say your prayer.

2. Feel deeply as you are speaking.

3. Speak with clarity and power.

4. Come to complete conviction in each section of your prayer before moving on to the next section.

These are sample prayers dealing with various areas of life: health, love, family, prosperity, spiritual development, and so forth. These examples can help you compose your own prayers using the nine-step method. Each of these steps is delineated by a separate paragraph.

Believe and trust that as it is easy for you to breathe the air and live by it, or to eat and drink, so it is easy and even still easier for your faith to receive all spiritual gifts from the Lord. Prayer is the breathing of the soul; prayer is our spiritual food and drink.

—JOHN OF CRONSTADT

You may use these prayers to heal yourself or to manifest goals that you want to achieve. Remember to speak the prayers in a strong, clear voice.

SELF-LOVE

This is a treatment for myself, (full name), for perfect self-love, self-worth, and self-acceptance or better now.

I recognize that God is divine, unconditional love. God is the source of love. God's perfect love brings peace and content. God is the all-forgiving, the source of compassion, mercy, and understanding now. God is the loving parent of this cosmos, and God's perfect work is done through love.

I AM a beloved child of God, held in the arms of God—loved, cherished, and nurtured. Precious in the sight of God, I AM one with God's unconditional love now. God shines the light of forgiveness, mercy, compassion, and understanding upon me now. God's love enfolds me and fills my heart with peace. God's love is doing its perfect work in and through me now. I AM the love that God is.

I, therefore, claim for myself, (full name), perfect self-love, self-worth, and self-acceptance or better now.

I now heal and release all negative thoughts that interfere with this claim, whether known or unknown, conscious or subconscious. My thoughts are now one with, the same as, and in tune with God's thought. I dispel from my mind any and all need to punish myself. I forgive myself completely, for I know that I have done the very best I could do in every situation. I let go of all shame, embarrassment, and fear of exposure now. I release all judgment of self now. I now welcome self-acceptance and self-expression now. I AM free to express myself in my own unique way. I boldly express myself the way I AM now, for I AM an expression of

God in human form. I release all fear of making a mistake and not being right. I AM perfect for me for now. I AM on my perfect path of unfoldment. I dissolve all self-condemnation now. I release all guilt now. I allow myself to be myself without criticism and judgment. There is nothing in the universe that holds anything against me now, and I hold nothing against myself now. I AM a perfect being of divine light, and I surrender all my limitations to God. I dispel any and all belief that others are better than, greater than, worse than, or less than myself. I know that all beings are equal in God's sight. I rejoice in God's perfection in every living being. Therefore I like myself, I accept myself, and I forgive myself fully, completely, and unconditionally right now. I AM perfect exactly the way I AM now.

I now fully accept in consciousness my perfect self-love, self-worth, and self-acceptance or better now.

I thank God for manifesting this good in my life now, under grace, in God's own wise and perfect ways.

I release this treatment fully and completely into the Spiritual Law of perfection everywhere now, knowing that it is accepted and demonstrates in my life now, under grace, in perfect ways. SO BE IT.

SELF-AUTHORITY

This is a treatment for myself, (full name), for perfect self-authority or better now.

I recognize that God is the one power and presence in the universe. God is the ultimate authority and has supreme dominion. God is the director and manager of the entire cosmos. God is the one sovereign and the only power. God is perfection everywhere now.

I AM one with the authority and dominion of God now. I AM the sovereign and director of my life now. I AM perfection everywhere now. I AM in control of my life now. My life is in perfection and power now.

I, therefore, claim for myself, (full name), perfect self-authority or better now.

I now heal and release all limiting ideas that interfere with this claim, whether known or unknown, conscious or subconscious. My thoughts are now one with, the same as, and in tune with God's thought. I dissolve from my mind now any and all need to be controlled or dominated by anyone or anything. There is no person, place, thing, organization, situation, circumstance, memory, or addiction that can possess me or hold me in bondage. I belong to God and to myself alone. I AM free. I dissolve any and all reluctance to take responsibility for my own decisions. I AM in dominion of my life now. I dispel all feelings of dependency on others. I AM independent and in command of my own life. I release any and all fear of expression, and I boldly express myself exactly the way I AM. I let go of feeling unworthy, undeserving, or unacceptable. I know now that I AM the expression of God, that I AM the perfection of God, and that I AM perfect for me for now. I AM worthy, deserving, and acceptable now. I AM in control. I AM the only authority in my life. I AM divinely protected by the light of my Being. I close off my aura and body of light to all but my own God self.

I now fully accept in consciousness my perfect self-authority or better now.

I thank God for manifesting this good in my life now under grace in perfect ways.

Thank you, God, and SO IT IS.

PERFECT DIVINE ORDER AND TIMING

This is a treatment for myself, (full name), for perfect divine order and timing in every phase and aspect of my life now.

I recognize that there is one divine lawgiver in the universe, God the good, omnipotent. God is the great organizing principle and power, the perfect former of true patterns, the perfect unfoldment of all true expression and action, now. God is the source of stability and order. God is the one perfection at work in the cosmos. God works through the power of divine order.

I AM one with God's absolute order and perfection now. I AM one with the Law of Divine Order and the Law of Right Action. God's highest good comes to me at the perfect right time, in the right way, and in divine order. The orderly divine rule of the universe orders my life now. God's Law of Divine Order is now established in my mind, body, and affairs. Divine order is at work in my life now, and I AM harmoniously tuned to this Law of Divine Order in every phase and aspect of my being. The inflow and outflow of everything in my life is established in divine order and harmony.

I, therefore, claim for myself, (full name), perfect divine order and timing in every phase and aspect of my life now.

I accept in consciousness perfect divine order and timing now. I now heal and release all thoughts that interfere with this claim, whether known or unknown, conscious or subconscious. My thoughts are now one with, the same as, and in tune with God's thought. I discharge from my mind any chaotic or unclear thinking. I release all disorder, chaos, unworthiness, disarray, discord, confusion, lack, incoherence, and inconsistency now. These thoughts are now released into God's sphere of perfection everywhere now. I now welcome and embrace thoughts of divine order, divine timing, divine perfection, precision, logic, intelligence, clarity, wisdom, strength, harmony, and coherence now. I AM in control. I AM the only authority in my life. I AM divinely protected by the light of my being. I close off my aura and body of light to all but my own God self. Divine order is the law of my mind, body, and affairs. I AM always in the right place, doing the right thing at the right time. My every desire has its perfect right time and place for fulfillment. I trust in God and in myself now. All is well in my life now. My life is in perfect divine order and timing now.

I now fully accept in consciousness perfect divine order and timing in my life now.

I thank God for divine order and timing now.

I release this treatment into the perfect order of God's divine law now, knowing that it demonstrates now, under grace in perfect order. Thank you, God, and SO IT IS.

INNER PEACE

This is a treatment for myself, (full name), for perfect inner peace now.

God is peace. God is the source of all stillness and tranquility. God is at rest and at peace even in the midst of the turbulent seas of life. God is perfect quietude, like the stillness and depth of the water at the bottom of the ocean. God is the constant source of peace.

I AM one with God's peace now. I AM peace. I AM stillness, quietude, and tranquility now. I AM at rest and at peace in the midst of all activity now. Knowing that God is my constant source of peace, I AM serene and confident. I AM an instrument of God's perfect peace in my world now.

I, therefore, claim for myself, (full name), perfect inner peace now.

I now heal and release all limiting concepts that interfere with this claim, whether known or unknown, conscious or subconscious. My thoughts are now one with, the same as, and in tune with God's thought. I renounce and release all anxiety, worry, fear, turbulence, and confusion from my mind now. These negations are dissolved by God's light and flow into the ocean of God's peace. I dissolve all thoughts of straining to accomplish. I dispel any feeling of compulsion or obsession now. I lift all tension from my mind and body now. I allow my mind and body to settle down to a state of perfect peace. I allow God to fill my mind and heart with quietude as I open myself to God's healing love. God's peace is at work in my life now, bringing me tranquility and stillness. I AM confident, stable, and my stability comes from within. I let go and let God do perfect, peaceful work through me now. I relax and turn over the results of my actions to God. I trust in God now. I AM in harmony and peace.

I now fully accept in consciousness my perfect inner peace or better now.

I thank God for bringing inner peace now.

Thank you, God, and SO IT IS.

SPIRITUAL ENLIGHTENMENT

This is a treatment for myself, (full name), for perfect spiritual enlightenment or better now.

I recognize that God is the source of light and of love. God is absolute wisdom and truth and the conqueror of ignorance. God is the perfection of being, perfection everywhere now. God is the all-seeing, all-knowing source of wisdom, knowledge, truth, and intelligence. God is the one source of supreme knowledge. God is the release from all bondage of the world and the ultimate freedom in God consciousness.

I AM one with God's light, love, wisdom, and truth now. In silence, I AM totally immersed in the presence of God. I AM merged, united, and one with God's holy presence. I AM one with the perfection of being. I AM the source of wisdom, knowledge and truth. I AM one with God's all-seeing, all-knowing intelligence now. I AM the light that God is. I AM the love that God is. I AM the perfect divine intelligence that God is. God's supreme knowledge dawns in my mind now. I AM released from all bondage and I AM free in God consciousness now.

I, therefore, claim for myself, (full name), perfect spiritual enlightenment or better now.

I now heal and release all negative thoughts that interfere with this claim, whether known or unknown, conscious or subconscious. My thoughts are now one with, the same as, and in tune with God's thought. Let there be light. Let there be light. Let there be light in my mind now. Let there be light. Let there be light. Let there be the light of God in my heart now. I dissolve from my mind all thoughts of separation from God, unworthiness, and undeserving now. I AM one with God and one with the truth of my being. I AM worthy and deserving now. I AM filled with God's love and I release all thoughts of negation, confusion, fear, anger, guilt, and blame. I AM filled with non-judgment, perfection, wholeness, oneness, peace, truth, knowledge, wisdom, enlightenment, and God awareness now. I AM open to accept spiritual enlightenment now. I AM perfection everywhere now. I AM divine light, love, and truth now. All ignorance and bondage is lifted by God's perfect grace now. I AM released from all fetters of illusion, and I AM the ultimate freedom of God consciousness now. I AM fully enlightened now.

I now fully accept in consciousness my perfect spiritual enlightenment or better now.

I thank God for manifesting this good in my life now. My word does not go forth void but returns that which has been spoken right now.

Thank you, God, and SO IT IS.

PERFECT MATE

This is a treatment for myself, (full name), for my perfect mate and companion with compatible likes, interests, desires, appetites, values, purpose, career, and ideals or better to be with me in an intimate, committed, monogamous relationship now. This perfect mate is compatible with me in every way: spiritually, emotionally, socially, morally, intellectually, mentally, geographically, financially, physically, and sexually or better now.

I recognize that God is all-loving, the wellspring of love, the fountain of good, the river of strength. God is the incarnation of divine love, the one true source of unconditional love. God is perfect fulfillment, contentment, and joy. God sees love and perfection in every particle of creation.

God is the fountain of my good, the river of my strength. God fills and surrounds me with love now. God's love opens my heart to all joy and blessings. I AM the contentment and fulfillment that God is now. I AM one with the source of love—God the good, omnipotent. I AM filled with unconditional divine love now. I AM created in the likeness and image of God. Thus, I AM a child of God, and God loves me exactly the way I AM.

I, therefore, claim for myself, (full name), my perfect mate and companion with compatible likes, interests, desires, appetites, values, purpose, career, and ideals or better to be with me in an intimate, committed, monogamous relationship now. This perfect mate is compatible with me in every way: spiritually, emotionally, socially, morally, intellectually, mentally, geographically, financially, physically, and sexually or better now.

I fully accept my perfect mate in consciousness now. I now heal and release all negative ideas that interfere with this claim, whether known or unknown, conscious or subconscious. My thoughts are now one with, the same as, and in tune with God's thought. I dispel from my mind now any and all thoughts of unworthiness, fear of intimacy, fear of abandonment, fear of rejection, sadness, bitterness, resentment, anger toward the opposite sex, and negative memories of past relationships. I give these thoughts over to the Holy Spirit now. I now wholeheartedly accept in my life unconditional love, peace, deserving, intimacy, self-love, self-acceptance, self-worth, fulfillment, inner strength, self-authority, and forgiveness of past relationships, forgiveness of the opposite sex, forgiveness of all past memories. I call upon the Holy Spirit to cut all psychic ties between myself and all past memories of relationships now. I also cut all psychic ties between myself and all past romantic attachments now. All these psychic ties are now lovingly cut, lifted, loved, healed, released, and let go in the name of God. I AM now free of these past experiences and free to welcome my perfect mate into my life now.

I now fully accept in consciousness my perfect mate and companion or better under grace in perfect ways.

I thank God for manifesting my perfect mate now.

Thank you, God, and SO IT IS.

HARMONIOUS HOME-LIFE

This is a treatment for myself, (full name), for the perfect loving, peaceful, harmonious home-life and family relationships or better now.

I recognize that there is one source of harmony, peace, and love in the universe—God, the good, omnipotent, and omnipresent. God is perfect unity, the wellspring of rest and continual renewal.

I AM one with this source of good, harmony, love, and peace now. God is my one power and the source of unity for my life now. I AM an instrument of God's peace and harmony in my home. At home with God, I find rest and renewal every day.

I, therefore, claim for myself, (full name), the perfect loving, peaceful, harmonious home-life and family relationships or better now.

I now heal and release all negations from my mind that interfere with this claim, whether known or unknown, conscious or subconscious. My thoughts are now one with, the same as, and in tune with God's thought. I now cut all psychic ties between myself and those who live with me now. These psychic ties are now lovingly cut, lifted, loved, healed, released, and let go into the light of God's love. I know that any dear ones influencing my home are now blessed, forgiven, and released into the love, light, and wholeness of divinity. You are unified with the true nature of your being. God's love and light fill and surround you now with love and peace. The earth plane no longer binds you. Fear and blame no longer keep you in chains. I call upon your higher self to take you into the light of God now. Go now in peace and love. I AM now free from all attachments that have prevented unconditional love in my home-life and family relationships now. I call upon the divine presence to dissolve from my mind all feelings of resentment, fear, coercion, domination, sadness, pain, rejection, and abandonment. They are released and healed by divine wisdom now. I instead welcome into my home and family: love, happiness, forgiveness, freedom, self-authority, joy, healing, self-love, self-acceptance, and self-worth now. I now free all persons in my home to express themselves in their own unique and perfect way, and I AM free to express in my own perfect way. I see only good in myself and in them.

I now fully accept in consciousness harmony, peace, and love or better in my home and in my family now.

I thank God for answered prayer.

Thank you, God, and SO IT IS.

PERFECT LOVING FRIENDSHIPS

This is a treatment for myself, (full name), for my perfect loving, intimate, dependable, reliable friendships or better in my life now.

I recognize that God is the source of all love in the universe. God is ever-giving, ever-present, always reliable, always stable, the rock and staff of life. God is unconditional divine love. God is perfect constancy and dependability.

God is my strength, my ever-present source of love at all times. God's love is dependable and reliable in my life. Wherever I AM, God always is, and all is well. God is the ever-abiding rock and staff of my life. I AM the unconditional love of God now.

I, therefore, claim for myself, (full name), my perfect loving, intimate, dependable, reliable friendships or better now.

I now heal and release all limited thoughts interfering with this claim, whether known or unknown, conscious or subconscious. My thoughts are now one with, the same as, and in tune with God's thought. I now free my mind from all memories and experiences of undependable and unreliable friends. I release all thoughts of loneliness and let go of all ideas of having no real friends. I release all beliefs in lack and limitation. I now let go of all feelings of self-pity, undeserving, and unworthiness. I now accept that I AM magnetizing to myself dependable, reliable, caring friends now. I welcome loving friends into my life and I AM never alone again. My heart is now open to love and I AM fulfilled with an abundance of friends. I now invite and welcome thoughts of self-love, acceptance of self, deservedness, self-authority, self-responsibility, and self-worth now. I like myself, I love myself, and I accept myself now. I forgive all past friends who have proved untrustworthy or unreliable now. I know that they did the best they could do and that there is no reason for guilt or blame. I, therefore, welcome wonderful, loving friendships into my life now.

I now fully accept in consciousness my perfect loving, intimate, dependable, reliable friendships or better now.

I thank God for my loving friendships now.

Thank you, God, and SO BE IT.

PERFECT RELATIONSHIP WITH CHILDREN

This is a treatment for myself, (full name), for the perfect loving, respectful relationships with my children or better now.

I recognize that God is the source of love and respect. God is the ever-loving, all-merciful, all-joyful, everlasting, eternal source of unconditional love and respect now. God is the wellspring of abundant love.

I AM one with God's unconditional love now. I AM unconditional love now. I AM unconditional respect now. I AM a source of constant joy. I AM the love that God is, now and always. I AM the abundance of God's love.

I, therefore, claim for myself, (full name), the perfect loving, respectful relationships with my children or better now.

I now heal and release all limiting concepts interfering with this claim, whether known or unknown, conscious or subconscious. My thoughts are now one with, the same as, and in tune with God's thought. I accept that my relationships with my children are filled with love and harmony now. I dissolve from my mind any thoughts of resentment and fear about my children now. I embrace unconditional love for my children now. I dispel any need to dominate, coerce, or control my children now. I dissolve the need to make all decisions for my children now. I release the idea that only I know what is best for my children. I free my children to follow their own heart and I AM divinely free to follow my own heart. I dissolve the idea that I possess my children and I let go of the fear that they will somehow be taken away from me. I know there is no limit to my good and God is my ever-present supply. Therefore, I need not possess anyone or anything. I release my children completely and know that I accept good and joy in all forms from the universe. I cut any and all psychic ties between myself and my children now. These psychic ties are now lovingly cut, lifted, loved, healed, released, and let go now by the Holy Spirit. I dissolve from my mind any feelings of lack of self-acceptance, lack of self-love, and lack of self-worth now. They are now let go, loosed, and released by God's divine light. I accept myself the way I AM and I AM free to express myself the way I AM. I accept my children the way they are and I free them to express themselves the way they are. I AM the perfection of God in human form, and I AM perfect for me for now. My children are also perfect for them for now. I AM filled with self-love, self-acceptance, and self-worth now. I AM now free to love and respect my children now and I accept their love and respect now.

I now fully accept in consciousness my perfect loving, respectful relationships with my children or better now.

I thank God for manifesting loving relationships with my children now, under grace in perfect ways.

Thank you, God, and SO IT IS.

PERFECT RELATIONSHIP WITH PARENTS

This is a treatment for myself, (full name), for the perfect relationship with my parents or better now.

I recognize that God is the everlasting, unbounded source of love. God is perfect love. God is wholeness, oneness, and peace. God is eternal harmony and joy. God is the source of humility, gratitude, and thanksgiving now.

I AM one with God's everlasting, unbounded love. God loves me unconditionally now and at all times. I AM wholeness, oneness, and peace. God's eternal harmony and joy saturate my life now. I AM filled with thanksgiving, gratitude, and humility now in the face of God's infinite love.

I, therefore, claim for myself, (full name), my perfect relationship with my parents or better now.

I now heal and release all negative beliefs that interfere with this claim, whether known or unknown, conscious or subconscious. My thoughts are now one with, the same as, and in tune with God's thought. I accept in consciousness that my relationship with my parents is healed and forgiven now. I dispel from my mind any and all feelings of unworthiness and guilt concerning my parents now. I dissolve all judgment toward my parents now. I release all thoughts that my parents are criticizing me now. I release all feelings of anger and resentment toward my parents now. I let go of the thought that my parents need to change in any way. I now embrace the knowledge that my parents are perfect the way they are now. I now accept my parents exactly the way they are without attempting to change them. I AM filled with self-worth, self-acceptance, and forgiveness toward my parents now. I know that they did the best they could do in every situation with me and that I did the best I could do in every situation with them. Therefore there is no guilt or blame. I forgive myself completely and I love my parents unconditionally now. I free my parents to express themselves in their own unique way, and I free myself to express in my own individual way. I call upon the Holy Spirit to cut all psychic ties between my parents and myself now. These psychic ties are now lovingly cut, lifted, loved, healed, released, and let go in the name of God. I AM free to love my parents with God's perfect love now.

I now fully accept in consciousness my perfect relationship with my parents or better now.

I thank God for manifesting this good in my life now.

Thank you, God, and SO IT IS.

HEALING OF RELATIONSHIPS

This is a treatment for myself, (full name), for the perfect healing of my relationship with (person) or better now.

I recognize that God is unconditional love. God is the all-loving, all-forgiving healing presence and healing power that dwells within us and around us. God is perfect forgiveness and divine restoration. God is the resurrection and the life, the all-loving, all-merciful, and all-embracing. God is oneness and harmony. God is the consummate relationship counselor.

God is the only power at work in my life now. God's all-loving, all-forgiving divine presence restores me to oneness and harmony. God's divine mercy and unconditional love fill and surround me with peace. I AM the perfect healing presence and healing power now. I AM healed and resurrected by God's perfect forgiveness. I AM one with God's perfect counsel now.

I, therefore, claim for myself, (full name), the perfect healing of my relationship with (person) or better now.

I accept this perfect healing in my consciousness now. I now release all limiting concepts that interfere with this claim, whether known or unknown, conscious or subconscious. My thoughts are now one with, the same as, and in tune with God's thought. Perfect love dissolves all fear and anger in our relationship. Love now unites us in perfect harmony. I forgive you now, dear (person), sending love from my heart, and I know you did the very best that you could do in every situation with me; therefore, there is no guilt or blame. I now call upon the power of God to cut all psychic ties between myself and (person). These psychic ties are now lovingly cut, lifted, loved, healed, released, and let go by the power and presence of almighty God. Dear (person), it is impossible for you to infringe upon my perfection. I recognize that you merely did what I invited, and that in reality neither you nor anyone else can hurt me. I AM perfect now, always have been, and always will be, and you cannot change that. I pour out my heart in unconditional love toward you. The divine self within me forgives you completely now. I visualize you before me in a beautiful sphere of golden divine light. Your inner beauty and radiance fills my being now with perfect forgiveness.

I now fully accept in consciousness the perfect healing of my relationship with (person) or better now.

I thank God for manifesting this healing in my life now.

I release this claim to God and to the natural laws of creation. My claim demonstrates now by the power and the presence of God. That is the nature of natural law. AMEN.

SEXUAL FULFILLMENT

This is a treatment for myself, (full name), for my perfect sexual fulfillment or better now with my consenting adult partner in a joyous loving relationship.

I recognize that God is the source of pleasure and fulfillment, the wellspring of satisfaction. God is unconditional love, acceptance, joy, and happiness. God is free from judgment and the source of pure love. God is the full expression of unconditional love now and always.

I AM one with God's love and nonjudging acceptance now. God's full expression of love permeates my life now. God's joy and happiness flood my heart with fullness. I AM replete with the pleasure of God's garden of joy and delights now. I AM unconditional love now.

I, therefore, claim for myself, (full name), my perfect sexual fulfillment or better now with my consenting adult partner in a joyous loving relationship.

I now heal and release all negations that interfere with this claim, whether known or unknown, conscious or subconscious. My thoughts are now one with, the same as, and in tune with God's thought. I dissolve from my mind any and all ideas of limitation, inhibition, fear, disgust, frustration, sexual guilt, and self-hatred now. I now welcome and accept freedom of expression, joy, uninhibitedness, love, fullness, fulfillment, forgiveness of self, and self-love now. I now release all negative ideas about sex from my upbringing. I release any ideas that sex is bad, dirty, or harmful. I now accept that sex is a beautiful, joyful expression of love. I accept that there is nothing wrong with my safe sexual expression with my consenting adult partner. I cut any and all psychic ties between myself and anyone who has made me feel guilty about sex. I cut, lift, love, heal, release, and let go of these psychic ties now, and they are dissolved in God's love and light. I now fully accept my body and my sexual expression with my consenting adult partner. I AM a loving, sexual, beautiful being of God, and my love is expressed sexually now in great joy and fulfillment. I AM filled with the joyous freedom of sexual pleasure and satisfaction now. My sexual expression is the expression of divine love. I AM perfect exactly the way I AM now, and I express myself freely the way I AM now.

I now fully accept in consciousness my perfect sexual fulfillment or better now with my consenting adult partner in a joyous loving relationship.

I thank God for manifesting this good in my life now under grace in perfect ways.

Thank you, God, and SO IT IS.

FREEDOM FROM CO-DEPENDENT RELATIONSHIPS

This is a treatment for myself, (full name), for perfect freedom from my co-dependent relationship with (person) or better now.

I recognize God as the fountain of unconditional love. God is divine love, truth, and joy. God is perfection everywhere now. God is perfect balance and wholeness. God is strength, invincibility, and supreme sovereignty.

I AM one with God's perfect unconditional love now. I AM the expression of God's divine love now. I AM truth and joy now. I AM perfection everywhere now. I AM one with God's perfect balance and wholeness now. I AM God's infinite strength, invincibility, and sovereignty now.

I, therefore, claim for myself, (full name), perfect freedom from my co-dependent relationship with (person) or better now.

I now heal and release all negative thoughts that interfere with this claim, whether known or unknown, conscious or subconscious. My thoughts are now one with, the same as, and in tune with God's thought. I dispel from my mind all feelings of being dependent upon anything or anyone now. I now release the idea that anything or anyone has control over me or that I have control over anything or anyone. I dissolve domination, coercion, control, and violence now. I discharge all feelings of being out of control now. I now welcome and embrace unconditional love, self-love, self-acceptance, self-worth, self-empowerment, and self-authority. I like myself, I love myself, and I accept myself now. I now welcome thoughts of inner dominion, inner strength, inner power, inner peace, divine control, joy, and stability. I let go of the need to be controlled. I renounce the need to be violated. I release the need to be abused. I dissolve all fear of rejection and fear of abandonment now. I give absolutely no power to anyone to create any negative experience for me. My self-direction is divinely guided and certain. I AM in command of my own life. I AM the only authority in my life. I AM divinely protected by the light of my being. I close off my aura and body of light to (person) and to all but my own God self. (Person) cannot in any way possess me or hold me in bondage. I AM responsible for my own life and my own mind. I belong to God and to myself alone. I can never possess anyone. I release the fear that anyone will be taken away from me. I know now that God is my ever-present supply and source of good. Therefore, I bless and release (person), and my acceptance is always open to my new and greater joy. I dissolve the notion that I must protect, hide, or save (person). I know that he/she is free and completely responsible for his/her own life. Therefore I allow him/her to take full responsibility for his/her own embarrassment, shame, problems, and addictions. I cut all psychic ties between myself and (person). These ties are now lovingly cut, lifted, loved, healed, released, and let go by the Holy Spirit in the name of God. They are released into divine light and love. I AM free to express myself now and he/she is free to express himself/herself now. I AM free to follow my heart and he/she is free to follow his/her heart now. I AM love. I AM light. I AM power and strength. I AM worthy of receiving love and of having a healthy, joyful, fulfilling relationship now.

I now fully accept in consciousness perfect freedom from my co-dependent relationship with (person) or better now.

I thank God for manifesting this good in my life now.

Thank you, God, and SO IT IS.

FREEDOM FROM SUBSTANCE ABUSE AND ADDICTION

This is a treatment for myself, (full name), for perfect mental health and for freedom from seeming substance abuse and addiction or better now.

I recognize that God is our rock and our strength. God is the pillar of strength and the fountain of good. God is all-powerful and almighty. God is perfection, truth, love, freedom, fulfillment, and complete contentment. God is wholeness and oneness now.

I AM one with God's strength. I AM filled with inner strength from the source of all power and all good—God the good, my rock and my staff. I AM one with the perfection of God. God's truth and love embrace my being with wholeness and oneness. I AM the freedom, fulfillment, and the contentment of God's holy presence now.

I claim, therefore, for myself, (full name), perfect mental health and perfect freedom from seeming substance abuse and addiction or better now.

I now heal and release all limitations that interfere with this claim, whether known or unknown, conscious or subconscious. My thoughts are now one with, the same as, and in tune with God's thought. I now accept in consciousness complete freedom from seeming substance abuse and addiction now. I let go and dissolve from my mind any and all ideas that anything outside of myself has any power or control over me. I AM free from the thought of bondage or possession, and I know now that nothing can possess me or hold me in chains. I belong only to God and to myself. I AM in control. I AM the only authority in my life. I AM divinely protected by the light of my being. I close off my aura and body of light to this addiction and to all but my own God self. I now cut any and all psychic ties between myself and this addiction. These psychic ties are lovingly cut, lifted, loved, healed, released, and let go by the Holy Spirit and God now. I AM free from all addiction now. I release the idea that I need anything other than my own divine light, my own divine love, and my own connection with the God-presence within me. I have no need for addictive substances, for I AM myself the source of all fulfillment and contentment within. I give no power to addictive substances to create any negative experience for me. I AM in command of my own life. My self-direction is divinely guided and sure. I release all self-hatred, disgust, and self-punishment. I dissolve all guilt and blame. I let go of suicidal tendencies and I embrace my life. I AM the source of love for myself. I love myself now and I forgive myself now. I cling to the feet of God, for I know that God is my salvation. I surrender my life to God and place my life into God's perfect hands.

I now fully accept in consciousness freedom from my seeming substance abuse and addiction or better now.

I thank God for manifesting this healing in my life in perfect ways.

AMEN.

HEALING OF A PHYSICAL AILMENT

This is a treatment for myself, (full name), for perfect physical health and for the perfect wellness of my (name the organ or body parts) or better now.

I recognize that God is perfect wholeness and strength. God's radiant light is the source of glowing health. God's love is the power of renewal, revitalization, and compassion. God is divine substance, the well of life, the quickening life of Spirit. God is the fountainhead of eternal, ever-renewing energy. God is the source of life, the only healer, the all-merciful river of well-being. God's vitalizing energy flows plentifully and unconditionally.

I AM one with the radiant living substance of God now. I AM filled with the quickening life of Spirit. I AM God's healing strength now. God's healing power works through me now in perfection. I AM the eternal fountainhead of ever-renewing energy. God's love, life, and healing power in me burst forth with the brilliance of glowing health right now.

I, therefore, claim for myself, (full name), perfect physical healing and the perfect wellness of my (name the organ or body part) or better now.

I now heal and release all negative thoughts that interfere with this claim, whether known or unknown, conscious or subconscious. My thoughts are now one with, the same as, and in tune with God's thought. I call upon the almighty divine presence to dissolve all weakness now. Any foreign elements that have seemingly attacked my body are now lovingly blessed, forgiven, and released into the love, light, and wholeness of the universal Christ. You are unified with the truth of being, your own divine nature. God's love and light pervade you now with love, peace, and blessings. The earth plane no longer binds you. Fear, pain, and anger have no control over you. I call upon your higher self to guide you into God's light. Go now in peace and love. I cut all psychic ties between my body and any seeming appearance of disease now. These psychic ties are now lovingly cut, lifted, loved, healed, released, and let go into the light of truth. I rebuke and relinquish all negative thoughts that have spawned this seeming disease now. I dissolve all thoughts of guilt, blame, punishment, anger, resistance, fear, frustration, and sadness now. They are released by God's love into divine light now. I now embrace and accept concepts of joy, forgiveness, acceptance of self, love, healing, flexibility, peace, and oneness. I AM free of all seeming appearance of disease, and my body expresses the truth of my being, which is perfect health, harmony, and wholeness. My body is God manifesting perfection now. Unlimited divine strength courses through my being at all times. God's vitalizing, life-giving energy floods every cell and atom of my body, and I AM renewed, refreshed, and rejuvenated. I AM made whole in body, soul, and consciousness. I AM a new creation through the healing, revitalizing life of the Christ. God's melody of life fills my being with resplendent health and vitality. The perfect life of God is my life now, and I AM whole and complete.

I now fully accept in consciousness the perfect physical health and wellness of my (name the organ or body part) in my life or better now.

Thank you, God, for my perfect health now.

SO BE IT.

PERFECT INCOME

This is a treatment for myself, (full name), for the perfect net income of $(amount) per month or better now.

I recognize that God is the source of all abundance and prosperity in the universe. God is the fountain of all bounty, all strength, and all good. God is the wish-fulfilling tree, the generous provider of all blessings and boons.

God's good is my good now. I welcome and accept God's blessings in my life now. God's bounty is mine now. There is no separation between God and myself; therefore a never-ending fountainhead of abundance flows freely into my life now with divine order and timing.

I claim for myself, (full name), my perfect net income of $(amount) per month or better now.

I accept in consciousness this perfect income now. I dissolve from my mind all limitations preventing me from having all perfect sources of income now, whether these limitations are known or unknown, conscious or subconscious. My mind is united with divine mind now. I, therefore, accept all perfect sources of income for myself now, including unexpected sources. I release all thoughts of denial of income from any avenues now. I release all belief of not being worthy to receive my good. I dispel the idea of not deserving prosperity. I release all beliefs that wealth is not spiritual and that money is the root of evil. All these thoughts are now lifted into God's love and released into divine light. I now know in my mind that money is divine, that it can be used for good, that I AM worthy and deserving to receive wealth and abundance, that God's immeasurable bounty flows into my life in a perpetual stream, without restriction. I open my mind and heart to all avenues of wealth, income, and abundance, even those that I previously never considered. I AM willing and open now to receive prosperity. My life is blessed with the free-flowing continual circulation of wealth and riches right now.

I now fully accept in consciousness my divine abundance now in the form of my net income of $(amount) per month or better now.

I thank God for answered prayer. I thank God for my perfect sources of income now, under grace in perfect ways.

I release this treatment into the spiritual law, knowing that it demonstrates now. Thank you, God, and SO IT IS.

PERFECT EMPLOYMENT

This is a treatment for myself, (full name), for the perfect employment for myself now, with a salary of $(amount) per week or better, that utilizes all of my talents and strengths of (talents) or better, and that I love doing now.

I recognize that God is the divine employer. God's will is at work in the universe and God's purpose is present within everyone and everything. God is the source of strength and the source of power. God is the generous benefactor of all life in this universe.

God is my divine employer now. God's divine will is at work in my life now. God's will is my will now. I AM in tune with the divine purpose of my life, which includes my true desires and true pathway now. I AM one with God's power and strength now. I AM open, receptive, and faithful to God's perfect divine plan for my life. I am the beneficiary of God's good will now.

I, therefore, claim for myself, (full name), the perfect employment for myself now, with a salary of $(amount) per week or better, that utilizes all my talents and strengths of (talents) or better, and that I love doing now.

I now accept in consciousness this perfect employment now. I now heal and release all thoughts that interfere with this claim, whether known or unknown, conscious or subconscious. My thoughts are now one with, the same as, and in tune with God's thought. I now free my mind and heart from any and all thoughts of unworthiness, lack, limitation, frustration, and fear. They are now dissolved by the light of God's love. I dispel and renounce from my mind now any and all beliefs that I cannot find employment in a job that I love and that utilizes my strengths and talents. I now open my mind to ideas of worthiness, abundance, prosperity, strength, ease, joy, fun, loving my job, being happy in my job, and finding the perfect employment for myself that utilizes my talents and strengths or better. I cut any and all psychic ties between myself and all previous jobs that I have had. These psychic ties are now lovingly cut, lifted, loved, healed, released, and let go by the power and the presence of God. I AM attuned to divine order and divine timing in finding this perfect employment now. God is my perfect employer now, and God now bestows upon me my perfect job in the perfect situation in my perfect career.

I now fully accept in consciousness my perfect employment now.

Thank you, God, for using me to fulfill your wonderful purpose now. I thank God for this perfect employment manifesting in my life now.

Thank you, God, and SO IT IS.

PERFECT ABUNDANCE

This is a treatment for myself, (full name), for the perfect divine abundance and prosperity or better manifesting in my life now.

I recognize that God is the cornucopia of abundance, the source of money, wealth, and prosperity. God is the fountainhead of all riches, divine unlimited bounty, and fulfillment. God is the reservoir of goodness, flowing in an eternal stream. God is the divine banker and supreme benefactor. God is the infinite source of all blessings and there is always a divine surplus. God's measureless wealth circulates freely throughout the cosmos.

I AM one with God's never-ending flow of abundance now. God sheds money, wealth, and prosperity upon me now in an endless stream. God's wellspring of limitless bounty floods into my life now. I AM filled to the brim and overflowing with plenty. I AM enriched and fulfilled through the infinite goodness of God. God is my divine investment banker. I AM the wealthy beneficiary of a loving God, and wealth is perpetually circulating throughout my life. God's love, through me, blesses and multiplies all that I have, all that I give, and all that I receive.

I, therefore, claim for myself, (full name), perfect divine abundance and prosperity or better manifesting in my life now.

I AM one with God's divine mind now. My thoughts are one with the thoughts of God. I now release all negative thoughts preventing me from receiving my divine bounty and prosperity now. I AM overflowing with the abundance of joy, of love, of money and of wealth now. I now release all ideas that money is evil and that wealthy people are materialistic and nonspiritual. I now release all ideas of being unworthy or undeserving of abundance. All these limiting thoughts are now lifted into divine light and let go by God's love. I now freely welcome the idea that I AM worthy of abundance, that prosperity is mine. I embrace thoughts that money is good, money is spiritual, and that a wealthy person can be Godly, divinely guided, and inspired. I, therefore, open my arms to receive the abundance of divine wealth now. Money, gems, jewels, luxuries, limitless possessions, assets, cash, and checks are showered upon me now. God's infinite wealth fills my bank account now and provides an unending source of credit. I place my bank account in God's hands, and God writes all my checks. I AM, therefore, now linked to an unlimited source of wealth and continual circulation of prosperity. I have all the wealth, money, assets, and riches that I could ever need. I circulate this wealth freely now. The abundant good and bounty of the universe is manifesting in my financial affairs now. There is no limit to my good, which is now flowing to me so richly and fully that I have a surplus of money to spare and share. I receive the abundant good that is mine by divine right now. Everything and everyone prosper me now, and I prosper everyone and everything now. I AM the wealthy beneficiary of a loving God, so I dare to prosper, right here and now.

I now fully accept in consciousness my perfect divine abundance and prosperity or better manifesting in my life now.

I thank God for unlimited wealth and prosperity.

I thank God that this is so now and SO IT IS.

PERFECT HOUSING

This is a treatment for myself, (full name), for the perfect housing for myself now in a comfortable and spacious new home with (number) bedrooms and (number) bathrooms in (place) or better, which is easily affordable for me, and which suits all my needs or better now.

I recognize that God is the only power and presence at work in the universe. God's perfect stability, prosperity, joy, and abundance fill the cosmos with divine love. God is the safe haven and perfect shelter from all storms.

I AM one with God now. God's holy sanctuary within my heart is the perfect place for me to dwell. God is my only dwelling-place. Right where I AM, I AM at home in the presence of God. The temple of God's love rests within my heart, and I AM secure in God's love. God's prosperity, abundance, and joy fulfill my life now. I am safe in God's perfect haven of love and shelter.

I, therefore, claim for myself, (full name), the perfect housing for myself now in a comfortable, spacious new home with (number) bedrooms and (number) bathrooms in (place) or better, which is easily affordable for me, and which suits all my needs or better now.

I now accept in consciousness this perfect place to live. I now heal and release all negative beliefs that interfere with this claim, whether known or unknown, conscious or subconscious. My thoughts are now one with, the same as, and in tune with God's thought. I denounce and dissolve from my mind any thoughts preventing me from accepting this perfect home now. I release all thoughts of fear, insecurity, unworthiness, instability, lack of commitment, guilt, sadness, and pain now. I now open my heart to embrace love, hope, faith, happiness, stability, commitment, fulfillment, forgiveness of self, and joy. I release all psychic ties and attachments with any previous dwelling-places I have lived in. These psychic ties are now cut, lifted, loved, healed, released, and let go by the power of the Holy Spirit. I AM in control of my mind now. I welcome with open arms my perfect, beautiful home now.

I now fully accept in consciousness the perfect housing for myself or better now.

I thank God for manifesting this new home in my life now, under grace, in God's own wise and perfect ways.

Thank you, God, and SO BE IT.

PERFECT VEHICLE

This is a treatment for myself, (full name), for the perfect vehicle with (number) doors, mechanically sound, safe, comfortable, enjoyable to drive, fuel-efficient, easily affordable for me, and operating perfectly or better now. My vehicle is ready to go whenever I AM. My mechanic does a good job for a fair price. Driving is a safe and pleasant experience for me and those who ride with me.

I recognize that God is the source of all abundance in the universe. God is the one power and the one presence that manifests all good now. God is the source of all creation. God is good, very good perfection now.

I AM one with the source of creation now. God is my ever-bountiful source of prosperity now. God is my unfailing, ever-present fountainhead of bounty now. I AM one with my good, very good perfection now.

I, therefore, claim for myself, (full name), the perfect vehicle with (number) doors, mechanically sound, safe, comfortable, enjoyable to drive, fuel efficient, easily affordable for me, and operating perfectly or better now. My vehicle is ready to go whenever I AM. My mechanic does a good job for a fair price. Driving is a safe and pleasant experience for me and those who ride with me.

I accept my perfect vehicle now, and I heal and release all old beliefs and thoughts that interfere with this claim, whether known or unknown, conscious or subconscious. My thoughts are now one with, the same as, and in tune with God's thought. I let go of all thoughts of fear, resistance, guilt, blame, confusion, and lack from my mind now. I dissolve from my mind all belief that I do not deserve the vehicle of my dreams now. I know now that I deserve my wonderful new vehicle now. I embrace thoughts of love, acceptance, abundance, forgiveness of self, openness to receive, divine order, and prosperity now. I let go of all vehicles that I have owned in the past, knowing that the past is gone and today is a new day of God's fresh, joyous opportunities and possibilities. With God as my wish-bestowing tree, I know now that my perfect vehicle of my dreams manifests now.

I now fully accept in consciousness and welcome my perfect vehicle or better now.

I thank God for manifesting this good in my life now in perfect ways. Thank you, God, and SO IT IS.

In the next section of this book, you will find practical prayer results in the form of scientific research and anecdotal evidence.

PART VI

CREATING MIRACLES
IN EVERYDAY LIFE

16 SCIENTIFIC RESEARCH ON PRAYER

EVERYONE PRAYS IN THEIR OWN LANGUAGE, AND THERE IS
NO LANGUAGE THAT GOD DOES NOT UNDERSTAND.

— Duke Ellington

*H*istorically, both religion and medicine worked together to heal disease. In fact, it is a recent development for these two branches of healing to diverge.

Pythagoras (560–480 B.C.), high priest of the ancient Orphic mysteries of Crete, merged healing with religion in his mystery school. Hippocrates (born 460 B.C.), "Father of Medicine," treated his patients by means of a spiritual restorative essence—the "healing power of nature." Maimonides, a twelfth-century rabbi, was also a renowned physician.

Hospitals were first established in monasteries, and then spread by missionaries. In native cultures, the shaman is both spiritual leader and healer. In India, the Ayurvedic physician is both priest and doctor.

However, in recent Western medicine, religion is no longer an adjunct to healing. In the twentieth century, the chasm between religion and medicine is increasingly divided. Yet, in the last few decades, prayer is once again considered a viable healing tool.

Since 1995, Harvard Medical School has annually held conferences on "Spirituality and Healing in Medicine." Duke University has established a Center for the Study of Religion/Spirituality and Health. In 1999, 48% of America's medical schools offered spirituality and health courses, in contrast to .02% in 1994.[1]

"The Healing Power of Prayer" was covered in an article in *Woman's Day* magazine on December 7, 2004. Paula Spencer reported that 37% of doctors surveyed have prayed with patients. Of these, 89% felt it helped. A

CNN poll found that 64% of Americans want their physicians to pray with them. Researchers at Harvard, Duke, Columbia, and other prestigious universities are now exploring the link between religion and medicine.

The rest of this chapter is a brief review of recent scientific research on prayer.

IN VITRO FERTILIZATION

Dr. Roger Lobo, Columbia University's Chairman of Obstetrics and Gynecology, found highly significant results in a study on pregnancy and prayer at Cha Hospital in Seoul, Korea, where 199 women, 26 to 46 years old, underwent in vitro fertilization and were enrolled into this blind randomized trial between December 1998 and March 1999.

Patients were categorized by: (1) age, (2) length of infertility, (3) type of infertility, and (4) number of prior attempts. They were then randomized into two equal groups to test the potential effects of intercessory prayer. Patients and their providers did not know they were participating in this study.

Groups from the U.S., Canada, and Australia prayed for some of these women to get pregnant. Adjusting for pregnancy loss data, 46.6% of the women who were prayed-for got pregnant, whereas only 22.2% of the women who were not prayed-for got pregnant more than 100% increase in the rate of pregnancy.[2]

CANCER PATIENTS

In 2002, Elizabeth Johnston Taylor, Ph.D., R.N., and Frieda Hawkins-Outlaw, DNSC/R.N., found that cancer patients decrease the physical and emotional stresses of illness with prayer. Most patients believed prayer helped them feel better dealing with the effects of cancer and find prayer a valuable coping strategy. The way one prays is unique to each individual. Therefore, strategies for facilitating prayer must be designed with sensitivity to each patient. Naïve advice to those experiencing the painful effects of cancer could significantly increase their emotional pain and stress.[3]

GENERAL HEALTH CONCERNS

In 2004, a Harvard Medical School study, "Prayer for Health Concerns: Results of a National Survey on Prevalence and Patterns of Use," by Dr. Anne McCaffrey, M.D. and colleagues found 35% of respondents used prayer for health concerns: of these, 75% prayed for wellness, 22% prayed for specific medical conditions, and 69% of those found prayer very helpful. Only 11% of respondents using prayer mentioned it to their physicians.[4]

SELF-ESTEEM, ANXIETY, AND DESPRESSION

In 1997, Dr. Sean O'Laoire, Ph.D., studied the "Effects of Distant, Intercessory Prayer on Self-Esteem, Anxiety and Depression." Participants improved markedly on all eleven measures in the study. The agents (those praying for study participants) improved markedly on ten measures. A significant, positive correlation was found between the amount of prayer the agent engaged in and agents' scores on the five tests. Agents had significantly better scores on all objective measures. Improvement on four objective measures was significantly related to subjects' beliefs in the power of prayer for others. Improvement on all eleven measures was significantly related to participants' convictions concerning whether they had been assigned to a control group or to an experimental group.[5]

RHEUMATOID ARTHRITIS

Dr. Dale Matthews, M.D., and colleagues studied the effects of intercessory prayer on patients with rheumatoid arthritis at the Arthritis Pain and

Treatment Center, Clearwater, Florida. Patients who were given face-to-face intercessory prayer displayed marked overall improvement at the one-year follow-up.[6]

CORONARY PATIENTS

At the Mid-America Heart Institute, St. Luke's Hospital, Kansas City, Missouri, in 1999, Dr. William Harris, Ph.D. and colleagues performed a "Randomized Controlled Trial of the Effects of Remote, Intercessory Prayer on Outcomes in 990 Patients Admitted to the Coronary Care Unit." Community volunteers offered four weeks of daily prayers for an uncomplicated, speedy recovery. None of the patients had knowledge of the experiment, but all had previously indicated belief in God's responsiveness to prayers for healing.[7] Adverse outcomes were lower for those patients assigned to the prayer group compared to those randomly assigned to the standard care group. Intercessory prayer produced measurable improvement in the medical outcomes of critically ill patients.[8]

Between August 1982 and May 1983, in San Francisco General Hospital's Coronary Care Unit, Dr. Randolph Byrd, M.D./P.O. studied the therapeutic effects of intercessory prayer in a coronary care unit population. Byrd studied 393 patients. All participants in the study, including patients, doctors, and Byrd, remained blind throughout the study. The results indicated that patients receiving prayer were healthier than those in the control group, who received normal treatment. The prayed-for group had less need of CPR (cardiopulmonary resuscitation) and less need for mechanical ventilators. They had a diminished need for diuretics and antibiotics, less occurrences of pulmonary edema, fewer episodes of pneumonia, fewer cardiac arrests, less need to be intubated and ventilated, and fewer deaths. It was determined that 16% of variance in overall outcome could be attributed to prayer.[9]

HIGH BLOOD PRESSURE

The August 31, 1998, issue of *Jet* magazine reported a study conducted by Duke University Medical Center in Durham, North Carolina with 4,000 participants over the age of 65. Those who pray and attend religious services on a weekly basis, especially between the ages of 65 and 74, had lower blood pressure than their counterparts who did not pray or attend religious services. The more religious the individual, particularly those who prayed or studied the Bible weekly, the lower the blood pressure. These people were 40% less likely to have high diastolic pressure or diastolic hypertension than those who did not attend religious services, pray, or study the Bible.

Dr. David B. Larson, president of the National Institute for Health Care Research in Rockville, Maryland, who co-authored the study, said, "The at-risk population of people with illnesses, such as the elderly seem to be helped if they have faith and religious commitment...Faith brings a calming state which helps decrease nervousness and anxiety with coping with day to day stress."[10]

DEPRESSION AND ADDICTIONS

The December 1998 issue of *McCall's* magazine reports a study of 1,902 twins at the Virginia Commonwealth University Medical College of Virginia, in Richmond. They found that those who were committed to their spiritual lives tended to have less severe depression and a lower risk of addiction to cigarettes or alcohol. The healthful lifestyles of the spiritually faithful clearly contribute to their well-being. They tend not to smoke or drink, or at least not excessively. Their marriages are more stable and their spiritual communities form a network that can support people when they are ill.[11]

PSYCHOLOGICAL WELL-BEING

To delve into religious attitudes and their impact on health, Kenneth Paragament, Ph.D., professor of psychology at Bowling Green State University in Ohio, studied 577 hospital patients, age 55 and older. One 98-year-old woman with pneumonia and congestive heart failure saw her illness as God's plan for her. She prayed often for the health and well-being of her family and friends. These attitudes were associated with a serene response to stress and low levels of depression. While positive feelings toward a higher power seemed to foster well-being, negative thoughts about a deity had the opposite effect. A woman in her late fifties with lung cancer left her church in her twenties, became involved with drugs, and now feels her illness must be a sign of divine disapproval. Her test scores that measured quality of life and psychological health were lower than the 98-year-old woman.[12]

MICROORGANISM GROWTH

Larry Dossey states in his book *Be Careful What You Pray For* that skeptics often dismiss the results of prayer studies because the control group gets contaminated. The reason is that those who are ill generally pray for themselves, or others pray for them. However, microbes, bacteria, plants, and yeast obviously cannot influence an experiment through their thoughts, by praying for themselves, or by praying for their fellow microbes or plants, or using the power of suggestion. So, in such studies, the problem of extraneous prayer is eliminated.

Jean Barry, a physician-researcher in Bordeaux, France, studied a destructive fungus, *Rhizoctonia solani*. He asked ten subjects to try to inhibit its growth through their intentions at a distance of 1.5 meters. The laboratory conditions were carefully controlled regarding the genetic purity of the fungi, composition of the culture medium, relative humidity, and conditions of temperature and lighting.

255

The control petri dishes and the influenced dishes were treated identically, except for negative intentions directed toward them. When the growth in 195 experimental dishes was compared to their corresponding controls, it was significantly retarded in 151 dishes. The possibility that these results could be explained by chance was less than one in a thousand.[13]

William H. Tedder and Melissa L. Monty from the University of Tennessee replicated the fungus experiment. In their study they inhibited the growth of fungus from a distance of one to fifteen miles. Two groups participated: Group 1 was made up of Tedder and six others who knew him personally; Group 2 consisted of eight unknown volunteers.

When the growth differential between the experimental and control dishes were compared, Group 1 was highly successful. The likelihood of explaining their results by chance was less than 3 in 100,000. Group 2 was less successful. Their likelihood of a chance explanation was 6 in 100. The researchers theorized that Group 1 might have had greater expectation and motivation of a positive outcome than Group 2. In a post-experiment questionnaire, the Group 1 subjects responded more positively to questions about how they perceived their ability to inhibit the fungal cultures at a distance.[14]

GERMINATING PLANT SEEDS

A 1959 controlled experiment on germinating seeds was performed by Dr. Franklin Loehr, a Presbyterian minister and scientist. Out of three pans of various types of seeds, one pan received positive prayer, the second received negative prayer, and the third was the control pan. Loehr found that positive prayer speeded germination and produced more vigorous plants. Negative prayer halted germination in some plants and suppressed growth in others.

In another experiment, one container of spring water received prayer, and the control received no prayer. The water was then used on corn seeds, with one pan receiving the prayer water and the other receiving the control water. The pan receiving the prayer water sprouted a day earlier than the other pan. The prayer seeds had a higher germination and growth rate.[15]

SPINDRIFT EXPERIMENTS

Beginning in 1969, the father-and-son team of Bruce and John Klingbeil studied the effects of prayer and wrote the controversial "Spindrift Papers." Their main experiments occurred between 1975 and 1993. Using hundreds of thousands of beans, seeds, yeast cells, and mold, and dividing them into control (non-prayed-for) groups and treated (prayed-for), Spindrift subjected the above to stress and measured and compared the responses of the organisms.

In seventy experiments, Spindrift's most well-known contribution is its two prayer styles: (1) goal-directed prayer, and (2) non-goal-directed prayer, which embraces the subject with pure qualities of holiness that promotes healing. Spindrift's research in the laboratory indicated the effectiveness of prayer.[16]

LONGEVITY

In 1996, Jeremy Kark and colleagues compared death rates for 3,900 Israelis in eleven religiously orthodox and in eleven matched, nonreligious collective settlements (kibbutz communities). The researchers reported that, over a sixteen-year period, in every age group, the death rate for those belonging to the religious communities was about half of their nonreligious counterparts, a result not explained by age or economic differences.[17]

In 1972, a study of 91,909 persons in one Maryland county found that the death rate for those who attended religious services weekly was less than those who did not—53% less from coronary disease, 53% less due to suicide, and 74% less from cirrhosis.[18]

A study published in 1999 followed 5,286 Californians over 28 years. Frequent religious attendees were 36% less likely to die in any year after controlling for age, gender, ethnicity, and education.[19] Another study published in 1999 followed 3,968 elderly North Carolinians for six years. It found that 23% of those attending religious services at least weekly had died, compared to 37% of infrequent attendees.[20]

A "National Health Interview Survey" followed 21,204 people over eight years. After controlling for age, sex, race, and region, nonattenders of religious services were 1.87 times more likely to die than those attending more than weekly.[21] This translated into a life expectancy of 83 years for frequent attenders and 75 years for infrequent attenders.

In a national health survey financed by the U.S. Centers for Disease Control and Prevention, religiously active people had longer life expectancies. In recent American studies, about 75% longevity difference remains in religiously active people compared with others, after controlling for unhealthy behaviors, such as inactivity and smoking.[22] Even after controlling for gender, unhealthy behaviors, strong social support, and preexisting health problems, the mortality studies find much of the mortality reduction remaining. The conclusion is that there is healthier immune functioning and fewer hospital admissions among religiously active people.[23]

There is cross-cultural evidence of prayer's efficacy. Prayer is not local, it functions at a distance, and spatial separation does not diminish the effect. It is nonintrusive and without harmful side effects. While the faithful will always believe there is no need for physical evidence of the power of prayer, science has come a long way toward showing that prayer is real, and it works.[24]

In the next chapter, you will find inspirational Scientific Prayer miracle stories.

EVERYDAY 17
PRAYER MIRACLES

FOR VERILY I SAY UNTO YOU, THAT WHOSOEVER SHALL SAY
UNTO THIS MOUNTAIN, BE THOU REMOVED, AND BE THOU
CAST INTO THE SEA; AND SHALL NOT DOUBT IN HIS HEART,
BUT SHALL BELIEVE THAT THOSE THINGS WHICH HE SAITH
SHALL COME TO PASS; HE SHALL HAVE WHATSOEVER HE SAITH.
—*Jesus Christ*[1]

CHANGING THE WEATHER

Susan Shumsky, D.D.

In September, 1989, I had sold my house in Iowa. A few days before the closing, I advertised a garage sale for the hours of 8 A.M. to 3 P.M. The weathercaster predicted huge thunderstorms for the entire day. At 6 A.M., low-hanging, dark gray, gloomy clouds loomed everywhere. It looked, smelled, and felt as though rain would deluge in buckets any second. I did a Scientific Prayer treatment, claiming that the rain delay until 3 P.M. I had unquestioning conviction in my prayer, so I set up the tables outside. Under dark, pregnant clouds, I had a successful garage sale. It was a busy day, so I forgot about the prayer.

At 2:45 P.M. a friend showed up and we went inside for a snack, since no customers were coming that late in the day. Suddenly, at precisely 3 P.M., the clouds ripped apart. A violent thundershower arose and rain poured down in torrents. I ran outside in a panic, remembering my prayer and laughing. I quickly pulled the tables into the garage, although everything had been soaked during the first two minutes of the storm. It was both miraculous and hilarious all at once.

GRAND CANYON MIRACLE

Susan Shumsky, D.D.

In September 1997, I was scheduled to speak in Sedona, Arizona. My higher self guided me to visit the Grand Canyon on my way to Sedona. Across the desert, it rained all day and night on the heels of hurricane Nora. I camped close to the canyon, which I planned to view in the morning. I woke up to rain still falling intermittently.

When I entered the national park, there was zero visibility. The entire Grand Canyon was blanketed in fog. A British couple walked by, snapping pictures of the white nothingness, declaring, "We'll show photos of our trip to the Grand Canyon to all our friends back home in England!"

Since it seemed this Grand Canyon visit was a bust, I sat on the nearest bench and asked God why I had been guided to come here. I received a strange message from my higher self: "Go have lunch. The fog will lift by two o'clock." I left the park and found a buffet luncheon at a nearby hotel. But I was concerned, since I would have to leave the Canyon at 2 P.M. in order to arrive in time in Sedona.

I returned to the Canyon at 1:30, only to encounter that same white nothingness. Through the thick fog I spotted the vague outline of tourists on an observation point. I joined them but could see no more than before—fog everywhere.

After gazing into the blankness awhile, I began to lose faith, though I was chanting, "fog lift, fog lift" repeatedly. As I leaned over the railing, straining to see something—anything—I spotted the wristwatch of a nearby tourist, which showed 12:45 P.M. "What time zone are we in?" I asked. "Pacific Time," he answered. It turned out that Arizona did not follow daylight savings time. I was elated. I exclaimed, "Great! I have one more hour to lift this fog." The tourists stared at me in disbelief.

I began to chant more vigorously, "fog lift, fog lift." Then I realized that I had to call on some real ammunition. So, I got out the big guns. I stood up really straight and demanded in a loud and clear voice, "God, lift this fog RIGHT NOW!"

Amazingly, within ten minutes all the fog lifted from the entire Grand Canyon, the sun shone, and the Canyon appeared in all its glory. The tourists cheered. I drove around the rim of the Canyon, stopping at various viewing points until it was time to leave for Sedona. Just as I entered my van to drive out of the park, the fog rolled right back into the canyon, blanketing it again in a relentless sea of whiteness.

Spirit had told me the fog was going to lift by 2:00 P.M. That is exactly what happened.

DELIVERED FROM IRAN

Mussa

Mussa had not seen his mother since he left Iran, many years before. As part of his class assignment in Scientific Prayer, he decided to write a prayer treatment for his mother to visit him in California. Soon after writing the treatment, his brother called to say that his mother was on a plane, flying to California. This was incredible, because when his mother applied for her visa, there were five hundred people applying to come to the United States, and only two people were granted visas. When she arrived, she told her son that it seemed she was delivered by the hand of God.

LOVE IS THE HEALER

Judy Cali, Boynton Beach, Florida

"My psychic and healing gifts started catching my attention at age three, after a near death experience. At age seven in 1953, in Reseda, California, I met Dr. Ernest Holmes and studied at the Church of Religious Science.

"In 1990 I was volunteering at Children's Hospital in L.A.—five hours on Thursdays in the playroom with kids and five hours on Sundays holding babies in the neo-natal unit. Each time, I would do a prayer treatment and ask the soul of the child to direct me. I told the children that I was there to honor their soul and purpose—to welcome them into the world, to validate them and their courage.

"A four-month-old baby had been in the hospital since birth. Her brain was two to three times normal size and was being drained once a month. I had been holding this sweet baby for about two hours when the head nurse came in. She told me the baby I was holding was due to have her head drained early next morning. After the nurse thanked me for volunteering ten hours every week, she said, 'I am glad you are holding her, since her mom cannot be with her before surgery. She works full-time.'

"That day, I spent the entire five hours seeing the little girl's head normal and knowing the divine perfection of her soul and body expressed.

"Three weeks later, I returned to the same neo-natal room. I noticed the little girl was not in her crib and a new child was in her space. I asked the head nurse where the baby was. She grinned from ear to ear. 'The most amazing thing happened. The nurses had shaved her head and were prepping her for surgery, when they noticed the baby's head was normal. The doctor sent her home that day.'

"I thanked all of Heaven's assistance, the little girl's higher self, guides, guardian angels, and God. I AM an instrument of love and God's healing energy flowed through me into the child to remind her who she was— love expressed."

PRAYING FOR POSITIVISM

Rev. Carmela Vuoso-Murphy, Unity Church, Boonton, New Jersey

"I have a prayer partner. We exchange lists of people that affect us in a negative way, and we pray for each other's list, along with our own. I had no idea how powerful this would be. Most of the people on our lists have had amazing positive reactions.

"One person who had not spoken to my prayer partner in three years called her for reconciliation. I had to attend compulsory monthly conferences with a group of people who were negative, closed, and dwelled on problems instead of solutions. After four weeks of partner prayer, the attitudes of the members of that group changed dramatically.

"I was totally amazed! Prayer does not have to be detailed. It can be very simple. My prayer partner and I simply prayed for joy for these people."

GOD IS MY ORTHOPEDIC SURGEON

Carolyn Hanson, Fresno, California

"One day I was walking my dog Arthur, an afghan, with my bike. Instead of putting his lead on the bike, I put it on my left wrist. As we turned the first corner, Arthur made a beeline for a bush to pee on, and he cut in front of my bike. Not wanting to injure him, I slammed on my brakes and flew off my bike to the left. I thought my arm was broken. After several attempts to get up, I finally managed to get my dog home before going to the emergency clinic.

"The doctor at the clinic x-rayed the arm and said it was severely separated and would require surgery. He further stated: 'You won't be able to lie down to sleep for two weeks (I thought, 'cancel, cancel'). You will be in severe pain for a year ('cancel, cancel'), and that step on your shoulder will never go away ('cancel, cancel'). This is how I handle it: I get up in the morning, have a pain pill, a cigar, and a coke.' (Now I really thought, 'cancel, cancel.') His last statement made me realize this wasn't what I wanted to create, so I separated my reality from his.

"My appointment with the orthopedic surgeon was in three days. Driving home, I reminded myself that the doctor told me the 'facts,' but it wasn't the 'truth'. I went into meditation and prayed for perfect healing. I saw my shoulder perfect. I repeated a prayer treatment morning and night. That night I taped my arm to my side and went to bed lying down. During the day when the pain was severe, I calmly said, 'Thank you God, that every cell in my body knows its perfection and now manifests that perfection.' The pain left.

"When the surgeon looked at my x-rays three days later, he asked whether I had the right x-rays, because they did not match my shoulder. I thrust my seemingly separated arm it into the air saying 'YES.' My doctor still calls it a miracle—I simply call it the Truth.

"We are constantly creating our reality and have the power to change the effects by simply realizing they aren't the truth about us—just the facts."

RECOVERING LOST PROPERTY

Jan Sloan, Unity Fellowship, Newport News, Virginia

"I left my purse on a shelf at the Post Office. When I realized what I had done, I claimed Divine Order and prayed that someone honest would find it. I returned to the Post Office, but no one had turned it in.

"Two hours later, the phone rang. The gentleman was calling to return my purse. He did not turn it in to the Post Office, because he was not sure everyone was as honest as he. I drove to the mall to meet him and, of course, everything was intact in the purse. The man would not accept a reward. He said God had already blessed him adequately."

GOD'S FINANCIAL ASSISTANCE

Laura Hager, Los Gatos, California

"One time I wrote a prayer treatment to help my financial situation. Several days afterward, my landlady came to me and said, in an agitated tone, 'I need to talk to you, I don't know what you are doing but...' I thought I was in trouble. My mind was racing to figure out what my daughter and I might have done.

"My landlady continued, 'God woke me up in the middle of the night and told me to take $200 off of your rent.' I looked into her eyes with gratitude and simply said, 'Thank you.' I felt like exploding with excitement. She walked off looking agitated that she had been woken up and baffled why she was telling me this. I went back inside my home and did my happy dance of gratitude, thanking the universe for the wonderful gift.

"I continued in my meditations, prayer, and thankfulness. A month later, ends were still not meeting. So I prayed again, knowing I must need to clean out my closet more. Once again, my landlady knocked at my door, in the same agitated manner. 'Honestly I don't know what you are doing over here, but God woke me up again last night and told me to take more money off your rent.'

"Once again, I said my thank-yous, shut the door, and did my happy dance. The following month she approached me, saying, 'I sold a painting today; you know what that means, don't you?' I had no clue what she was suggesting. She said 'I sold a painting, so you do not pay rent this month.' I was in shock, but extremely thankful. It was the most amazing example of how prayer treatment really works."

GOD IS MY AIRLINE PILOT

Connie Fisher, Galisteo, New Mexico

"In December, I was flying to Aspen from Denver. We were flying through a winter storm and it was bumpity bump all the way. If we couldn't land in the tiny mountain airport of Aspen, we would have to return to Denver where the airline had arranged buses to drive us five hours from Denver to Aspen. I prayed and prayed. The intensity of my prayer was extreme. It was a long day already and I didn't want to have to ride on a bus from Denver to Aspen. A hard way to start my much deserved mountain holiday.

"I later learned that ours was the only plane that landed in Aspen that day."

SOURCE OF UNLIMITED INCOME

Akasha Noelle, D.D., Saratoga, California

"In 1978, I was divorced and had taken over a retail jewelry business from my ex-husband. I was totally immersed in learning about healing and was using several Scientific Prayer treatments to help me get over the divorce.

"One day, a thief robbed the store at gunpoint. He took all my cash and all my coins from my coin store. The robber said, 'Well, you know you're covered by insurance.' I replied, 'I am not.' More than $75,000 in cash and coins was stolen. The robber had depleted me of all the money that I needed to continue my business.

"I called a New Thought minister and told him what happened. He advised me, 'Just claim it back.' So, I did a Scientific Prayer treatment. I claimed back the money and put white light around the thieves. I knew the money didn't have to come back in the form that it was stolen, but I wanted it back in some form. I claimed my good.

"When I did that prayer treatment, I had no money. It was really scary. Before I was robbed, I had just made a deposit on a house. So, there were mortgage payments and two kids to raise. Yet all the money was gone.

"I was depleted, but I wasn't depleted in my faith—I was highly attuned to Spirit. I went for counseling and asked a prayer therapist to do a prayer treatment for me. For the treatment and counseling, I exchanged a coin worth over $250.

"People suggested that I sell the house, but I had faith and knew everything would be all right. We moved the jewelry store from our small office to a larger office complex across the street. We worked there day and night. I felt really high, and I didn't know why. I put much more enthusiasm into answering the phone and being there for the customers.

"Within three months, we made up our loss. That's because I listened, and I believed, and I did my Scientific Prayer treatments. When I got upset, I constantly reverted to the prayers. The important thing was that I maintained my consciousness, and I really believed that it came from God. That's how I operate my business."

GOD IS MY INTERIOR DESIGNER

Marg Hux, Chaplain, Christ Church Unity, Hamilton, Ontario, Canada

"I had done much renovation on the small, out-of-date house that we bought. I wanted a dishwasher, but since the countertops were shorter and narrower than regulation, to install a dishwasher would require replacing the base cabinets. This would necessitate replacing all the upper cabinets to match. Then I would have to replace all the small, old appliances. This would mean re-doing the floor, which would require removing the wall between the kitchen and the small den.

"This became a mini-obsession. I researched all kinds of dishwashers and found no portable size that would fit the small space. Installing a built-in would escalate into removing a support wall and paying for a huge renovation.

"I finally decided the dishwasher was not worth it. Weary of the mental struggle, I did a spontaneous prayer and gave up this focus. It interfered too much with my peace of mind and my ability to love. But since I hate doing dishes regularly, I asked to have a dishwasher as a place to hide the dirty dishes. Then I totally left my kitchen in God's hands and forgot about it.

"One month later, we were at a family party. My sister-in-law's mother said she was renovating her kitchen and she had a small portable dishwasher in excellent condition that she would hate to throw out. We had come to her mind, as she knew our kitchen was small (we had not talked about our renovation dilemma with anyone in the family). If we would like, she would arrange to deliver it to us the following week. We would be welcome to it for free. It turned out this size fit the kitchen in color and size, and it was perfect to solve the problem."

TREATMENT COOLS ANGER

Marg Hux, Chaplain, Christ Church Unity, Hamilton, Ontario, Canada.

"My friend Gary was talking to me on the phone. Earlier that day, Gary had given notice to leave his apartment in one month. Since he had refinished the floors in the apartment, and painted and repaired it, he requested that his landlord waive the required two months termination fee. The landlord had yelled at Gary and threatened him. Gary was furious.

"While we were on the phone, someone knocked on Gary's door, and I heard an angry voice calling Gary. Gary said the landlord was there and said a quick goodbye. I immediately started a Scientific Prayer treatment about Gary and the landlord being one with God. I cut psychic ties and did a prayer that Gary was filled with certainty of his divine nature and awareness of his self worth, and that the landlord acknowledge him and allow a generous benefit for the renovations done.

"When I called back ten minutes later, Gary said he had gone to the door and just stood there looking at the landlord. At first he looked mad. Then he just said that he did not want to fight. If Gary would write up his notice for one month, he would accept it and not require the second month's rent."

MIRACLE FROM SAINT JUDE

Curt de Groat, New York, New York

"My father had a breakdown and was institutionalized after my mother died. He was not responding to medication. His money from insurance was running out that week and he would have to be moved. Since he was not responding to drug therapy, his doctor said he would need shock therapy. I was overwhelmed and didn't know what to do. So, I went to a church and was led to the shrine of Saint Jude, patron of impossible causes. I found a paper with a novena to him. I looked at that paper and knew I had to do it. This would mean coming every day for nine days to do the prayer nine times and leave nine copies each day.

"On the ninth day the hospital called and said he was responding to drugs and didn't need shock therapy. Also, they would give him an extra week in the hospital for free. Then $2,500 came in the mail and my sister called to say she was coming up to give him a place to live. Praise God and Saint Jude.

"I did not know what to pray for but put all in God's hands. After I finished the novena, on the original copy I finally saw this sentence: 'It never fails.' I have since learned that Saint Jude is the most popular and prayed-to saint in the U.S."

FORGIVENESS WORKS WONDERS

Frieda Kirk, Center for Spiritual Living, Seattle, Washington

"My right knee was injured three times in ten years, and the doctors say this is the cause of the arthritis. I have used a walking stick since a car accident in 1992. In 1995, the doctors said I would be back for new knees in two years because of the pain. But with lots of prayer treatment, this did not happen. I live pain free, but am getting slower.

"At our church, Center for Spiritual Living Seattle, Rev. Kathianne said that if an area seems stuck, usually it is associated with someone we have not yet completely forgiven. She suggested praying and meditating to discover who it might be.

"After spending a week on forgiveness, I had not come up with a person, situation, or group with whom I had not already worked. So, Sunday morning (in exasperation) I focused on praising and raising 'whoever or whatever still needed forgiving.' Then, I went off to church.

269

"My mind was on the people I was greeting. It was not until I arrived at the Ministry of Prayer room that I realized I had walked all the way from the car comfortably without even noticing that I was walking, with no thought of a cane. I continue to walk more easily and farther and continue to pray with intention of forgiveness associated with my knees."

NOTHING IS LOST

Diann Rollins, Religious Science Practitioner, Philadelphia, Pennsylvania

"At a Religious Science conference, I lost the key to my room on Monday. It would cost $25 to replace the lost key, and I would not have enough cash to get home from the conference. I repeated the affirmation 'Nothing is lost in time and space.' The key appeared in the Lost and Found, and I retrieved it at the front desk on Thursday."

GOD IS MY INSURANCE ADJUSTER

Luzette M. Rivera-Diez, Director, Prayer and Pastoral Care, Licensed Unity Teacher, Unity on the Bay, Miami, Florida

"When I leased my car, I asked the insurance company to waive the 'uninsured motorist' from my coverage. The rate was more than I wanted to pay, and being a 'safe driver,' no accidents in over twenty years, it was a calculated risk.

"The insurance company made a mistake and tried to debit my account for the full amount, including the coverage I had waived. There was not enough money in the account for that extra coverage. I called the insurance company twice to make a phone payment so I would not lose coverage, but they insisted everything was okay—I did not need to pay. I insisted that the electronic debit would bounce. They told me to wait, as it appeared to be paid.

"I went to Unity Village for two weeks and returned home to find my insurance cancelled. On Monday morning, I decided to go personally to the insurance office and resolve this issue. As I was turning the corner to the insurance agency, I had an accident. I hit one car, which, in turn, hit two more.

"Before I even got out of the car, I called my daughter, who is a Unity Chaplain, and we prayed for divine order. No one was badly hurt, but the car that I hit was a total loss. I got home and called the Silent Unity Prayer Tower. We prayed for the best outcome for all involved. Then, I called the insurance company.

"I explained my case and asked for an investigation. They gave me very little hope, told me that I had already been sued, and warned me that I had no insurance. I told the adjuster that I had faith that it would be resolved.

"For about a week, in my prayer time, I affirmed the perfect resolution and inner peace, since I was in fear. Then, one morning, I woke up feeling deeply that the prayer work was completed and that I needed to allow Spirit to do its work. A great peace filled me and I knew 'It was done.' I said a prayer of thanksgiving and placed the insurance file under my 'God box' on my altar. (I have a little box where I place things I surrender to God.) Whenever anyone asked about the accident, I simply said, 'I surrendered it to God and I am allowing Spirit to do the work.'

"About a month later, I received a call from the insurance company saying that they randomly record their calls, and they found recordings of both of mine. The adjuster said that in nearly twenty-five years of service, she had only two cases like mine where they found the recordings and they were obligated to reinstate the insurance at the right cost (originally requested by me) and to cover the accident. Everyone got paid, and the suit was resolved for a minimum amount."

SILENT UNITY PRAYER MIRACLE

Rev. Julie Montague, Unity of the Valley Church, White Rock, British Columbia, Canada

"My child contracted cancer at about four years old. We called the Silent Unity Prayer Tower, and my mother and I prayed. My child went into spontaneous remission within twenty-four hours and has never had any sign of the disease again. He will be 29 years old this year in November."

FAITH IN PRAYER

Rev. Roberta Croddy, D.D., Creative Living Fellowship, Phoenix, Arizona

"I have been a Religious Science Practitioner and Minister for seventeen years. I have had so many answered prayers that it is just a way of life for me. I have every expectation that every time I do an affirmative prayer, it will be answered. Sometimes the simplest stories have taught me that prayer is always answered.

"One time I was driving around a large parking lot, frustrated that there were no parking places. In fact, I was so upset that I was ready to cry. Suddenly, the thought came, 'Why don't you pray?' So I put my head down on the steering wheel and said a brief prayer. When I looked up, three cars were pulling out of spaces at the same time. Now, this took only a few seconds, and not a living soul was walking around the parking lot when I started. I laughed, because God was showing me trust and abundance. I just said, 'Okay, God I get it, and I really only needed only one space!'

"Another time I prayed with a girl who had just been diagnosed with a brain tumor by CAT scan. She was going to have another scan a few days later. When she had the next scan and saw her doctor, there was no evidence of the tumor.

"Another time a couple asked me for assistance with their car. They said they were feeling insecure that the car did not always start and did not run well. They had no money to fix it or to buy a new one. After I prayed for their car, needless to say, they have not had a moment's trouble with the car since.

"Every day, I notice how God is working in my life, from the simplest things to big things. If I forget and become emotionally involved, I call another practitioner to remind me who I am and to do prayer support for me."

HEALING ALCOHOLISM

Michelle Engel, Medford, Oregon

"I prayed for my friend Heather and her two sons. Heather's ex-husband had died of alcoholism almost two years before. Heather had been drinking a lot daily, and I thought perhaps her ex-husband was influencing her.

"Amazingly, Heather quit drinking right after I started praying for her. She has had a complete turnaround. Her oldest son had been picked up for DUI and put in jail. In fact, he had several drinking offenses. I prayed for him and now he quit drinking. He is on the mend."

SELLING PROPERTY

Rev. Roy Ayers, Unity Church, Mount Vernon, Washington

"My wife and I moved from Michigan to Mount Vernon, Washington. Yet we still owned a five-family unit in Michigan. We tried to sell it for three years. We owned the home together and were at odds about how to effectively sell it. One day, we gave up trying to work on it. We turned it over to prayer when I became part of a Mastermind prayer group at Unity Church of Today. The property sold quickly for the full asking price.

"The home had been on the market since 2000, then off the market, then back on the market. We told the agent we needed a miracle and asked him to expect one for the sale of the place. He got the miracle out of the blue—a cash offer. It sold in 2003 and closed in January 2004."

SPIRITUAL LOVE STORY

Barbara Torresen, Vancouver, British Columbia

"In 1960, my husband deserted our family and I was a single mom with four children for eight years. My early years of church were not satisfying my needs. So I searched for a meaning to life other than working at two jobs and caring for my children. In my search, I was directed to meditation. Almost immediately my life changed. I gave up smoking within two weeks. Within three months, I met my future husband. Eighteen months later, we were married and have had a wonderful life together for the past thirty-five years.

"Spirit guided us to reading *Science of Mind* magazine. Eventually, in 1981, we discovered the Science of Mind Church in Vancouver. We found our spiritual home and we attend every Sunday. I have been a practitioner for sixteen years and my husband has been on the Board of Trustees and is a constant volunteer.

"I believe the Divine Spirit within me opened me to accepting my good through my meditations and returning to my Source of all Good. When my husband met me, he was a lifelong bachelor. So we often joke with him about becoming a husband, father, and grandfather in the space of fifteen minutes, the time it took for the marriage ceremony. He in turn found a loving wife, children, grandchildren, and now we have two beautiful great grandchildren. We are so grateful for all our many blessings."

PRAYING FOR PSYCHIC EXPERIENCES

Andrew Sanderson, Auckland, New Zealand

"I used the Scientific Prayer formula for the first time, and I got great results. I prayed for psychic powers and deep, clear, pure psychic experiences. The next night, I had a profound, vivid experience that showed me, in a very clear way, the collection of all the experiences, impressions, thoughts, and feelings that I have ever had as an individual I AM. It was like a complex web, where all the experiences are meshed together and continually moving. It was like looking at my DNA from very close up. It was so alive and colorful! So vital! It was a very clear experience, but difficult to describe. I am definitely going to use the Scientific Prayer formula more and hopefully have more experiences like this."

A CALL FROM MY SON

Elizabeth Wilson, Westminster, California

"In Wednesday night's Scientific Prayer circle, you all prayed for our healing from the separation between my son Kyle and me during my period of addiction. I just want to express our gratitude and hope. Kyle called me, for the first time in weeks, on Thursday night. Your prayers work!"

GETTING MY NEW HOME QUICKLY

Junette McBryde Parker, Temple Terrace, Florida

"I started attending the Religious Science Church in 2000. I wanted a new home because ours felt too small for my two sons and me. So, in November 2001, I wrote a prayer treatment. I got the boys expensive gifts for Christmas, which I paid for out of my savings. God had provided, and I was relaxed enough to stop living in fear.

"I continued my prayer treatment through the beginning of the new year. On February 8, 2002, I found a house. On February 22, we moved in. I had some doubt whether I could pay the down payment, pay for moving expenses, and make arrangements to rent out my old house. I had spent most of my savings during Christmas, not anticipating I would find my new home so quickly. But it manifested perfectly. Four bedrooms, two-and-a-half baths, brand new, and in the same school area so I did not have to disrupt my sons' lives.

"I met and married my husband quickly like that also. It is as though, once the resistance is gone—bam! Manifestation."

THE DOCTOR IS NOT ALWAYS RIGHT

Dionn Rollins, Religious Science Practitioner, Philadelphia, Pennsylvania

"I was disabled, receiving financial aid for a psychiatric diagnosis. I was told I would never work again. But I did not believe that diagnosis. My desire was to enhance my R.N. degree by getting a B.S.N. degree so I could teach family members of the ill and nursing assistants how to take care of sick.

"At the Religious Science church, through practitioners in counseling sessions and classes, and through prayer treatments, the means to fulfill my goal came to fruition. My entire education was subsidized by the Office of Vocational Rehabilitation, and I repaid the loan promptly after graduation. I had a job interview before I graduated. I got paid for the job interview and was hired on the spot to teach nursing assistants. Later, because of my B.S.N., I was asked to teach licensed practical nurses."

GOD BLESS THE ANIMALS

Reverend Lauren McLaughlin, Port Richey, Florida

"In 1979, an experiment was conducted in Lee's Summit, Missouri, by six female Seminary students concerned about finding homes for animals in a local animal shelter. For a period of six weeks, several times each day, they repeated an affirmation: 'God, as Divine Order, is moving in and through the Lee's Summit Animal Shelter. Peace, Love, and Joy abound.' The shelter tracked its activity during those six weeks. At the end of the period, the City of Lee's Summit reported the adoption rate in their shelter raised appreciably. At one point, a line of people extended outside their doors, waiting to adopt a pet. Impressed with this experiment, one of the graduating students began an Internet prayer ministry for animals: www.godblesstheanimals. com."

The following are a couple of the many reports from visitors to the website whose animals benefited from prayer:

Betty Jazyk: "Over a week ago, I wrote and asked you to pray for my diabetic orange tabby, Jack, who was having a hard time. Within a couple of days, Jack became very vibrant. He is his old self again. This morning I found a tooth, a fang on the floor. It belongs to Jack, I believe he had a bad tooth and I have no idea how but it is now out of his mouth. God must have pulled it out, root and all."

Annette Hebert: "Whitey survived eighteen hours in a blizzard and returned safely home to us at 11 P.M. on Sunday night. I know that he returned to us because of prayer! Thank you."

SELLING A HOME

Joan Grant, Ocala, Florida

"I moved out of my mobile home and purchased a house. The mobile home had been for sale for several months, with a lot rent of $350, payable monthly, even though it was vacant. After many frustrating discussions on what to do with it, I decided to do a prayer treatment with my partner one morning last week. Within five hours, we received an offer on the sale. We close in two weeks. Treatment works!"

GOD IS MY PLUMBER

Manuel Zambrano, Norwalk, California

"I was trying to unclog the bathtub and was having a hard time. Then, I took a break. I looked up and invoked the angels, saying: 'Archangel San Gabriel, you that are famous for bringing messages from God as you did to

Virgin Mary, please plant the divine message in my head, the knowledge to unclog this bathtub for the benefit of my family and myself. I ask you in the name of God.' (By this time, I was already frustrated, because I could not unclog the stupid thing.)

"I was about to try to pass the snake again through the drain, when suddenly I started to get thoughts in my head about trying from outside of the house. I found a main seal that goes directly to the main pipe connected between the bathtub and the sewer, and bingo! *En un dos por tres!* It was done. *Aleluya Gloria Dios.*"

SHE WILL "NOT LEAVE THE HOSPITAL ALIVE"

Rev. Dean Van Wie, Unity Church of Christianity, Moline, Illinois

"Several years ago, I was contacted by a couple in Arizona. Their daughter Angela was passing through the Quad Cities and had been involved in a bad accident. They asked if our church members would 'adopt' Angela, as they lived so far away and would not be able to visit her. The doctors had said Angela would not leave the hospital alive because her injuries were so bad.

"I went to the hospital to see Angela, about age 25. She had been raised in the Unity Church, but had grown away from it. Now she was running with a bad crowd, doing drugs, and in a contentious relationship with her parents for several years.

"The first time I saw her, she had a tracheotomy and could only whisper. Several members of our congregation volunteered to visit Angela during the next few weeks. We read Unity's *Daily Word* to her and prayed with her. She was very familiar with the *Daily Word* and our Prayer of Protection and Prayer of Faith. In less than two weeks, the tracheotomy was completely removed, and she was wheeling herself around the hospital in her wheelchair.

"Instead of dying in the hospital as her doctor had predicted, in approximately two months Angela flew home to Arizona, sitting up in her seat, spent a few weeks in a nursing home, and is now living with her parents, doing very well, and living a normal life. The nurses in the hospital were amazed at her quick recovery and called it a 'miracle.'"

GOD'S LOVE

Kate Peppler, Licensed Unity Teacher, Rochester, Minnesota

"Once I was sitting on a chair and ottoman with my 'Unity 12 Powers' thrown on it, in my favorite prayer place, overlooking our little pond with its trees and waterfowl. I was trying to get into the flow of sitting in the silence. At the time, I was troubled about feeling a lack of enough love to go around.

"Suddenly, I felt like I was a well being filled with the continuous, over-flowing unconditional God Love. Tears streamed down my cheeks. At that moment, I understood that there is no such thing as lack. God's love is continuous, within us, always. I realized that everything we should ever need is ever-present.

"I learned that God's love is like a Christ candle shining brightly. Whether we have one or ten people who seek our love, it is like lighting a candle for each person from that Christ candle. All candles shine fully, and of course the Christ candle (me, you, each of us) burns just as brightly as before the other candles were lit. The beauty is that now all candles create an even brighter light—together!"

LETTING GO

A woman from Menlo Park, California

One woman from Menlo Park, California, expressed fear due to the uncertainty of letting go of an old career and starting a new one. She asked, "How will I know what steps to take?" Jesus answered her question through Rev. Rian Leichter, president of Teaching of Intuitional Metaphysics, Woodside, California: "When you were a child you did not know how to dance, so you danced on your father's feet as he guided you across the floor to the music. Then, as now, you may not know the steps, but you can dance on your Father's feet, for He surely knows the way."

APPENDICES

NINE STEPS OF SCIENTIFIC PRAYER IN THE JUDEO-CHRISTIAN TRADITION

The *Shemoneh Esrei*, otherwise known as the *Amidah* ("to stand"), is the most sacred prayer in Judaism. This eighteen-step formula is similar to Scientific Prayer, although its format differs. This ancient prayer is the basis of the Lord's Prayer, which was composed by the Jewish rabbi, Jeshua ben Joseph (Jesus). The twenty-third Psalm, written by King David, is one of the most quoted prayers of the Bible. The prayer of Jabez from I Chronicles has become a very popular, affirmative, results-oriented prayer today, due to the publication of *The Prayer of Jabez: Breaking Through to the Blessed Life*.

As you read these prayers, do your best to identify the corresponding steps of Scientific Prayer. See what I have chosen in the Table at the end. There are no right or wrong answers. Please feel free to agree or disagree.

THE LORD'S PRAYER

1. *Our Father which art in heaven, Hallowed be thy name.*
2. *Thy kingdom come, Thy will be done in earth, as it is in heaven.*
3. *Give us this day our daily bread.*
4. *And forgive us our debts, as we forgive our debtors.*
5. *And lead us not into temptation, but deliver us from evil.*
6. *For thine is the kingdom, and the power, and the glory, forever.*
7. *Amen.*

PSALM 23

23:1 The LORD is my shepherd; I shall not want.

23:2 He maketh me to lie down in green pastures: he leadeth me beside the still waters.

23:3 He restoreth my soul: he leadeth me in the paths of righteousness for his name's sake.

23:4 Yea, though I walk through the valley of the shadow of death, I will fear no evil: for thou art with me; thy rod and thy staff they comfort me.

23:5 Thou preparest a table before me in the presence of mine enemies: thou anointest my head with oil; my cup runneth over.

23:6 Surely goodness and mercy shall follow me all the days of my life: and I will dwell in the house of the LORD forever.

PRAYER OF JABEZ

4:10 And Jabez called on the God of Israel, saying,
Oh that thou wouldest bless me indeed,
and enlarge my coast,
and that thine hand might be with me,
and that thou wouldest keep me from evil,
that it may not grieve me!
And God granted him that which he requested.

SHEMONEH ESREI (AMIDAH)

My Hashem, open my lips that my mouth may tell Thy glory.

PATRIARCHS

1. *Blessed art Thou, Hashem, our God and God of our forefathers, God of Abraham, God of Isaac, and God of Jacob. The great, mighty and awesome God, the supreme God, Who bestows great kindness and creates*

283

everything, Who recalls the kindness of the Patriarchs, and brings a Redeemer to their children's children, for His name's sake, with love. O King, Helper, Savior and Shield. Blessed art Thou, Hashem, Shield of Abraham.

GOD'S MIGHT

2. *Thy might is eternal, my Hashem, Resurrector of the dead, Great in salvation, who makes the wind blow and the rain fall, who sustains the living with kindness, who revives the dead with great mercy, supports the falling, heals the sick, frees the confined, and keeps faith with the dead. Who is like Thee, Almighty, and who resembles Thee, O King who can bring death, gives life, and makes salvation sprout. Blessed art Thou, Hashem, who resurrects the dead.*

HOLINESS OF GOD'S NAME

3. *Thou art holy, and Thy name is holy, and holy ones shall praise Thee every day. Blessed art Thou, Hashem, the holy God.*

INSIGHT

4. *Thou grantest knowledge to man, and teach insight to humans. From thine own self, favor us with knowledge, insight, and wisdom. Blessed art Thou, Hashem,*
Giver of knowledge.

REPENTANCE

5. *Return us, our Father, to Thy Torah, and bring us near, our King, to Thy service, and make us return in perfect repentance. Blessed are Thou, Hashem, who desires repentance.*

FORGIVENESS

6. *Forgive us, our Father, for we have erred, pardon us, our King, for we*

have willfully transgressed, for Thou art pardoner and forgiver. Blessed art Thou, Hashem, gracious One who pardons abundantly.

REDEMPTION

7. *Behold our affliction, take up our grievance, and redeem us speedily, for Thy name's sake, for Thou art a mighty Redeemer. Blessed art Thou, Hashem, Redeemer of Israel.*

HEALTH AND HEALING

8. *Heal us, Hashem, and we shall be healed, save us and we shall be saved, for Thou art our praise. Bring complete recovery for all our ailments, for Thou, Divine King, art the faithful, compassionate Healer. Blessed art Thou, Hashem, who heals the sick of His people Israel.*

YEAR OF PROSPERITY

9. *Bless this year for us, O Hashem our God, and all its varied crops for the best; give a blessing on the face of the earth, satisfy us with Thy bounty, and bless our year like the best years. Blessed art Thou, Hashem, who blesses the years.*

INGATHERING OF EXILES

10. *Sound the great shofar for our freedom, raise a banner to gather our exiles, and gather us from the four corners of the earth. Blessed art Thou, Hashem, who gathers the dispersed of His people Israel.*

RESTORATION OF JUSTICE

11. *Restore our judges as in early times, and our counselors as at first, remove from us sorrow and groaning; reign over us, Thou alone, Hashem, with kindness and mercy, and vindicate us in judgment. Blessed art Thou, Hashem, King, who loves righteousness and judgment.*

THE RIGHTEOUS

12. *On the righteous and the devout, on the elders of Thy people, the house of Israel, on their surviving scholars, on the righteous converts and on ourselves, let Thy compassion flow, Hashem our God. Grant good reward to all who sincerely trust in Thy name; place our lot with them forever, and let us not feel ashamed, for in Thee do we trust. Blessed art Thou, Hashem, who supports and safeguards the righteous.*

REBUILDING JERUSALEM

13. *And to Jerusalem Thy city, return with compassion, and dwell within it as Thou promised; rebuild it soon in our day as an eternal structure; and speedily establish the throne of David within it. Blessed art Thou, Hashem, builder of Jerusalem.*

DAVIDIC REIGN

14. *The offspring of Thy servant David, swiftly make flourish, and exalt his honor through Thy salvation; for Thy salvation do we constantly hope. Blessed art Thou, Hashem, who raises the ray of salvation.*

ACCEPTANCE OF PRAYER

15. *Hear our voice, Hashem our God, have compassion and mercy for us, accept our prayers with mercy and favor, for Thou art a God who hears prayers and supplications. King, turn us not away empty-handed. Mercifully hear the prayer of Thy people Israel. Blessed art Thou, Hasham, Who hears prayers.*

TEMPLE SERVICE

16. *Be favorable, Hashem our God, toward Thy people Israel and their prayer, restore the worship to the Holy of Holies of Thy Temple. Accept with love and favor the fire-offerings of Israel and their prayer, and may*

the service of Thy people Israel always be favorable to Thee. May our
eyes behold Thy return to Zion in mercy. Blessed art Thou, Hashem,
who restores His Presence to Zion.

THANKSGIVING

17. We give thanks unto Thee who art Hashem our God and God of our
forefathers forever. Thou art the rock of our lives and shield of our salvation in every generation. We shall thank Thee and declare Thy praise for
our lives that are in Thy hand, and for our souls that are in Thy care,
and for Thy miracles that are with us daily, and for Thy wondrous deeds
and favors that occur at all times, evening, morning, and noon. The
Benevolent One, for Thy mercies are never exhausted, and the
Compassionate One, for Thy merciful deeds never end, always we place
our hope in Thee. For all these, may Thy name be always blessed and
exalted, our King, forever and ever. All the living will forever thank Thee
and praise Thy name in truth, O God, our salvation and help, Selah!
Blessed art Thou, Hashem, whose name is the Beneficent One; it is
fitting to give thanks to Thee.

PEACE

18. Establish peace, well-being, blessing, grace, loving kindness, and mercy
upon us and upon all Israel, Thy people, for Thou art King, Master of
all peace. For by the light of Thy presence have you given us, Hashem
our God, a Torah of life, love of kindness, justice, blessing, compassion,
life, and peace. It is good in Thy sight to bless Thy people Israel at all
times and every hour with Thy peace. Blessed art Thou, Hashem, who
blesses His people Israel with peace.

NINE STEPS OF SCIENTIFIC PRAYER

SCIENTIFIC PRAYER	SHEMONEH ESREI	THE LORD'S PRAYER
1. REQUEST	(See Resolution)	(See Resolution)
2. RECOGNITION	Sec. 1: Patriarchs Sec. 2: God's Might Sec. 3: Holiness of God's Name	Our Father which art in heaven, Hallowed be thy name
3. RAPPORT	Sec. 4: Insight Sec. 5: Repentance	Thy kingdom come, Thy will be done in earth [the outer world], as it is in heaven [the inner realm of Spirit]
4. RESOLUTION	Sec. 9: Year of Prosperity Sec. 10: Ingathering of Exiles Sec. 11: Restoration of Justice Sec. 12: The Righteous Sec. 13: Rebuilding Jerusalem Sec. 14: Davidic Reign	Give us this day our daily bread [sustenance of all kinds]
5. RENEWAL	Sec. 6: Forgiveness Sec. 7: Redemption Sec. 8: Health and Healing	And forgive us our debts, as we forgive our debtors. And lead us not into temptation, but deliver us from evil [error]:
6. REALIZATION	Sec. 15: Acceptance of Prayer Sec. 16: Temple Service	For thine is the kingdom, and the power, and the glory, forever.
7. REWARD	Sec. 17: Thanksgiving	
8. RELEASE	Sec. 18: Peace	Amen
9. REPOSE	(See Release)	(See Release)

IN THE JUDEO-CHRISTIAN TRADITION

PSALM 23	PRAYER OF JABEZ
(See Resolution)	(See Resolution)
23:1 The LORD is my shepherd; I shall not want.	4:10 And Jabez called on the God of Israel,
23:2 He maketh me to lie down in green pastures: he leadeth me beside the still waters.	and that thine hand might be with me,
23:3 He restoreth my soul: he leadeth me in the paths of righteousness for his name's sake.	saying, Oh that thou wouldest bless me indeed, and enlarge my coast,
23:4 Yea, though I walk through the valley of the shadow of death, I will fear no evil: for thou art with me; thy rod and thy staff they comfort me.	and that thou wouldest keep [me] from evil, that it may not grieve me!
23:5 Thou preparest a table before me in the presence of mine enemies: thou anointest my head with oil; my cup runneth over.	that which he requested.
23:6 Surely goodness and mercy shall follow me all the days of my life:	And God granted him
and I will dwell in the house of the LORD for ever.	
(See Release)	(See Release)

NEW THOUGHT LUMINARIES

- Emanuel Swedenborg (1688–1772): *Heaven and Hell*.

- Franz Anton Mesmer (1734–1815): *Mesmerism*.

- Henry David Thoreau (1817–1862): *Walden, or Life in the Woods*.

- Phineas Parkhurst Quimby (1822–1866): *The Complete Writings*, father of New Thought.

- Ralph Waldo Emerson (1803–1882): "On Self-Reliance," founder: Transcendentalism.

- Warren Felt Evans (1817–1889): *The Mental Cure*.

- Henry Drummond (1851–1897): *The Greatest Thing in the World*.

- Madam Blavatsky (1831–1891): *The Secret Doctrine*, and Col. Henry Steel Olcott (1832–1907), founders: Theosophical Society.

- Julius A. Dresser (1838–1898): *The True History of Mental Science*, student of Phineas Quimby.

- Swami Vivekananda (1863–1902): *Raja-Yoga*, founder: Vedanta Society.

- Malinda Cramer (1844–1906): *Divine Science and Healing*, founder: Divine Science.

- Mary Baker Eddy (1821–1910): *Science and Health with Key to the Scriptures*, founder: Christian Science.

- Helen Wilmans (1831–1907): *Home Course in Mental Science*.

- William James (1842–1910): *The Varieties of Religious Experience*.

- Wallace Delois Wattles (1860–1911): *The Science of Getting Rich*.

- James Allen (1864–1912): *As a Man Thinketh*.

- Frank Channing Haddock (1853–1915): *Power of Will*.

- Thomas Troward (1847–1916): *Edinburgh and Dore Lectures on Mental Science*.

- Genevieve Behrend: *Your Invisible Power*, founder: The School of the Builders.

- Ella Wheeler Wilcox (1850–1919): *Heart of the New Thought*.

- Ursula N. Gestefeld (1845–1921): *How We Master Our Fate*, founder: Science of Being.

- Frederick L. Rawson (1859–1923): *Life Understood*, founder: Society for Spreading the Knowledge of True Prayer.

- Orison Swett Marden (1850–1924): founder: *Success Magazine*.

- Annie Rix Militz (1856–1924): *Master Mind* magazine, founder: Home of Truth.

- Russell H. Conwell (1843–1925): *Acres of Diamonds*, founder: Temple University.

- Emma Curtis Hopkins (1853–1925): *Scientific Christian Mental Practice,* founder: Emma Hopkins College of Metaphysical Science.

- Rudolf Steiner (1861–1925): *How to Know Higher Worlds*, founder: Antroposophy, Waldorf Schools.

- Emile Coué (1857–1926): *My Method*, founder: The Coué Method.

- William Walker Atkinson, aka, Yogi Ramacharaka (1862–1932): *Secret of Success*.

- Annie Wood Besant (1847–1933): *Thought Power*.

- Charles Brodie Patterson (1854–1936): *The Measure of a Man*, editor, *Arena* and *Mind* magazines.

- Florence Scovel Shinn (1871–1940): *The Game of Life and How to Play It*.

- Harriette Emilie Cady (1848–1941): *Lessons in Truth*.

- Albert C. Grier (1864–1941): *Truth and Life*, founder: The Church of Truth.

- Brown Landone (1847–1945): *How to Turn Your Desires and Ideals into Realities*.

- Nona L. Brooks (1861–1945): *In the Light of Healing*, co-founder: Divine Science.

- Alfred North Whitehead (1861–1947): *Process and Reality*, founder: Process Philosophy.

- Frank B. Robinson (1886–1948): *Psychiana*, founder: Psychiana.

- Charles (1854–1948) and Myrtle (1845–1931) Fillmore: *The Twelve Powers of Man*, founders: Unity Church.

- Charles F. Haanel (1866–1949): *The Master Key System*.

- Alice A. Bailey (1880–1949): *Esoteric Psychology*.

- Rebecca Beard (1885–unknown): *Everyman's Search*.

- Robert Collier (1885–1950): *Secret of the Ages*.

- Emmet Fox (1886–1951): *The Sermon on the Mount*.

- Claude M. Bristol (1891–1951): *The Magic of Believing*.

- Paramahansa Yogananda (1893–1952): *Autobiography of a Yogi*, founder: Self-Realization Fellowship.

- Horatio Willis Dresser (1866–1954): *Health and the Inner Life*, founder: *Journal of Practical Metaphysics*.

- Dale Carnegie (1888–1955): *How to Win Friends and Influence People*.

- William H. Danforth (1870–1956): *I Dare You*, founder: Ralston Purina Company, and American Youth Foundation.

- Glenn Clark (1882–1956): *The Soul's Sincere Desire*, founder: Camps Farthest Out.

- George S. Clason (1874–1957): *The Richest Man in Babylon*.

- Ralph Waldo Trine (1866–1958): *In Tune with the Infinite*.

- Henry Thomas Hamblin (1873–1958), *Within You Is The Power*, founder: *The Science of Thought Review*.

- Fenwicke Lindsay Holmes (1883–unknown): *Healing at a Distance*.

- Ernest Holmes (1887–1960): *The Science of Mind*, founder: Religious Science.
- Carl Jung (1875–1961): *Man and His Symbols*, founder: Analytical Psychology.
- Walter Russell (1871–1963): *The Message of the Divine Iliad*, founder: University of Science and Philosophy.
- Joel S. Goldsmith (1892–1964): *The Infinite Way*, founder: The Infinite Way.
- Walter Clemow Lanyon (1887–1967): *Thrust in the Sickle*.
- Napoleon Hill (1883–1970): *Think and Grow Rich*, founder: The Science of Success.
- Frederick W. Bailes (1889–1970): *Your Mind Can Heal You*.
- William Griffith Wilson (1895–1971): *Alcoholics Anonymous*, founder: AA.
- Reginald C. Armor (1903–unknown): *Thought Is Power*.
- Mildred Mann (1904–1971): *How to Find Your Real Self*, founder: Society of Pragmatic Mysticism.
- Neville Goddard (1905–1972): *The Law and the Promise*.
- Joseph Murphy (1898–1981): *The Power of Your Subconscious Mind*.
- Peace Pilgrim (1908–1981): *Peace Pilgrim*.
- Agnes Sanford (1897–1982): *The Healing Light*.
- Dr. Masaharu Taniguchi (1893–1985): *Truth of Life*, founder: Seicho-No-Ie.
- Joseph Campbell (1904–1987): *Hero With a Thousand Faces*.
- Brother Mandus (1907–1988): *The Healing Science*, founder: World Healing Crusade.
- Earl Nightingale (1921–1989): *The Strangest Secret*, founder: Nightingale-Conant.
- Manly Palmer Hall (1901–1990): *The Secret Teachings of All Ages*, founder: The Philosophical Research Society.

- Ervin Seale (1909–1990): *Mingling Minds*, founder: The Quimby Memorial Church.

- Norman Cousins (1912–1990): *Anatomy of an Illness*, founder: Center for Psychoneuro-immunology.

- Vernon Linwood Howard (1918–1992): *The Mystic Path to Cosmic Power*, founder: New Life Foundation.

- George Bendall (1919–1992): *Now the Time*.

- Norman Vincent Peale (1898–1993): *The Power of Positive Thinking*, founder: *Guideposts* magazine.

- Ken Keyes, Jr. (1921–1994): *Handbook to Higher Consciousness*, founder: Ken Keyes College.

- Marcus Bach (1906–1995): *The World of Serendipity*, founder: The Fellowship for Spiritual Understanding.

- Og Mandino (1923–1996): *The Greatest Salesman in the World*.

- William Samuel (1924–1996): *A Guide to Awareness and Tranquility*.

- Donald Curtis (1915–61997): *Your Thoughts Can Change Your Life*.

- Jack Ensign Addington (–1998): *Your Needs Met*, founder: Abundant Living Foundation.

- Stuart Grayson (–2001): *Spiritual Healing*.

- William Clement Stone (1902–2002): *Success through a Positive Mental Attitude*.

- James Dillet Freeman (1912–2003): *Happiness Can Be a Habit*, "Poet Laureate" of Unity.

- Eric Butterworth (1916–2003): *Discover the Power Within You*, minister of Unity Church, New York City.

- Maxwell Maltz (1927–2003): *Psycho-Cybernetics*, founder: Psycho-Cybernetics Foundation.

- Alexander Everett (1921–2005): *The Genius Within You*, founder: Mind Dynamics.

- M. Scott Peck (1936–2005): *The Road Less Traveled*.

- Gerald Gershan Jampolsky (1925–): *Love is Letting Go of Fear*, founder: Center for Attitudinal Healing.

- Maharishi Mahesh Yogi (1918–): *Science of Being and Art of Living*, founder: Transcendental Meditation.

- Zig Ziglar (1926–): *See You at the Top*.

- Robert Harold Schuller (1926–): *Tough Times Never Last, but Tough People Do*.

- Richard Nelson Bolles (1927–): *What Color Is Your Parachute?*

- Jim Rohn (1930–): *7 Strategies for Wealth and Happiness*, founder: Jim Rohn International.

- Roy Eugene Davis (1931–): *Life Surrendered in God*, founder: Center for Spiritual Awareness.

- Stephen R. Covey (1932–): *The 7 Habits of Highly Effective People*.

- John Randolph Price (1932–): *The Superbeings*, founder: Quartus Foundation for Spiritual Research.

- Dennis Waitley (1933–): *The Psychology of Winning*, founder: The Waitley Institute.

- Richard Bach (1936–): *Jonathan Livingston Seagull*.

- Ken Blanchard (1939–): *The One Minute Manager*, founder: Blanchard Training and Development.

- Terry Cole-Whittaker (1939–): *How To Have More in a Have Not World*, founder: Adventures in Enlightenment.

- Wayne Dyer (1940–): *Your Erroneous Zones*.

- Thomas J. Peters (1942–): *In Search of Excellence*.

- Brian Tracy (1944–): *Maximum Achievement*.

- Les Brown (1945–): *Live Your Dreams*, founder: Les Brown Unlimited.

- Mark Victor Hansen (1948–): *Chicken Soup for the Soul*.

- Shakti Gawain (1948–): *Creative Visualization*, founder: New World Library.

- Marianne Williamson (1952–): *A Return to Love*.

- Anthony Robbins (1960–): *Awaken the Giant Within*.

- Lillian DeWaters: *The Christ Within*.

- Raymond Charles Barker: *The Science of Successful Living*, founder: First Church of Religious Science, New York City.

- Uell S. Andersen: *Three Magic Words*.

- Charles E. Jones: *Life Is Tremendous*, founder: Life Management Services.

- John C. Maxwell: *The 21 Irrefutable Laws of Leadership*, founder: INJOY Group.

- Catherine Ponder: *The Dynamic Laws of Prosperity*.

- Edwene Gaines: *The Four Spiritual Laws of Prosperity*, founder: Rock Ridge Retreat Center.

- David J. Schwartz: *The Magic of Thinking Big*, founder: Creative Educational Services.

- Bernie S. Siegel: *Love, Medicine, and Miracles*.

- Barbara Sher: *Wishcraft, How to Get What You Really Want*.

- Rev. Dr. Johnnie Coleman: *Open Your Mind and Be Healed*, founder: Christ Universal Temple.

- Louise Hay: *You Can Heal Your Life*, founder: Hay House.

NOTES

CHAPTER 2

1. John 5:19.
2. John 12:50, 51.
3. John 8:28.
4. John 14:10.
5. Philippians 2:5–6.
6. Luke 18:27.
7. Matthew 19:26.
8. Luke 17:21.
9. Matthew 6:33.
10. Matthew 7:7–8.
11. John 14:12.
12. Matthew 5:48.
13. Luke 6:40.
14. Matthew 8:22.
15. Acts 1:8.
16. John 14:26.
17. Matthew 5:14, 16.
18. Luke 17:21.
19. John 10:34, Psalm 83:6.
20. Romans 8:14, 16, 17.
21. 1 Corinthians 2:9–10.
22. John 14:12.
23. Psalms 46:10.
24. Albert Einstein Quotes: giga-usa.com.
25. Matthew 21:22.
26. John 14:12.

CHAPTER 3

1. *Dhammapada* 1:1: en.wikiquote.org.
2. Proverbs 23:7.
3. John 14:12.

CHAPTER 4

1. Luke 6:38.
2. Luke 6:31, Matthew 7:12.
3. Galatians 6:7.
4. Matthew 8:13.
5. Matthew 8:13.

CHAPTER 5

1. Obadiah 1:15.

CHAPTER 6

1. Hebrews 4:16.
2. Matthew 19:26.
3. Galatians 5:18.
4. *Khandogya Upanishad*, VI:2, Upanishads: sacred-texts.com.
5. Isaiah 45:22.
6. Deuteronomy 6:4.
7. Jeremiah 23:23–24.
8. Joshua 1:5.
9. I Corinthians 3:16.
10. Luke 17:21.
11. Acts 17:27–28.
12. *Qur'an*, Das, *The Essential Unity*, 98.
13. *Qur'an*, Perry, *A Treasury*, 845.
14. Sufi Writings, Das, *The Essential Unity*, 103.
15. Ibid., 99.

16. Mumonkan 30, Wilson, *World Scripture*, 74.
17. *Mahaparinirvana Sutra* 214, Wilson, *World Scripture*, 147.
18. Chan, Wing-tsit. Chapter 26, The Platform Scripture 30.
19. Kwan-Yin-Tse, Das, *The Essential Unity*, 147.
20. *Adi Granth*, Dhanasari, M.9, Wilson, *World Scripture*.
21. *Adi Granth*, Majh Ashtpadi, M.3, 116, Wilson, 72.
22. *Amita-Gati*, Samayika-patha, Das, *The Essential Unity*, 146.
23. *Jeevan Mukta Gita* 1. Keshavadas, *Sadguru Dattatreya*, Chapter 4, page xx.
24. *"Aham Brahma, Tat tvam asi, Esha ma Atma antar-hrdaye, Hrdi ayam tasmad hrdayam."* (Sanskrit). Arabic maxim (Sufi), Das, *The Essential Unity*, 107.
25. *Hermetica Libellus* V.2, Perry, *A Treasury*, 748.
26. Deuteronomy 6:5.
27. Exodus 33:13.
28. Psalms 91:1–2.
29. Psalms 23:6.
30. John 5:30.
31. John 6:38.
32. Romans 12:2.
33. Ephesians 3:16.
34. 1 Kings 19:12.
35. Matthew 8:13.
36. Romans 8:2.
37. Besant, *Bhagavad Gita* 4:37.
38. Romans 6:14.
39. Genesis 2:16–17.
40. Genesis 3:7.
41. Mark 5:28.
42. Mark 5:34.
43. Exodus 33:11.
44. Matthew 19:26.
45. Matthew 7:7.
46. Matthew 6:12.
47. Deuteronomy 15:1–2.
48. Leviticus 25:10.
49. Ephesians 2:8–9.
50. Holmes, *Science of Mind*, 1926, Part III: Special Articles.
51. Numbers 6:24–26.

CHAPTER 7
1. *Khandogya Upanishad*, II:8, Upanishads: sacred-texts.com.
2. Genesis 1:3.
3. John 1:1.
4. Genesis 1:1.
5. *Katha Upanishad*, II:14–16, Upanishads: sacred-texts.com.
6. Holmes, *Science of Mind*, 1938, 30.
7. Exodus 3:8.
8. Exodus 3:14.
9. Exodus 20:7.
10. Luke 11:2.
11. Miller, *Zohar*, Vol. 1, Beresheet A, Section 1.
12. Aranya, *Yoga Philosophy: Yoga Sutras*, 44.

CHAPTER 8

1. James 1:4–7.
2. Holmes, *Science of Mind*, 1938, 283.
3. Matthew 17:20 and 13:31–32.
4. Holmes, *Science of Mind*, 1938, 280.
5. Ibid., 149.
6. Parker, *Prayer Can Change*.
7. Prayer as Therapy, ficotw.org.
8. James 4:3.
9. Psalms 27:8.
10. 1 John 4:8.
11. 1 Thessalonians 5:17.
12. 1 Peter 5:7.
13. Proverbs 6:2.
14. Luke 11:9.

CHAPTER 9

1. Matthew 7:7.
2. Psalms 18:30.
3. Psalms 19:7.
4. Matthew 8:13.
5. Matthew 9:22.
6. Holmes, *How to Use*, 16.
7. Deuteronomy 6:4.
8. Genesis 1:22.
9. Isaiah 55:11.
10. Luke 6:38.
11. Luke 12:6–7.
12. Galatians 6:7.
13. Genesis 1:4.

14. Ecclesiastes 3:1.
15. Genesis 1:31.
16. Ecclesiastes 3:14.
17. Matthew 7:1–2.
18. 1 Corinthians 13:12.
19. Holmes, *How to Use*, 8.
20. Holmes, *How to Use*, 23.
21. Holmes, *How to Use*, 16.
22. Holmes, *How to Use*, 18.
23. Holmes, *How to Use*, 18.
24. James 4:3.
25. Holmes, *How to Use*, 6.

CHAPTER 10

1. Braden, *Spirits in Rebellion*, 14–18.
2. Emanuel Swedenborg: swedenborg.newearth.org.
3. Theosophy Library: theosophy.org.
4. Emerson: plato.stanford.edu/, Transcendentalists: transcendentalists.com, American Transcendentalism: vcu.edu.
5. Dresser: website.lineone.net.
6. New Thought Movement: websyte.com/alan.
7. Scientific Christian: emmacurtishopkins.wwwhubs.com.
8. Mary Baker Eddy Library: marybakereddylibrary.org.
9. Religious Movements: New Thought: religiousmovements.lib.virginia.edu.

10. Scientific Christian: emmacur-tishopkins.wwwhubs.com.

11. Introduction, Emma Curtis Hopkins: desert.xpressdesigns.com.

12. Birth Divine Science: divine-sciencecommunitycenter.org.

13. Ibid.

14. Ibid.

15. Divine Science, divinescience.com.

16. Ibid.

17. Religious Movements: New Thought: religiousmovements.lib.

18. Religious Movements: Unity: religiousmovements.lib.

19. Ibid.

20. Religious Movements: New Thought: religiousmovements.lib.

21. Religious Movements: United: religiousmovements.lib.

22. Holmes, *Science of Mind*, 1938, 638.

23. Ibid., 281.

24. Fox, *The Golden Key*.

25. Affiliated New Thought: newthought.org.

26. Holmes, *Science of Mind*, pg. 149.

27. Holmes, *How to Use*, 24.

CHAPTER 11

1. What Is Spiritual Mind: reli-giousscience.org.

2. Psalms 33:9.

3. What Is Spiritual Mind: reli-giousscience.org.

4. Matthew 19:26.

CHAPTER 12

1. Matthew 21:22.

2. Matthew 4:10.

3. Holmes, *Science of Mind*, 1938, 187.

4. Holmes, *How to Use*, 33.

5. Holmes, *How to Use*, 80.

6. Romans 12:2.

7. Matthew 7:7.

8. Matthew 18:20.

9. James 5:16.

10. Matthew 21:21.

CHAPTER 13

1. Lamsa, Psalms 118:6.

2. Lamsa, Matthew 5:39.

3. Matthew 5:45.

4. Psalms 115:14–15.

5. Psalms 19:7–8.

6. Jeremiah 33:3.

7. Psalm 142:7.

8. John 8:32.

9. Psalms 73:23–24.

10. Psalms 133:1.

11. Psalms 25:1–2, 4–5.

12. Psalms 27:1, 3.

13. Psalms 121:1–2, 8.

14. Psalms 23:4.

15. Mark 4:39.

16. Psalms 46:10.

17. Psalms 26:3, 5–6.

18. Psalms 145:18.

19. Psalms 15:1, 3.

20. Psalms 56:13.

21. Psalms 91:1–2.

22. Psalms 51:1–2.

23. Lamsa, Psalms 16:7–9.

24. John 10:10.

25. John 11:25.

26. Psalms 147:3–5.

27. Psalms 55:22.

28. Lamsa, Psalms 146:1–2.

CHAPTER 14

1. Matthew 19:26.

2. Matthew 6:10.

3. Psalm 91:11.

CHAPTER 16

1. Levin, "Religion and Spirituality in Medicine."

2. Kwang, reproductivemedicine.com.

3. Taylor, *Holistic Nursing Practice*.

4. McCaffrey, "Prayer for Health Concerns."

5. O'Laoire, " An Experimental Study of the Effects."

6. Matthews, "Effects of Intercessory Prayer."

7. On Assessing Prayer: davidmyers.org.

8. Harris, "A Randomized Controlled Trial."

9. Byrd, "Positive Therapeutic Effects."

10. Williams, plim.org.

11. Ibid.

12. Ibid.

13. Ibid.

14. Ibid.

15. Ibid.

16. Sweet, *A Journey*.

17. Kark, "Does Religious Observance?"

18. Comstock, "Church Attendance and Health."

19. McCullough, "Religious Involvement."

20. Koenig, "Does Religious Attendance?"

21. Hummer, "Religious Involvement."

22. Musick, "Attendance at Religious Services."

23. Koenig, "Attendance at Religious Services."

24. Williams, plim.org.

CHAPTER 17

1. Mark 11:23.

BIBLIOGRAPHY

BOOKS

Aranya, Swami Hariharananda. *Yoga Philosophy of Patanjali*. Calcutta, India: University of Calcutta, 1963.

Baba, Prem Raja. *Transform Your Life*. McCloud, California: Prem Raja Baba, 1991.

Baba, Prem Raja. *Seven Steps to Joy in a Changing World*. McCloud, California: Affirmations International, 1991.

Besant, Annie. *The Bhagavad Gita*. Adyar, India: Theosophical Publishing House, 1973.

Braden, Charles S. *Spirits in Rebellion*. Dallas, Texas: Southern Methodist University Press, 1963.

Chan, Wing-tsit. *A Source Book in Chinese Philosophy*, Princeton, New Jersey: Princeton University Press, 1963.

Das, Bhagavan. *The Essential Unity of All Religions*. Wheaton, Illinois: Quest Book, The Theosophical Publishing House, 1969.

Fox, Emmet, *The Golden Key*. Unity Village, Missouri: Unity School of Christianity, 1931.

Holmes, Ernest. *How to Use the Science of Mind*. New York: Dodd, Mead and Co., 1950.

Holmes, Ernest. *The Science of Mind, Original 1926 Text, 1988 Edition*. Encino, California: Hi Productions, 1998.

Holmes, Ernest. *The Science of Mind*. New York: Dodd, Mead and Co., 1938.

Holy Bible. Iowa Falls, Iowa: World Bible Publishers.

Karyalaya, Gobind Bhawan. *The Bhagavadgita*. Gorakhpur, India: Gita Press, 1984.

Keshavadas, Sadguru Sant. *Sadguru Dattatreya*. Oakland, California: Vishwa Dharma Publications, 1988.

King, E. Wesley. *Your Indwelling Presence*. San Gabriel, California: Willing Publishing, 1951.

Lamsa, George M. *Holy Bible from the Ancient Eastern Text*. San Francisco, California: Harper & Row, 1957.

Mahesh Yogi, Maharishi. *Bhagavad Gita, a New Translation and Commentary with Sanskrit Text*. Los Angeles, California: International SRM Publications, 1967.

Makeever, Ann Meyer. *Self Mastery in the Christ Consciousness*. Lemon Grove, California: Dawning Publications, 1989.

Meyer, Ann P. and Peter V. Meyer. *Being a Christ!* Lemon Grove,

California: Dawning Publications, 1988.

Miller, Moshe, trans. *Zohar*. Chicago, Illinois: Fiftieth Gate Publications, 2000.

Parker, Dr. William R. and Elaine St. Johns. *Prayer Can Change Your Life*. Englewood Cliffs, New Jersey: Prentice Hall, 1957.

Perry, Whitall N. *A Treasury of Traditional Wisdom*. Cambridge, England: Quinta Essentia, 1971.

Ponder, Catherine. *Prosperity Secret of the Ages*. Englewood Cliffs, New Jersey: Prentice Hall Trade, 1974.

Ponder, Catherine. *Prospering Power of Prayer*. Marina del Rey, California: DeVorss & Company, 1983.

Ponder, Catherine. *Prospering Power of Love*. Marina del Rey, California: DeVorss & Company, 1984.

Ponder, Catherine. *Dynamic Laws of Prosperity*. Marina del Rey, California: DeVorss & Company, 1985.

Ponder, Catherine. *Dynamic Laws of Prayer*. Marina del Rey, California: DeVorss & Company, 1987.

Prabhavananda, Swami, and Christopher Isherwood. *Shankara's Crest Jewel of Discrimination*. Hollywood, California: Vedanta Press, 1975.

Shinn, Florence Scovel. *The Writings of Florence Scovel Shinn: The Game of Life and How to Play It, Your Word Is Your Wand, The Secret Door to Success, The Power of the Spoken Word*. Marina del Rey, California: DeVorss & Company, 1988.

Shumsky, Susan G. *Divine Revelation*. New York: Fireside, 1996.

Shumsky, Susan G. *Exploring Meditation*. Franklin Lakes, New Jersey: New Page Books, 2001.

Shumsky, Susan G. *Exploring Chakras*. Franklin Lakes, New Jersey: New Page Books, 2003.

Shumsky, Susan G. *Exploring Auras*. Franklin Lakes, New Jersey: New Page Books, 2005.

Sweet, Bill. *A Journey into Prayer*. Xlibris, 2003.

Waterhouse, John B. *Five Steps to Freedom, An Introduction to Spiritual Mind Treatment*. Burnsville, North Carolina: Rampart Press, 2003.

Wilson, Andrew, ed., International Religious Foundation. *World Scripture*. New York: Paragon House, 1991.

Zubko, Andy. *Treasury of Spiritual Wisdom*. San Diego, California: Blue Dove Press, 1996.

PERIODICALS AND PROCEEDINGS

Byrd, Randolph, MD, PO. "Positive Therapeutic Effects of Intercessory Prayer in a Coronary Care Unit Population." *Southern Medical Journal*, Vol. 81, 71, 826–829.

Comstock, G.W. and K.B. Partridge, "Church Attendance and Health," *Journal of Chronic Disease*, 25 (1972), 665–672.

Duckro, P.N., and P.R. Magaletta, "The Effect of Prayer on Physical Health—Experimental Evidence." *Journal of Religion and Health*, 33, (1994) 211–219.

Harris, William S., PhD; Manohar Gowda, MD; Jerry W. Kolb, MDiv; Christopher P. Strychacz, PhD; James L. Vacek, MD; Philip G. Jones, MS; Alan Forker, MD; James H. O'Keefe, MD; Ben D. McCallister, MD, "Randomized Controlled Trial of the Effects of Remote, Intercessory Prayer on Outcomes in Patients Admitted to the Coronary Care Unit." *Archives of Internal Medicine*, Vol. 159, (October 25, 1999) 2273–2278.

Hummer, R.A., R.G. Rogers, C.B. Nam, and C.G. Ellison, "Religious Involvement and U.S. Adult Mortality." *Demography*, 36 (1999), 273–285.

Kark, J.D., G. Shemi, Y. Friedlander, O. Martin, O. Manor, and S.H. Blondheim, "Does Religious Observance Promote Health? Mortality in Secular vs. Religious Kibbutzim in Israel," *American Journal of Public Health*, 86 (1996), 341–346.

Koenig, H.G. and D.B. Larson, "Use of Hospital Services, Religious Attendance, and Religious Affiliation," *Southern Medical Journal*, 91 (1998), 925–932.

Koenig, H.G., H.J. Cohen, L.K. George, J.C. Hays, D.B. Larson, and D.G. Blazer. "Attendance at Religious Services, Interleukin-6, and Other Biological Indicators of Immune Function in Older Adults," *International Journal of Psychiatry in Medicine*, 23 (1997), 233–250.

Koenig, H.G. et al. "Does Religious Attendance Prolong Survival? A Six-year Follow-up Study of 3,968 Older Adults." *Journal of Gerontology: Medical Sciences*, 54A (1999), M370.

Levin, J.S., D.B. Larson, and C.M. Puchalski, "Religion and Spirituality in Medicine: Research and Education," *Journal of the American Medical Association*, 278 (1997), 792–793.

Matthews, Dale MD, Sally Marlowe, and Francis MacNutt, "Effects of Intercessory Prayer on Patients with Rheumatoid Arthritis." *Southern Medical Journal,* Vol. 93 No. 12, (December 2000), 1177–1186.

McCaffrey, Anne M., MD, David M. Eisenberg, MD, Anna T. R. Legedza, ScD, Roger B. Davis, ScD, and Russell S. Phillips, MD. "Prayer for Health Concerns: Results of a National Survey on

Prevalence and Patterns of Use." *Archives of Internal Medicine*, Vol. 164, (April 2004), 858–862.

McCullough, M.E., W.T. Hoyt, D.B. Larson, H.G. Koenig, and C. Thoresen. "Religious Involvement and Mortality: A Meta-analytic Review." *Health Psychology*, Vol.19, No. 3, (2000), 211–222.

Musick, M.A., J.S. House, and D.R. Williams. "Attendance at Religious Services and Mortality in a National Sample." Paper presented at the American Sociological Association Convention, 1999.

O'Laoire, Sean, MD. "An Experimental Study of the Effects of Distant, Intercessory Prayer on Self Esteem, Anxiety and Depression." *Alternative Therapies*, Vol. 3, 6, (November 1997), 54–61.

Taylor, Elizabeth Johnston, PhD, RN, and Frieda Hawkins-Outlaw, DNSC/RN, *Holistic Nursing Practice*, Vol. 16 No. 3, (April 2002), 46–60.

INTERNET SITES

Affiliated New Thought Network, Practitioner: www.newthought.org/practitioner.html.

Albert Einstein Quotes compiled by GIGA: www.giga-usa.com/quotes/authors/albert_einstein_a008.htm.

American Transcendentalism Web: www.vcu.edu/engweb/transcendentalism.

Birth of Divine Science: www.divinesciencecommunity-center.org/sermons/birthof.html.

Dhammapada: Wikiquote (trans. F. Max Muller): http://en.wikiquote.org/wiki/Dhammapada.

Divine Revelation: www.divinerevelation.org.

Divine Science History: http://divinescience.com/beliefs/ds_history.htm.

Dresser, Horatio W.: *A History of the New Thought Movement*. New York: Thomas Y. Crowell, 1919. http://website.lineone.net/~newthought/ahotntinx.htm.

Emanuel Swedenborg (1888–1772): New Church: New Jerusalem: http://swedenborg.newearth.org.

Introduction to Emma Curtis Hopkins: http://desert.xpressdesigns.com/ech.html.

Kwang Y. Cha, MD, Daniel P. Wirth, JD, MS, and Rogerio A. Lobo, MD "Does Prayer Influence the Success of in Vitro Fertilization–Embryo Transfer? Report of a Masked, Randomized Trial." *Journal of Reproductive Medicine*, Vol. 46, No. 9, (September 2001). www.reproductivemedicine.com/Features/2001/2001Sep.htm.

305

Mary Baker Eddy Library for the Betterment of Humanity: http://www.marybakereddylibrary.org/marybakereddy/bio.jhtml.

New Thought Movement Home Page: http://websyte.com/alan.

New Thought Related Authors: http://cornerstone.wwwhubs.com/corner.htm.

On Assessing Prayer, Faith, and Health: www.davidmyers.org/Brix?pageID=54.

Positive Thinking Timeline: www.steamboats.com/hobbies/positivethinkingtimeline.html.

Prayer as Therapy: www.ficotw.org/prayerastherapy-lesson.html.

Ralph Waldo Emerson: http://plato.stanford.edu/entries/emerson/.

Religious Movements Homepage: New Thought Movement: http://religiousmovements.lib.virginia.edu/nrms/Newthoug.html.

Religious Movements Homepage: United Church of Religious Science: http://religiousmovements.lib.virginia.edu/nrms/ucrs.html.

Religious Movements Homepage: Unity School of Christianity: http://religiousmovements.lib.virginia.edu/nrms/unity.html.

Scientific Christian Mental Practice, Chapter One: http://emmacurtishopkins.wwwhubs.com/scmp1.htm.

Theosophy Library Online, Great Teacher Series, Franz Anton Mesmer: http://theosophy.org/tlodocs/teachers/FranzAntonMesmer.htm.

Transcendentalists…Dial Magazine: http://www.transcendentalists.com/.

Upanishads, Part I, Khandogya Upanishad: VI:2: http://www.sacred-texts.com/hin/upan/index.htm.

What Is Spiritual Mind Treatment: http://www.religiousscience.org/practitioners/about_prac_what_is_treat.html.

Williams, Debra, D.D. "Scientific Research of Prayer: Can the Power of Prayer Be Proven?" 1999 PLIM Retreat, 1999 PLIM REPORT, Vol. 8, No. 4. Theme: Inner Journey, Part 5. www.plim.org/PrayerDeb.htm.

World Ministry of Prayer Treatment Builder: http://www.religiousscience.org/wmop_site/forming_prayer_builder.html.

ABOUT THE AUTHOR

Susan Shumsky, D.D. is the author of *Divine Revelation*, now in its ninth printing with Simon & Schuster and published in several foreign countries. She is also the author of *Exploring Meditation*, *Exploring Auras*, and the award-winning book *Exploring Chakras*.

Dr. Shumsky has practiced meditation and self-development disciplines since 1967. Her personal mentor was enlightened spiritual master from India, Maharishi Mahesh Yogi, founder of Transcendental Meditation and guru of the Beatles and Deepak Chopra. Dr. Shumsky lived in Maharishi's ashrams in secluded areas, including the Himalayas and the Alps, for twenty-two years, where she spent many months in deep meditation and complete silence. She served on Maharishi's personal staff for seven years. After 1989, she studied New Thought and metaphysics with other enlightened masters.

Since 1970 Dr. Shumsky has taught meditation, self-development, prayer, and intuition to thousands of students worldwide. A highly-acclaimed, greatly respected professional speaker, teacher, healer, spiritual coach, counselor, and prayer therapist, she has authored many seminars and classes and published several video and audio programs.

Dr. Shumsky received a Doctor of Divinity degree from Teaching of Intuitional Metaphysics, founded by Dr. Peter Meyer of San Diego. She is the founder of Divine Revelation®, a complete technology for contacting the divine presence and listening to the inner voice. Divine Revelation is not a theory, but a proven system that has worked for thousands of students.

To invite Dr. Shumsky to speak to your group, for information about her itinerary, Divine Revelation teachers in your area, a complete description of the Divine Revelation curriculum, retreats and tours to sacred places, for a private session by phone, or to order books, audio and video products, please visit the following web site: www.scientificprayer.com. When you join our mailing list online, you will receive a free, downloadable, guided meditation.

We want to hear from you. Please write to us your personal Scientific Prayer demonstrations, stories of answered prayer, and everyday miracles: Teaching of Intuitional Metaphysics, P.O. Box 7185, New York, NY 10116, 212-946-5132, or email divinerev@aol.com.

INDEX

Note: figures are indicated by *f*